Restoring the Glory

Discovering the Keys to Unlock Inner Healing and Deliverance

LAURA GAGNON

ISBN: 1979257930
ISBN-13: 978-1979257930

CONTENTS

TESTIMONIES AND REVIEWS

Here are some comments from various individuals that left comments on our webpage, **Beyond the Barriers,** regarding a prayer to break generational curses. This one is known as our **Breakthrough Prayer**.

"I want to appreciate God and Laura Gagnon for the breakthrough prayer. It has delivered me from generational and self-inflicted curses." – Kena Charles, February 3, 2017

"I want to thank you for providing such powerful prayers, may God bless you. Every time I recite a prayer I feel closer and closer to God. Thank you so much, may God be with you. " – Anonymous, Dec. 4, 2016

"Effectively powerful; a yoke-breaking prayer. Thank you." Michael Ajari, April 19, 2016

"I thought I didn't need this, but since you covered everything, there it was! Thank you, and God bless your ministry." Linda Sommers, Sept. 6, 2015

"I read this prayer yesterday and it manifested today. My passport was detained for 8 months. I had applied for a visa to the embassy, they responded for the first time. May God continue to give you more revelations. God bless you." Nguebih Anastasie, Sept. 7, 2015

"Thanks for mentioning that salvation is not the same as deliverance. I also believed it but for some reasons I couldn't explain it from the scripture. For a long time I thought if one is born again, he/she is automatically delivered from every curse but somehow my reality was saying something else." Clive Nzama, June 20, 2016

"Without mincing words, these prayer points are sure weapons of mass destruction to the kingdom of hell. The teaching that preceded the prayer was just so on point. Just prayed it and I can tell things are already happening in the realm of the spirit." … "When you use the word restore it means you are taking it back to how it is originally. You were born a winner already the devil stole it and he must give it back. The Devil just lost another battle. WE ARE VICTORIOUS." Franklin, Oct. 10, 2016

"Thank you Norm and Laura Gagnon for this thorough prayer and others in this blog. May the LORD Jesus Christ bless you abundantly. I believe everyone here has been mightily blessed by these prayers. I know I am." Yosief Kesete, Oct.17, 2016

"WOW!!! This is such a powerful prayer. I just prayed it and immediately felt the release! Thank you for sharing. May the Lord continue to bless you and keep you." Esther Chayil, Mar. 19, 2017

The following reviews are from Amazon.com from the book **Prayers for Impossible Situations:**

"This book "Prayers for Impossible Situation" exceeded my expectations. I pray this prayers almost every day, I find the prayers very helpful and it touches specific areas in my life, which is why I don't go without this book for long. This book taught me how to pray, it speaks the words on my heart. I feel God hears me when i pray using the prayers in this book. Get this book if you can, you will not regret it and it will bless your life. Laura did a wonderful job in this book." – Happy Blessing, March 10, 2016

"This book was written for a time like this in my life! Sometimes in prayer I could not articulate in words what I wanted to ask the Lord- this was definitely written from a humble heart! I thank God for the author and for her obedience to write it!" – Andrea G., January 17, 2016

"Excellent Prayers! I used the Prayer for Sight on my 70+ Spiritual Mother and God RESTORED HER SIGHT! She called and left me a voice message saying, "I can READ!!!!". Thank you Jesus and Thank you Laura Gagnon." – Anonymous, March 20, 2017

These reviews are from Amazon.com from the book, **Seduced into Shame: Finding Freedom from Sexual Sins.**

"This book should be read by every believer! I was in turmoil to say the least. Tormented and troubled just about on every side because I had opened the wrong doors. I was led to Sister Gagnon's website and she had amazing prayers. I saw this book, brought it, and through faith in Jesus.... the chains have been broken! This book was very helpful. Where it seems all of my prayers had been held up, everything seemed to be released almost immediately once I prayed and turned my heart back to Jesus Christ and Him only. HE IS THE ONLY WAY!!!! This book is a must-have." – M.J., April 30, 2018

"This is a must read for anyone feeling trapped in bondage by the enemy. It has helped me tremendously and thankful for God that Laura shared her struggles and wrote this book to help others!" – Amazon Customer, Jan. 23, 2018

"An effective tool every deliverance team should have in its resource pool!"
– Amazon Customer, May 28, 2018

"This past 5 months has honestly been the most challenging and darkest seasons of my life, and I've been in the shadow valley of death a few times! I cried out to God with everything I had, a few times! I heard His voice so many times and received scripture that was so spot on with the last few seasons and including this one - Ps 41 - 45, seeing God move in all other areas of my life but yet still being tormented, it honestly really drove me insane!!! I hear so clearly from God and He confirms it so powerfully through scripture and yet these things keep going! I see people get healed and radically touched by the Father and yet Authority exercised against these things and nothing happens..... Goodness it was so confusing, and really have to be honest, I pursue walking clean and in purity with Him (being an ex-drug addict which have pushed the limits of God's grace on my life. Just being very honest) as I can't afford any open doors. And I couldn't figure out if it was an authority problem or open door, And I did seek counsel from my Spiritual Leaders which are very anointed and specially equipped for deliverance, But they wanted me to RISE UP and walk in complete dependence with Father! It was very frustrating, and I seriously had to get extremely serious about seeking God and meeting Him in the Secret Place with all this going on around me, I got distracted a few times, and actually gave in to the spirit of fear (And have battled this thing a few times, so it was a few TIMES 7) and it opening doors to other defeated fo's! Anyway, Im going to be very honest, This season was about getting completely dependent on God and really breath, sleep and live out of the secret place and letting Him direct your every footstep, and seriously its like God set this season up this way that I could only get the nescary keys straight from Him! I got lead through a very specific google search and found laura's blog, and it was DIVINE, not only was it everything I was going through and facing, but she knew what she was talking about regarding deliverance and the demonic realms, and I say that cause I have seen these things operate (in my past and when I was on drugs. when 3rd eye was open) and through personal experience and seeing how strong and anointed Deliverance Ministers operate with Holy Spirit in these realms.

It was crucial for me that I find someone who knew these realms and deliverance, and honestly, all these boxes were ticked when I came across Her website. I did the prayers, and did experience something, but it kept coming, I reached out to her, and was so relieved and excited for her to reach back and offer her complete support and counsel to find the open door, get me free and see these things scater like lightning! I could and can truly sense a true yearning, desire and compassion from her to see me get free and by looking at her interaction on her website and FB others aswell. She never asked me for money or anything! she was truly set on seeing me get free! Anyway, she gave me the right tools and things to look for in finding the open door, I truly searched and seeked and stood, and it got better, actually throught I found the open door. but it a day or two later came back and stronger!! This time round I was seriously desperate and wanted this breakthrough and was willing to go to whatever measure with God to get this breakthrough, I messaged Laura and boooooom, her book was available, SO DIVINE!!! I started fasting and was dead set willing to go till death, to get this breakthrough!!! and dove into this book with absolutely DIVINE EXPECTATION of getting free and seeing revenge on these defeated foes!!! This book was divinely structured and orchestrated by Holy Spirit, reason I say that is.. She started the book out with how these spirits operate individually, strategically, corporately and to what doors each of these are attracted too, detecting their behavior and attributes. It's like Holy Spirit used this structure as puzzles to further allow me to effectively identify - what, why and who was operating. After it was identified, it is like I had a ROCKET OF TRUTH to close those doors and see them scatter with tails between their legs.

Glory to God, I received my breakthrough and learned so much about my past and behaviors and really, really experienced and encountered God's Love, Goodness and really seeing Him come through for me as a FATHER!." – Rudy, Feb. 23, 2017

"I believe that anybody who is a Christian should read this book. Even if your life is perfect you probably know some Christians who are stuck in life and it seems like there is no answer to their prayers… there is no explanation why this things keep happening..... well, this book will shine the light right to the roots of the problems.... this book is not just about sexuaal sins, sexual problems it touches everything in life and gives you clarity about many things." – Amazon Customer, May 22, 2017

INTRODUCTION

We all have a great burden to fulfill the great commission. Matt 28:18 instructs us, "Therefore go and make disciples of all nations, baptizing them in the name of the Father, and of the son, and of the Holy Spirit, and teaching them to obey everything I have commanded you".

Preaching the word, leading nations to Christ and teaching them to obey the Lord's words have very different challenges and obstacles. As a Pastor for 20 years and a street evangelist for 5 years, the preaching and baptizing part of the commission was the easy part. Raising disciples who were obedient to God's word and coming under the authority of the Holy Spirit was a very different challenge. Laura's teaching on freedom and prayer brings a fresh release and anointing to establish every believer in truths that will transform them.

The key to freedom in Christ is through obedience. Jesus found complete victory over the evil one through His obedience. This is why Jesus could proclaim that the prince of this world had no claim to him and no power over him, in John 14:30. After being tested in the wilderness Jesus started his ministry by proclaiming from the Book of Isaiah, "The Spirit of the Lord is upon me... He has sent me to proclaim freedom to the prisoners and recovery of sight to the blind... to set the oppressed free. "

Many leaders feel overwhelmed at seeing so many people coming to Christ at altar calls, being baptized yet dealing with people who don't have the freedom to pursue a deeper relationship with the Holy Spirit or to walk in their purpose and calling. As a pastor, I personally lacked important answers regarding people's bondages, struggles and oppression. I wanted my flock to obey the word and my teaching and quit struggling, but my approach was backward. They needed freedom from their shackles so they could run after God without hindrance before they would be able to listen and obey the Holy Spirit.. My congregation and I would all have benefited greatly if I had the understanding and revelation that is found in this book. The prayers are powerful and liberating for all people and nations to help bring God's children into the fullness of their calling in Christ. God took my wife and I on a journey to learn about the importance of deliverance that heals the issues of the soul. Many of those truths are in this book. This is what leads people into freedom, peace and joy

Norm Gagnon

CHAPTER ONE

AWAKENING AND ALIGNMENT

When God spoke from Mount Sinai his voice shook the earth, but now he makes another promise: "Once again I will shake not only the earth but the heavens also. The words "once more" indicate the removing of what can be shaken--that is, created things--so that what cannot be shaken may remain.
Hebrews 12:26,27

A new season of revival and awakening is upon us. Whether it concerns economic systems, financial security, the political realm or religious structures, God is shaking the foundations of structures and systems. What is at stake is the moral foundations of nations and many issues concerning social justice. As we transition from one era to another, whether as a nation, a family or an individual, we must let go of certain things in order to embrace something new, however, in the process we must recognize that the enemy plays a key role just as much as God does, because ultimately everything is directly connected to our identity, dominion and what kingdom will prevail. Will it be the kingdom of darkness or the kingdom of light? The shaking of beliefs, the confrontation of injustices and the cry of the oppressed is necessary to wake people up to their own need for change so that they can come into a place of proper alignment with God.

When people forsake their Creator and turn to their own ways, they will go into captivity and suffer at the hands of their enemies. On a corporate level it could mean the invasion of a foreign enemy, or even government oppression that takes unfair advantage over its people. In the life of an individual, an enemy is defined as something that binds a person to sin, shame, guilt, a curse of poverty, infirmity, loss or emotional wounds. An enemy is something that harms or weakens the individual. Miriam Webster Dictionary defines an enemy as someone that is antagonistic towards another person; one who seeks to injure, overthrow or confound. All of these things serve to restrict a person's intimacy with their heavenly Father and others.

In order to successfully make it through transition, we must learn to unload the baggage from our past and embrace the truth that frees us.. God operates in times and seasons. When God is preparing people to close out one season and enter a new one, they will often find themselves confronting things that have been left unresolved or unhealed. He allows us to feel the pain of old issues rise to the surface, and we may feel like suddenly we have entered a time machine, going back to revisit certain events where wounding occurred. God allows us to experience these things so that we have another opportunity to surrender those old offenses, wounds and let him heal them. They must be cleansed before they can heal.

"For He wounds, but also binds; He strikes, but His hands also heal." Job 5:18

It is human nature to stuff our pain deep down inside where no one else can reach it. It is like dropping our pain into a deep, dark well where we try to ignore that it is there, but God sees what is hidden in our soul. His love and justice demands that every enemy to our future is dealt with so that we can live free and healed. The problem is, most people are reluctant to face the issues of their past that have left them with painful, unresolved emotions. Sometimes that means we must get intimately acquainted with the pain until we are willing to do what is necessary for our healing. The great physician lances the wound so that it can be drained properly and remove the infection. He wants to heal us from fear of rejection, shame, guilt, and the lies the enemy has told us. Memories of certain events can be painful. The memory itself is just stored data. It has no ability to hurt us, but twisted perceptions and lies that we've believed concerning those memories can cause us pain. Sometimes the lie we believe makes us feel as though we must absorb shame or injustice because of how other people's actions have impacted us, or we absorb rejection because someone else's negative actions are projected towards us. It doesn't matter what others may say or what they feel about us; feelings and opinions are not equal to truth. God's word is truth, and He says that we are loved and accepted in the Beloved, through Christ our Lord.[1] We must come to learn that the character flaws of others are not a true indicator of our value. Our value does not diminish because someone else fails to

---

[1] Ref. Eph. 1:1-11.

demonstrate the good fruit of love, acceptance, grace or forgiveness towards us. Why then do we allow other people's weaknesses, false judgments and criticisms define how we see ourselves? Our value is assigned by our Heavenly Father. Our ability to walk in confidence is because our position is secure as a child of God. Our true identity in Christ is found in Him, not in other people's ability to love or affirm us. Therefore, as we can learn to understand this truth, we also understand that our Father's justice looks like forgiveness, freedom, peace and joy. The process of transition includes digging things out of our well (our soul) and learning to look at them through new eyes. When we can truly surrender our pain, we can leave it with Jesus and be ready to transition into a new season. Because ultimately, if we do not let go of the pain, disappointment, and the lies in our belief system, our emotions will end up ruling our heart and directing all our decisions.

Our heavenly Father's love and commitment to us is so loyal and longsuffering in spite of our many failures. It is His unwavering commitment towards us that compels Him to awaken us to our identity so that we may walk in our God ordained purpose. This is why people (and nations) go through seasons of intense shaking. It is to remove those things man has made for himself that oppose God's rulership and His kingdom. The purpose of transition is to lead people out of something that is no longer useful or necessary, (or something that has served its purpose) so that they can enter into the new thing He wants to bring forth. The process, however, can be a challenge.

As I contemplated writing this book, I knew I wanted to incorporate large portions of my previous book, ***Unmasking the Culture***, because the information in it is vital to so many different nations. It was originally written as a teaching resource for missionaries and ministry leaders to Mexico, but the information contained is important due to the ethnicity, culture and traditions. Although the book was written specifically with missions to Mexico and Spanish speaking nations in mind, so much of the cultural influences and religious practices have migrated to other nations and are connected with one another. I could not see a way around this issue, therefore I have incorporated a great deal of ***Unmasking the Culture*** into this book, but I have also included new teaching and additional prayers. The first half of the book tackles the issues of religious and cultural influences, family upbringing and generational curses, and the second half of the book explores deeper levels of inner healing, spiritually rooted issue and how they pertain to physical healing, and transformation.

One of the first things we must come to terms with is our belief system. People have a variety of beliefs that include man-made philosophies and a smorgasbord of beliefs that they have collected over time. Many people have made gods of their own understanding and have become disillusioned with their idols, and because of their disappointment they have either turned to false religions, the occult, agnosticism or declared themselves an atheist

Religion can become a subject of strong viewpoints. For some, their faith is directly tied to their morals, and perhaps with others religion is more aligned with an established set of rules and religious traditions. For others, their sense of spirituality is connected to attaining knowledge and enlightenment because it's equated to wisdom. In all religions, people interact with and worship a god or a variety of deities that can take on either male or female characteristics. Some people even worship animals, believing that animals play an integral role in teaching mankind valuable life lessons.

Many spiritual philosophies do not have a heaven or hell. Some religions believe that departed souls live among us, or there may be different spiritual realms but they all exist somewhere on earth. Organized religion can be viewed by some people as dictatorial and unyielding, and some prefer to be known as spiritual but not religious. The ambiguity and lack of structure has a romantic appeal, especially among Millennials and Gen Xers, who often resist what they view as restrictive beliefs. The various forms of spirituality, New Age philosophies and occult practices can seem preferable because they are flexible, more suited to personal preference and allow for more creative expression. In fact, many of those who prefer to be known as spiritual but not religious would go so far as to label themselves as agnostic or atheist simply because the idea of being pegged into a religious group doesn't appeal to them. The things that are important to them, however, include a sense of personal value, identity, self-esteem and a spiritual connection that makes them feel loved and accepted. How wonderful it is indeed that all of those core values – love, acceptance, forgiveness of sins, personal worth, identity and belonging are all encompassed in a relationship with Jesus Christ. Through Christ, we are reconnected with our Heavenly Father, who assures us of our value as a child of God.

Another aspect of what people find appealing is having a sense of power over their circumstances. When I was younger the thing that motivated me to look to witchcraft for answers was a sense of hopelessness over certain circumstances in my life. I wasn't seeking a relationship with God. I wasn't looking for identity, a sense of purpose or love; I was desperate for the power to change certain aspects of my life that were very much out of control. I hated feeling powerless. Witchcraft offered me what I thought was an immediate answer to pressing needs. I had no idea that I was actually inviting even more problems into my life because I had invited a curse.

Witchcraft appeals to many young people for exactly the same reasons. It can seem like a quick solution to a bully or an adversary, turn a romantic interest into something more, or any number of things. Many people desire fast answers, and magic seems like a quick fix. The Bible teaches that looking for answers outside of God and engaging the occult realm for assistance is forbidden by God. Those 'practices' carry a curse. As I discovered, and I'm sure others have too, the lure of witchcraft always comes with strings attached. People don't realize that they're signing a contract with Satan, but once that door has been opened, it's a legally binding contract in the spirit realm. Those that try to use devils as their servants **will** pay the price.

There are many reasons why people search for truth and answers. Some may be looking for freedom from negative labels and stereotypes, freedom from religious shame or they have negative experiences with a church or religious group. As a result, they ended up pulling away from all organized religion. It can start out as trying to maintain a sense of self-preservation, but if the person doesn't allow inner healing to take place, those negative judgments can end up convincing them that they have no need for others. Isolation produces an independence from God and others, and disdain for God and the church body can leave a person disconnected from their Creator as well as the life source that can heal them. It can also leave people disconnected from the plans and purposes of God. Rejection leaves people broken with a deep dissatisfaction and disappointment, causing a sense of suspicion and criticism of God and others. When people are cautious and distrustful of God, rebellion follows.

There is an openness in various quests for spirituality that allows for many spiritual practices because of the belief that it encourages happiness, but in many situations people are running away *from something* instead of *running to* the One that can heal them and set them free. Doing what we want with no thought to the rewards that we will reap leads people straight into captivity. Our entire world is framed by the spiritual laws that God has established. If we break them we must be willing to accept the consequences. Yes, we have the free will to make our own decisions, but we are not free from the consequences of our choices.

One thing I am sure of: no one that is bound by witchcraft is truly happy because they are bound by pain. Demons, by their very nature, are intent on deceiving and destruction. They are energized by anger, bitterness, and other negative emotions. Their assignment is never peace; it is to kill, steal and destroy without exception. As a matter of fact, one sure sign that a person has demonic influences in their life is a lack of peace and joy. Demons are entirely evil, void of all love, compassion or concern for others. It is not harmless to conjure up spirits to act as one's servants. Witchcraft binds people to a curse and a tyrannical master that has no capacity for mercy.

Insisting on living by various man-made philosophies is not wisdom or enlightenment. It is making a willful choice to live in self-deception, because to not choose Christ is by default making a choice to serve Satan. There is no in-between or place of neutrality. There is no place in the spirit realm for the procrastinators and undecided. The choice is either become a child of God, have your sins forgiven and receive God as your heavenly Father ; or, allow Satan to assume the role of a false father and master. No one needs to live with the fear of eternal damnation because their sins are not forgiven . You get to choose, but why in the world would you want to choose the second option? And yet, people waiver between those two decisions every single day, sometimes without making any decision at all.

"For God expressed His love for the world in this way: He gave His only Son so that whoever believes in Him will not face everlasting destruction, but will have everlasting life. Here's the point. God didn't send His Son into the world to judge it; instead, He is here to rescue a world headed toward certain destruction.

No one who believes in Him has to fear condemnation, yet condemnation is already the reality for everyone who refuses to believe because they reject the grace available to cleanse them from sin. Why does God allow for judgment and condemnation? Because the Light, sent from God, pierced through the world's darkness to expose ill motives, hatred, gossip, greed, violence, and the like. Still some people preferred the darkness over the light because their actions were dark. Some of humankind hated the light. They scampered hurriedly back into the darkness where vices thrive and wickedness flourishes. Those who abandon deceit and embrace what is true, they will enter into the light where it will be clear that all their deeds come from God." John 3:16-21 The Voice Translation

Don't wait until it's too late and procrastination has made the decision for you! The wisdom of man is not greater than the wisdom of our Creator. God does not want pain, torment, sickness and disease, poverty and misery for you. Those are characteristics of living apart from God. This is the broad road that Jesus warns us about in Matthew 7:13 and 14. He contrasts the two paths available in life. One path is very broad and has a great many people on it, but it leads to destruction. The other path is very narrow and few people choose it even though it leads to life.

In considering the choice people make and the way it affects nations, we must consider our ancestors, the cultural effect, and the historical impact of settling nations. All those events and influences become key components in how they affect the beliefs of those that live in certain places. Many spiritual practices and religions were birthed out of resistance because of what affected their ancestors, but those same events or situations are not necessarily true today. Thousands of years ago, when nations were being settled and explorers were conquering lands, it was common to force those who were conquered to adapt to the culture and beliefs of those that dominated them. People rebelled against proselytization and resisted forced religious conversion. As a result, organized religion was viewed by some people as objectionable. In an attempt to hold on to their own culture, traditions and a sense of identity, many various people groups including Africans, Mexican, Asian and various native tribes brought their own spiritual beliefs with them, syncretizing them with existing religions, in particular, Catholicism. As people were dispersed through various diasporas this caused the spread of cultural beliefs and traditions to migrate to other lands. That is one of the reasons why there is a large portion of this book that examines Catholic traditions and compares them to scripture. We will examine those things in greater detail in a later chapter.

Many people have adopted certain customs and beliefs because that is all they've known, but it might not be true to God's original design. If we are going to settle our identity issues we must first make sure we ask the right questions. What foundation are we using to determine truth? The world and a philosophy of humanism would try to tell us that everything is subjective. At the whim of man, we can decide what it true or not true. When a people or a nation does not know foundational principles of where they came from, to whom they belong, or in whose image they are created; it causes them to be vulnerable to deception. "My people perish for lack of knowledge..." Hosea 4:6.

A person's identity can be molded and shaped by influences in their family, the spiritual and emotional health of those around them, religious expectations and other factors. These things are all influencers that attempt to mold people into someone else's image and expectations, but those beliefs, customs and traditions may not be the person God wants them to become. A person's true identity is discovered when they realize that they are made in the image of God. Our identity, calling and the purpose for which we were created can only be revealed through personal relationship with Jesus Christ because He is the bridge back to our Heavenly Father. Only the voice of our Father who created us can call us into our truest identity, destiny and purpose.

Satan, ever the accuser, twists people's perception to create confusion and a false belief that loyalty to Jesus Christ is subjecting oneself to the belief that we must identify with sin and shame. Initially, this part is true; **we should** understand that we are sinners in need of God's grace and mercy, but we don't need to retain a shame based identity. Jesus set us free from the stain of guilt and shame associated with our sin. However, we should not cheapen the significance of the cross by trying to make it more comfortable for people. Jesus Christ poured out His life blood for us and the price He paid cost Him everything. His sacrifice should never be treated lightly. The reality is every person on earth ends up trying to cover their sin and shame. When a person feels guilt, the first thing they often do is attempt to either make excuses or shift the blame onto someone else, because experiencing guilt, shame and embarrassment from our own sin is uncomfortable. Every person on earth ends up trying to cover their mistakes in order to try and avoid feelings of guilt, condemnation, embarrassment, failure and disappointment. The good news is that Jesus died to take our sin upon himself. He has removed our sin and shame and we do not need to live under the weight of that guilt. We need only to acknowledge Him as the risen Son of God that died in our place upon the cross, covering our sins in His blood. When we invite Him to be our Lord and Savior, it is with the acknowledgement that we cannot save ourselves. We cannot be holy enough on our own merit to justify God allowing us into His heaven. Heaven is holy. Someone had to pay the price for our sin so that we could once again be restored to relationship with our Creator, and because of Jesus' sacrifice our Heavenly Father welcomes us with open arms as His sons and daughters. We become heirs to all that is in His kingdom. We no longer have to live as slaves to the evil one that comes to kill, steal and destroy us. We have been given access to every spiritual blessing our Father has for us. This is indeed good news!

Every aspect of God whether in the form of Father, Son or Holy Spirit is as a person. Read the Bible and you'll see this is true. God never represents Himself as someone He is not. He has emotions; He has feelings, character, integrity, standards and a value system. Christianity promotes a humble Father/child relationship. One can never deny the person of Jesus Christ and expect to enter into God's holy heaven, for it is written, "nor is there salvation in any other, for there is no other name under heaven given among men by which we must be saved," Acts 4:12. The Bible tells us the wages of sin is death. We are eternally separated from God if our sins are not atoned for by the shed blood of Christ. This is the **only** way to the Father and into relationship with God.

"If you confess with your mouth the Lord Jesus and believe in your heart that God has raised Him from the dead, you will be saved. For with the heart one believes unto righteousness, and with the mouth confession is made unto salvation. For the scripture says, 'Whoever believes on Him will not be put to shame." Romans 10:9-11.

In every other religion in the world, righteousness is self-made through good works, not imputed through a Holy God. In every other religion, there is a demand to earn acceptance or favor from gods or goddesses that 'keep score,' and mete out punishment. In no other religion except Christianity did God – Jesus Christ – pay the price for our punishment with His own life, then raise himself from the dead 3 days later. Hundreds of people witnessed and testified to His death and resurrection. God demanded a penalty for sin and His own Son paid the requirement in His blood. What other god or goddess can say the same? Not one! In no other religion has man or a so-called god given their life to redeem mankind from their sins. They have no power or authority to do so. Given the evidence, why would anyone want to serve Satan, knowing that Jesus took the keys of Satan's domain away from him and gave them to God's very own blood-bought children?

"Jesus came and told his disciples, "I have been given all authority in heaven and on earth." Matt.28:18 Then Jesus said to His disciples:

"Look, I have given you authority over all the power of the enemy, and you can walk among snakes and scorpions and crush them. Nothing will injure you." Luke 10:19

Most people who feel there is no God usually deny Him as a result of deep disappointment or a feeling that if God existed and if He cared for them, certain circumstances would never have occurred. Most would argue that if God exists, the world would not be full of pain, suffering and disappointment or characterized by evil occurrences. Yet pain, suffering and evil are the result of what happens when people fail to trust in God or turn to Him for help. Sin causes suffering, disease, poverty and much more. Evil is simply the absence of God in the soul of mankind. **Evil is the result of what happens when people reject the Lordship of God and choose to rule themselves.** The existence of evil does not disprove God's existence; it simply proves what man becomes where God's love is absent.

One cannot serve Jesus Christ among other gods. He alone paid the price for our sin and He alone deserves our loyalty. Tony Reinke, in an article titled, *"We Become What We Worship"* writes, "The pagan worship of an image is an act of God replacement. Idols are twisted versions of reality. Whenever we worship an object, person or animal, we are acting unnaturally toward the Creator. Through this act of unnatural worship towards a created thing, the life of the worshipper takes on increasingly unnatural characteristics as well…" [12]

A humble spirit that honestly desires truth will yield to the Holy Spirit. If in doubt, pray and ask Holy Spirit to reveal truth as you read through the pages of this book. Ask Him to show you any areas where you might have unknowingly bought into a lie and adopted religious beliefs, cultural customs or family traditions that are forbidden by God. Holy Spirit is the Spirit of Truth. He has the ability to convict the heart of sin so that people will turn back to Him and practice a right way of life. When people turn away from the things that displease God, that is genuine repentance. Repentance is the key that unlocks breakthrough, blessing, revival and restoration. It is time for all people everywhere to wake up to truth and come back into proper alignment with their Heavenly Father.

I would be negligent if I did not pause to offer a prayer for salvation at this point. The rest of the book would not even make sense to people if they are not saved! If you would like to invite Jesus Christ into your heart so that you can become a child of God, please prayer the prayer below – or use it as a guide as you pray your own words from your heart.

Dear Heavenly Father,

Today I am taking a step of faith towards You. I give You my heart and my life. I give You my frustrations, limitations, fears and failures. I give You my family, my hopes, and dreams for our future. I choose to place my trust in You, God. Help me to truly know You as Father.

Father, please give me the revelation of Your love for me. I thank You for Your Son, Jesus, who gave His life in exchange for my sins. I thank You, Jesus, for Your sacrifice on the cross because You paid the price for my redemption. Jesus, I invite You to be my Lord and Savior. Please fill me with Your Holy Spirit and give me the power to live a life that honors You.

Forgive me for trying to play god of my own life. Forgive me for any areas where I have tried to maintain control instead of trusting You. Please take the veil away from my understanding. Show me any lies I have believed, and reveal what the enemy is using against me to obscure my vision of Christ and the power of His cross. Show me any areas where my life is aimed at ruin instead of restoration. Give me a heart that is open to truth and able to

---

[2] Reinke, Tony, "We Become What We Worship," DesiringGod.com, Aug. 22,2012 https://www.desiringgod.org/articles/we-become-what-we-worship, Accessed Feb. 2, 2018. (ref. Beale, Greg: We Become What We Worship).

understand Your word without confusion. I ask You to reveal my true identity and show me how You see me, Father. I ask You to bless me with the gifts of Your Spirit that help me to hear You more clearly, and to add strength and power to my prayer life. Holy Spirit, I yield to Your authority in my life, and I ask You to fill me with a hunger and thirst for righteousness. In Jesus name, Amen.

Note: All other prayers are in chapter nine.

CHAPTER TWO

CURSES

He brought them out of darkness and deepest gloom, and snapped
their chains. Let them praise the LORD for his great love and for
the wonderful things he has done for them.
Psalm 107:14,15

Before we get into the prayers in this book, I would like to offer some explanation regarding curses and deliverance. The subject of curses is greatly misunderstood and for some people it can be a stumbling block, so let's examine this further.

Galatians 3:13-14 tells us that Jesus became a curse for us and through His death and resurrection, He redeemed us from the curse of the law. There were many moral and ceremonial portions of the Mosaic Law that made it impossible to keep. No one could keep it perfectly, which is why Jesus was sent to redeem mankind and make a bridge back to our Heavenly Father. The meaning of this scripture is that anyone that attempts to attain their righteousness through self-effort is essentially rejecting the grace of God and has put themselves back under the curse. Jesus delivered us from the guilt and the penalty of sin, which is eternal separation from God. We are also instructed to 'live by faith,' for without faith it's impossible to please God. The question remains then, how can a person who has received Christ still have generational curses - or any curse for that matter, operating in their lives? **It has everything to do with how a person interprets scripture, and who you believe is enforcing the curse.**

There are many Old Testament scriptures that speak of curses. Deuteronomy 28 contains a whole list of curses due to breaking God's commands. One scripture, found in Exodus 34:5-7, states that the 'sins of the fathers will be passed down to the children to the third and fourth generation.' It is also found in the Ten Commandments. Take a look at

Exodus 20:4-6.

"You shall not make for yourself an idol of any kind, or an image of anything in the heavens above, the earth below, or the waters under the earth. You shall not bow down to them or worship them; for I, the LORD your God, am a jealous God, visiting the iniquity of the fathers on their children to the third and fourth generations of those who hate Me, but showing loving devotion to a thousand generations of those who love Me and keep My commandments...."

God put things in context by identifying His expectations. If you love Me, keep my commandments, but He also wants obedience to come from a willing heart. God doesn't want unfeeling, robotic slaves; He wants sons and daughters. His expectation both then and now is that His people enter into a covenant based on mutual love, honor and trust, and obedience to His laws would naturally follow. The first commandment God gave His people in Exodus 20: 2 is where God identified Himself as the God of the Israelites and told them they were to have 'no other gods.' This established the foundation of the covenant between God and His people. The people were to demonstrate their loyalty by refusing to worship other gods nor make any graven images to set before their eyes. He alone was to be the one true God in their lives. He would not tolerate other gods. Jesus also made a similar statement to His disciples in John 14:15 when He said, "If you love Me, keep my commandments." Here we see the intent and the expectation from God is that people that love Him will honor Him through their obedience.

Scripture tells us that it is the kindness of God that leads men to repentance. Repentance then becomes the fruit of His goodness and mercy towards us. Just as natural parents look for their children to honor their authority and obey their wishes, their deeper desire is that their kids would choose obedience out of love and submission. This is God's heart for His children, too, and that is the intent in scripture. However, when people choose disobedience over obedience, those decisions can have lasting effects on the individual as well as their family. Some people might ask, "Does a sin of the parents or grandparents or other previous family members really pass down to other generations? What about the scripture in Colossians 2:14 that says He canceled the record of the charges against us and took it away by nailing it to the cross? How then can Satan have any legal rights over people to hold them accountable for the sins of previous generations? It is because people **do** give Satan legal rights to be in their lives through choices and agreements they've made. Sins can be passed down by familiar spirits but they can also be passed down by learned behavior.

We know that sin is inherited because of Adam's disobedience. It was because sin passed down through the bloodline that a perfect sacrifice with innocent blood became necessary. If sin was not inherited, there would be no need for salvation, and if there is no need for salvation, then Christ died in vain. The reality is that every person of every generation must seek salvation for themselves. Every decision people make has a ripple effect, especially if it is a choice to sin or act with unrighteousness. Each person must confess their own sins and seek forgiveness for the iniquities that have been in their family line. Each person must likewise seek freedom and deliverance from the demonic spirits that have been on assignment to their particular family. In every area where Jesus is not made Lord in that person's life, it is a place where the enemy has authority.

We have absolutely been redeemed from the curse but it does not automatically just fall out of the sky and land on us. Many Christians think that the moment they accept Jesus as their Savior that they are immediately set free. In theory, yes - that freedom is available, but **each person must take action in order to receive what Christ has made available**. Every promise of God is received in seed form. If we are believing for healing, then we take up the promises of God and declare His word over our situation, but healing does not automatically happen. We have to do something to insure it comes to pass. Likewise, with curses we must take action to break any agreements that exist in the spirit realm that allows sickness, disease, poverty, ruin, addictions, and other evidence of a curse before we can receive the blessing.. Many Christians confuse the 'curse of the law' which refers to the Mosaic Law with other laws in God's word, but they are not the same thing. There are spiritual laws of cause and effect, too.

Scripture tells us we will reap what we sow. This means we will have to deal with the consequences of our actions. If we sow injustice, we will reap accordingly. If we sow wickedness, we will eat of the fruit of those actions.[3] Proverbs 5:22 reveals a principle of scripture. Evil deeds ensnare people and the power of sin holds them, or binds them, to that sin.. If we step outside of God's protection, then we will incur unpleasant results. **God no longer enforces a curse upon His children, but the enemy is certainly willing to do so**.

"Like a fluttering sparrow or a darting swallow, an undeserved curse will not land on its intended victim." Proverbs 26:2 (TLB)

The enemy is a legalist. He is always looking for areas of our life where

---

[3] Ref. Gal. 6:7; Prov. 22:8; Prov. 1:31; Prov. 5:22

we have broken a spiritual law or he has been granted legal rights to enforce some sort of penalty or punishment. The curse finds a place to land if it is 'deserved.' God's method of protecting us is through our obedience, but if we open a door to the enemy through disobedience, that can allow demonic spirits to come in and cause all manner of trouble. Disobedience on our part grants Satan a legal right to enter our life, and he always comes to rob us of our blessings.

Although a person can be saved, sometimes people still make wrong choices. Those choices carry a penalty for their actions. For instance, I have spoken with many Christian women that for a variety of reasons, chose to have an abortion even after they were saved. They violated one of God's commands, "Thou shall not kill." Does the fact that they are under grace mean that they can willfully sin without bearing any responsibility for their actions? Of course not. Murder is an act of injustice. It doesn't matter what the emotional justification behind those actions is, it is still a crime against another person. The blood cries out. Is there no need to acknowledge it before God? Yes, there is. If someone does something they know is wrong they need to acknowledge it and demonstrate genuine repentance. They need the mercy and forgiveness of God that comes by way of confessing their sin. I have seen what it does to those that try to cover their secret. They are eaten up with guilt, shame and pain. That pain manifests in how they treat their other relationships. Pain spills out in anger, accusation, unforgiveness, distrust, hard-heartedness, grief and other things. Sometimes it was the husband that pressured the woman into having the abortion. If this occurs between married couple it often becomes death to the relationship. Women especially cannot violate their God-given role of being the ones chosen to bear children without it bringing tremendous pain to their conscience, and they cannot escape the mental torment without the blood of Jesus erasing the pain and shame of their guilt. Even though the person wanted to be free from the responsibility of raising that child, they are not free at all. They are in bondage to the enemy.

What if the person takes that secret to their grave and never repents for it? A future generation may not necessarily bear the guilt of that sin, but because demonic spirits were not cut off and sent back to the abyss, it can manifest in other ways. It could show up as a murderous spirit in later generations, tormenting spirits, or even a spirit of infirmity and terminal disease because an agreement was made with the spirit of murder when the sin was committed. The curse of repeated injustice often travels down the family line.

Can Christians still be subject to a generational curse? Yes. Let me give you a couple more examples to clarify just how this works. If I choose to seek knowledge of my future outside of God, that is seeking answers from a source other than God's Holy Spirit. There are many ways to do so, such as consulting a medium, having tarot cards read, going to a palm reader, using a Ouija Board, a magic eight ball or even consulting horoscopes. It is all a form of divination. These are forbidden practices in scripture. If I choose to act in disobedience, even if it is in ignorance, I have still invited demonic spirits to speak to me. I have invited them to influence my future. They cannot predict the future, but they can try to entice me with secret knowledge, thereby gaining my cooperation into letting them direct my actions. They have been invited in, and they now have every legal right to harass, lie, trick me, toy with me and make me the object of their ridicule. They can curse me with poverty, illness, disease or something else, but they will not leave unless (and until) they are told they must go. **However, they will not leave unless I am truly submitted to God.** This requires repentance. James 4:6,7 reminds us that we must first submit to God before we can resist the devil, **then** he must obey. I have victory in my life to the degree that I willingly choose to submit myself under the authority of God. In order to walk in authority, one must be submitted to authority.[4] If I do not take authority over what I opened a door to while I have an opportunity to do so, then those spirits will remain as familiar spirits in the lives of my children, grandchildren, great grandchildren and so forth until someone deals with them.. My children and grandchildren do not have to bear the **guilt** for my sin (that's where grace comes in), but they will still be affected by the consequences of my sin because someone has to take responsibility for the spirits that were given a place to operate. Is this a generational curse? Absolutely. Does the punishment come from God? **No.** The enemy is the one enforcing the curse. Does the presence of a generational curse mean we are back under Mosaic Law? No. It is not our salvation that is in jeopardy; it is our ability to live in freedom, health and victory.

My mother was orphaned as a young child and bounced from home to home to live with various relatives because her father was not able to care for her. Some of the people that took care of her didn't treat her very well, and she grew up with an orphan spirit. She carried rejection, insecurity, a deep need to feel loved and a false sense of identity all her life. Her sense of identity was the direct result of a poverty spirit, and that influenced her belief system all her life. Those same spirits affected her children. It has been extremely difficult to be set free from those debilitating mindsets because I had to learn about deliverance and inner healing, and learn to identify what was present in my life. I also inherited spirits of lust, fear, witchcraft and rebellion.

---

[4] Ref. Matthew 8:5-13

Familiar spirits were always present. I could sense their presence. They became my 'imaginary friends.' I spoke to them, I told them my problems, and they in turn found ways to enforce anger, rebellion, and encourage sin. So, I inherited generational spirits that had been present in my mother's life, and most likely much further back than that, but because I didn't know what they were and I didn't realize I needed to tell them to leave, they were permitted to stay for a long, long time.. On my father's side were alcoholism, mental illness, depression, and many other things. Those spirits also influenced my beliefs and my actions, and were assigned to unravel any progress I made in life. This is another example of a generational curse.

The problem many people face is that they feel offended at the thought that God would allow punishment, affliction, disease or a serious health issue into their lives or in their children's lives when they feel it is undeserved. "I'm not a bad person," they say. "Why would God punish me?" Or, "Why would God punish a child by making them sick?" People always tend to blame God for the enemy's actions. That's when the hand goes up, "Stop right there! You're preaching legalism!" they say. A whole lot of other objections are usually close behind and the debate of whether or not this can be true can end up setting people on a defensive edge. Yet, if you examine your own family, you can probably identify some things that have repeated in your family line, such as divorce, adultery, or maybe your family can never seem to get out of poverty. Sometimes there is pregnancy outside of marriage that repeats over and over, or being drawn into New Age or occult practices. There may be a history of untimely death or being accident prone. Other families may have a history of certain diseases or being stubborn and unteachable to receiving the truth of God's word. All of these things can have spiritual roots.

People reject what they don't understand, or misunderstand what they think you're going to say because they have preconceived ideas of what they believe. Their minds are closed to receiving more truth. They reject the thought that they or their loved ones could be under a curse because they can't reconcile a loving God that allows suffering to occur. This is where we need to get some additional clarity. A generational curse means it will affect future generations if people do not stop to take responsibility for their sin. It is NOT God enforcing the curse as though we are still under some Old Testament Law; it is the enemy enforcing the curse because he was granted legal grounds to do so and no one evicted him out of the family. It is the parent's job to protect their children by renouncing their sins, putting them under the blood of Jesus, and through prayer and obedience, provide a hedge of spiritual protection over their family. If the hedge has holes in it because the parents have failed to do their part, don't blame God. He has given us everything we need to live a life of righteousness but we must still do our part to put away sin and enforce the laws of His kingdom.

Jesus left **us** – His followers and disciples – ALL **authority** over earthly affairs. God gave us **dominion**. He gave us **power** to enforce the laws of His kingdom. He also gave **us** the power to use the **gifts** He gave us to heal the sick, cast out devils, restore sight to the blind, restore hearing to the deaf, make the lame walk and power to resurrect the dead. If we are not using what He gave us, then whose fault it is? The fault does not lie with God. It is with our understanding. **Even when the curse is deserved,** He left us the means to reverse the curse and live a victorious life. He left us the means to cut off the works of evil and do the works that Jesus did. It is not God's fault if people have rejected relationship with Him. It is not His fault if they reject knowledge or refuse to grow in understanding of His word. We cannot plead ignorance, for He has left us His word. It's our job to search out the matter and put the axe to the root so that every door is closed to the enemy.

When considering the variety of generational curses, cultural influences and false gods that could be involved, it becomes very important to understand a person's ancestry. How can you break a curse if you don't know it exists? That was my problem many years ago. I knew something was resisting my ability to receive God's blessings. It felt like such a fight to get every answer to prayer! I couldn't identify what the problem was until the Lord told me to renounce Voodoo. I had no idea that was in my ancestry! Familiar spirits run in families. They can pass down the bloodline from one generation to another, even in Christian families. Everyone has generational curses because everyone has sinned. The curse can be broken through Christ but we still need to do something intentional to rid ourselves of the demonic spirits that have been a part of our life before we accepted Christ.

Let me reiterate, they do not automatically leave us when we pray a prayer of salvation. 1 John 3:8 tells us that Jesus came to destroy the works of the devil, yet James 4:7 tells us to resist the devil. Well, which is it? It is both. Jesus accomplished it all, but we must still do our part to implement the victory that has been won. We must implement repentance by asking God to forgive the sin that was committed, even if we were not the one to open the door to it, then apply the blood of Jesus to those sins. Familiar spirits know us; they know our weaknesses, our areas of vulnerability and how to trigger emotional responses. They are always looking for ways to manifest, and that includes reproducing the sins that grant them legal grounds to remain in a person's life. Most often, those sins are committed first with the mouth and agreements are made. These mistakes with the mouth often lead to broken relationships, violation of God's commands, and transgressing

God's laws. That is how demons continue to manifest emotional wounds, illness, disease, relationship failure, addictions, self-sabotage behaviors, death, destruction, poverty and other things.

When people and their ancestors have worshipped other gods, they know those gods by a certain name. Those spirits have been invited in to assume to role of a god. That means they have been given authority and power to act and enforce the laws of the kingdom of darkness. The people who worship these various gods understand the attributes associated with certain gods and goddesses because they have become familiar spirits that operate in a particular family, or even a geographic region. These spirits will reinforce certain beliefs, customs and traditions in a family line, in an ethnic group or the population in a certain geographic region. Those spirits have found a place of cooperation and dominion often for many, many years and can be very resistant. Many times demons associated with pride, racism, rebellion and bitterness are deeply rooted in people due to their ethnicity. These 'spiritual agreements ' become a marriage of sorts that operates in the spirit realm.

When people sin, it is an open invitation for demonic spirits to feel welcomed into a person's life. The spirits that have been invited become servants in that family line, but what they offer always comes at a price. These spirits have been given authority and dominion in the lives of those they have inhabited. Therefore, it is necessary to let those spirits know that their power, authority and dominion has been revoked and they have been served an eviction notice. Be specific in making your intentions known. Generic prayers are not always effective.

If you were sick and went to a general practitioner, most of the time that would be sufficient. However, when the general practitioner cannot figure out what is wrong, they will refer a person to a specialist because they know a specialist will run additional diagnostic tests and be much more thorough. When dealing with spiritual matters, it pays to be thorough. You might not know what lurks in the secrets of your parents and grandparents. You have no way of knowing what great grandpa or great grandma did that could have opened a door to the enemy. While it is impossible to try to renounce every single sin, sometimes you do need a specially crafted prayer to identify the exact place where the enemy is hiding. Oh, how he loves to operate in the safety of secret places! He gloats thinking you will never find out what door he is using to gain access to you! There are definitely times when we all need a more comprehensive prayer to destroy the blind spots and remove the enemy. That is why the prayers in this book are written in such detail. Demons must be openly rebuked and told you are no longer in a contract or covenant agreement with them, because if you do not verbalize your intentions, they will not leave. That is why every prayer included in this book is intended to be spoken out loud. We are to exercise the spiritual authority that God gave us.

This brings me to the question many people have in regards to why they should renounce the sins of their ancestors, because they claim that it is not found in the New Testament. So let's review. The entirety of God's word is useful for teaching, because it shows the intent of scripture.

In various place in the Old Testament the spiritual leaders told the people God's laws then had them renounce the sins of their ancestors. Some examples are as follows:

"But if they will confess their iniquity and that of their fathers in the unfaithfulness that they practiced against Me, by which they have also walked in hostility toward Me—" Leviticus 26:40

"Those of Israelite descent separated themselves from all the foreigners, and they stood and confessed their sins and the iniquities of their fathers...." Nehemiah 9:2

There are many other scripture references: Lev. 5:5, 1 Kings 8:33, Ezra 10:1-11, Daniel 9:1-21, Nehemiah 1:6, 1 Kings 8:30, Hosea 5:15, Isaiah 58:9, Isaiah 65:24, Psalm 32:5, Psalm 51:2, and Psalm 145:18 to name a few. This theme of confession and repentance as well as renouncing the sins of a person's ancestors was consistent throughout many books of the Bible and many generations. It shows the intent of scripture. Are we to completely disregard it because it occurred in the Old Testament? Of course not. Do you allow Old Testament to teach and instruct you in other matters, or do you disregard it because it's Old Testament? No, we do not just cut out half of the Bible, that would be ridiculous! However, the teaching must come through the grid of the cross. The verbiage changes from Old Testament to New also. The word 'curse' is not necessarily used as much in the New Testament but the principles of confession and repentance in order to receive cleansing and atonement is consistent throughout scripture. Where there is no application of the atoning blood, there is no remission of sins. [5]

The Old Testament was about the authority of God and the covenant between God and His people, while the New Testament reveals more about another aspect of His nature. In the New Testament we discover more about

_____

[5] Ref. Hebrews 9:22

the Father's heart for His children, His grace and mercy, and His desire to heal and deliver. Yet, Father never changed His mind about obedience and He didn't wipe out the consequences of disobedience just because we are under grace. The blood of Jesus delivers us from eternal damnation as a consequence of sin but it's also not a license to live in disobedience. Some New Testament scriptures that discuss confession and repentance are the following:

"If we say that we have no sin, we are deceiving ourselves and the truth is not in us. If we confess our sins, He is faithful and righteous to forgive us our sins and to cleanse us from all unrighteousness. If we say that we have not sinned, we make Him a liar and His word is not in us." 1 John 1:8-9

"Whoever conceals their sins does not prosper, but the one who confesses and renounces them finds mercy." Proverbs 28:13.

"Therefore confess your sins to each other and pray for each other so that you may be healed. The prayer of a righteous man has great power to prevail." James 5:16

In the Old Testament the word frequently used was 'renounce.' The KJV Dictionary defines it like this:

RENOUNCE, v.t. renouns'. L. renuncio; re and nuncio, to declare, from the root of nomen, name.

1. To disown; to disclaim; to reject; as a title or claim; to refuse to own or acknowledge as belonging to; as, to renounce a title to land or a claim to reward; to renounce all pretensions to applause.

2. To deny; to cast off; to reject; to disclaim; as an obligation or duty; as, to renounce allegiance.

3. To cast off or reject, as a connection or possession; to forsake; as, to renounce the world and all its cares.We have renounced the hidden things of dishonesty. 2 Cor. 4.

RENOUNCE, v.i. renouns'. To declare a renunciation.

RENOUNCE, n. renouns'. The declining to follow suit, when it can be done. [6]

---

[6] KJV Dictionary, accessed Aug. 7, 2018, https://av1611.com/kjbp/kjv-

The person renouncing the sins of their fathers as well as their own sins was to completely, 100% no-holds-barred reject the sin that separated themselves from God. The use of this word implies that they were not to hold anything back from doing the right thing. It was also a way of reminding the younger generation of the laws of God so that they would learn to keep His commandments. Repentance was also a prerequisite from God before He would restore their blessings. Of course, many people are familiar with the verse in 2 Chronicles 7:14 which says,

"…if my people, who are called by my name, will humble themselves and pray and seek my face and turn from their wicked ways, then I will hear from heaven, and I will forgive their sin and will heal their land."

In the New Testament, John the Baptist showed up preaching repentance, instructing people to bear fruits worthy of repentance. He was telling them in every sense of the word to renounce their sin. Do you know why? John was preparing people's hearts to receive Jesus as their Savior. They needed to change the way they viewed their relationship with God. Up until that point, they only had the law, and the law was unforgiving. John's message declared that people should turn from their sin and demonstrate genuine change, and helping people receive cleansing from sin was part of his assignment. He also prepared hearts to receive someone even greater than himself – the long awaited Messiah - that would come and cleanse them with spiritual fire and power. John's ministry was a sign post pointing to the imminent arrival of Jesus Christ, the One whose sacrifice and power could cleanse them from all sin and grant them eternal life.

There are many people today that believe that after an initial salvation prayer, grace covers every sin and there is no need for confession or repentance. This is a dangerous deception because it gives people the impression that a person can live however they please without truly having a proper understanding of what it means to work out your own salvation with fear and trembling before the Lord. The Bible says the fear of the Lord is the beginning of wisdom. The word 'fear' means to have a healthy respect for a Holy God, and that includes not being full of pride. Hebrews 12:14 reminds us to pursue peace and holiness, for without holiness no one can see the Lord. Salvation is a process that we work out on a daily basis until the day we go home to be with the Lord. Repentance then, must precede 'seeing the Lord' because it allows us to reject pride and draw close to God in true communion with Him. Repentance is the requirement that precedes our restoration. A person cannot stay in sin and expect the blessings to flow. God

_____

dictionary/renounce.html

wants to bless His kids! His heart is full of love for us because He is our Father! Devils, on the other hand, will always try to tempt us so that they can ensnare us and inflict pain, suffering and keep us captive to a curse. A curse is a loss of blessings.

Are the blessings flowing in your life? Are you in good health? Are your finances blessed? Are your relationships blessed? Do you have peace and joy? God doesn't want us to be wishy-washy when it comes to making a commitment to turn away from sin. He knows the harm it will do to us. We must learn to stand our ground and not repeat the same habits, sins and mistakes of our ancestors. There are many people who would agree.

What person would willingly choose to become like their parents if, for example, those parents abused them? What person would willingly choose to become an alcoholic or drug addict? What person would choose poverty or a life marked by brokenness, instead of a life of wholeness, peace and joy? What person would choose to repeat the sins of their parents, if they knew it would bring them heartache, shame, broken relationships or rejection? What parent would want to inflict any of those things upon their children, or leave them vulnerable to demonic attachments assigned to reproduce those curses upon their children? In light of this knowledge, doesn't it make perfect sense to renounce the sins of your ancestors so that you can be free from the demonic attachments that are assigned to destroy the lives of you and your family members? I hope the answer is so clear in your mind that you embrace repentance, confession and prayer with all that is in you. We are to hate evil and cling to what is good. Repentance breaks old cycles. Do you want to break the cycle for you and your family?

The word renounce is also used in another portion of scripture.

"…but we have renounced the things hidden because of shame, not walking in craftiness or adulterating the word of God, but by the manifestation of truth commending ourselves to every man's conscience in the sight of God." 2 cor. 4:2

The act of asking God's forgiveness for those sins applies the blood of Jesus over ungodly covenants and contracts in the spirit realm so that the person can be forgiven and cleansed. This is the first step in breaking the cycle. However, it needs to be stated that true freedom and healing occur as a result of coming into submission to God. As we gain deeper and deeper revelations of truth, it has the capacity to set us free. It doesn't happen automatically, but as our identity in Christ is revealed and we walk into that truth, we begin to come into alignment with God and willingly submit to His authority for our lives. Then we can stand on the principle of James 4:6,7. **First we submit** to God, **then we resist** the enemy and he must obey us.

Jesus told His disciples that whatever was permitted on earth was permitted in heaven, and likewise, what was bound on earth had already been bound in heaven. This act of binding is to make something inactive, inoperable or unable to move. Loosing involves freeing someone from something that has been tied up or bound upon them. The way we bind or loose is through our words. What we speak either enforces the laws of God's kingdom or it allows the kingdom of darkness to operate. Death and life are in the power of the tongue.

Many of the prayers in this book have been written as a result of studying historical, geographical, religious and cultural influences, then incorporated into a very specific prayer. The prayers of renouncements help to loose people from demonic attachments that may be clinging to their lives and thus enforcing curses, but deliverance and healing involves a great deal more. Consider the prayers a **starting point** that makes room for deeper levels of healing and freedom. It is simply one tool to help remove some of the legal rights the enemy has been using to remain in a person's life. There are also other prayers that make room for Holy Spirit to go deeper in the healing process. We can command the fruit of generational sin (and other curses) to die, and then we speak blessing over the situation.

You might be wondering if this type of prayer is effective. The answer is yes! Let me share a brief story about one woman's experience. This woman is of Mexican and Mayan descent, and also a prophetic minister and missionary. The night before she was preparing to leave to the mission field, she was in her room praying through the prayers to renounce the gods and goddesses of Mexico. She was very surprised to report feeling a dark presence swiftly leave the room as she prayed through the prayer!

Even though a person may have prophetic knowledge and insight, this story is proof that people can have spirits attached to them of which they are unaware. We can all have blind spots and we can all use deeper levels of healing, revelations of the Father's heart towards us, and understanding of our true identity. There is so much God wants to bless us with in order to make us whole. Yet, if we fail to realize this is God's heart towards us then it leaves us vulnerable to the blind spots we cannot see and demonic attachments that may be operating in our life without us knowing it. Sometimes we don't realize there is a something different we should pray. These prayers are written to help cover a lot of ground that people might not ordinarily think to pray, and they can be quite effective.

CHAPTER THREE

ALTARS AND THRONES

"It will come about in that day," declares the LORD of hosts, "that I will cut off the names of the idols from the land, and they will no longer be remembered..." Zecharaiah 13:2

When constructing a home, the builder cannot use a faulty foundation. If the foundation is cracked, unlevel or unstable, it affects the whole structure. He must take up the old foundation piece by piece and remove the rubble before he can pour a new foundation. It is also like this in the spiritual realm. Prayers of repentance, renouncing our former way of living, along with false gods, certain customs and traditions forbidden by God helps remove the old foundation in people's lives. We are to abandon the things that God calls sin and follow the Lord Jesus Christ. This enables people to build a new life built upon Christ. We cannot build an altar to the Lord in our life until we remove old foundations and the wrong sort of altars. He becomes our hope for a better future, our peace, our strength and stability.

ALTARS AND THRONES

The Hebrew word for altar is mizbeah. It is defined as :

Altar: "an elevated place or structure, as a mound or platform, at which religious rites are performed or on which sacrifices are offered to gods, ancestors, etc." "Altars are places where the divine and human worlds interact. Altars are places of exchange, communication, and influence. God responds actively to altar activity." ... "Altars were markers of place, commemorating an encounter with God (Gen 12:7), or physical signs of habitation." Sacrifices provided a form of exchange at the altar. Although

God didn't need them, man did, because the sacrifices established by God in the Old Testament provided atonement for sin. "The act of sacrifice also acted as an announcement to the spirit realm, that through the action of sacrifice a contract between man and God had been sealed. The act of putting a sacrifice on the altar moved it from the profane to that which became sacred and accepted in the eyes of God." The spiritual laws connected to altars work the same way in the demonic realm, too. Whenever an agreement is made in the spirit, something good, godly, pure and right is sacrificed and an exchange takes place. Altars are a place where an announcement is made to the spiritual realm when a contract or covenant had been made with a particular spirit." [7]

Throne in the Greek is the word 'thronos', and is defined as:

1.   The chair or seat having a footstool, such as what was assigned to kings or royalty; to God, as the governor of the world;
2.   To the Messiah, the partner and assistant in the divine administration
3.   To judges, equivalent to tribunal or bench (a seat)
4.   To Satan
5.   of one who holds dominion or exercises authority; thus in plural of angels:.

Both altars and thrones are very important because they establish who or what is exalted as the dominant spiritual power in a particular place (or region). Where we place our loyalties, and the authority that we exalt (either Christ or Satan) determines what type of throne is established in our lives, in our churches and in our communities. People don't always stop to consider the need to intentionally destroy the wrong sort of altars. Those altars may only exist in the spiritual realm due to some covenant that has been made with the enemy, but just because we can't see them doesn't mean they don't exist.

Many people do not understand how certain things work in the spiritual realm. God has established spiritual laws that are always in effect. The Bible says in Amos 3:3, "Can two walk in agreement unless they are agreed? The spiritual law of agreement is what the enemy uses to establish a covenant with us. Whether it is done knowingly or unknowingly, once he has our cooperation he has legal grounds to enforce a curse. The spirit we have come into agreement with will manifest everything that demon represents. Exodus 20:24 is a scripture that represents another spiritual principle.

---

[7]" Altar", Baker's Evangelical Dictionary,
https://www.biblestudytools.com/dictionary/altar/, accessed Aug. 10, 2018

"An altar of earth you shall make for Me, and you shall sacrifice on it your burnt offerings and your peace offerings, your sheep and your oxen. In every place where I record My name I will come to you, and I will bless you."

This is the law of the altar. God told Moses to make an altar to Him, to offer sacrifices and offerings, and that would be a place where His name would be recorded. His promise of blessing came to those that built an altar to the Lord and worshipped Him according to His pattern. This spiritual law works the same way in the demonic realm, too. When someone gives the enemy a foothold through some sort of sin, they give devils legal grounds to enslave them or enforce some curse. Spirits are invited to remain in that person's life, and through either neglect (failing to resist the enemy and take authority over him) or through disobedience to one of God's laws, an altar is constructed in that person's life.

An altar is a place of contact where a covenant or agreement is made in the spirit realm. In the place where a specific name or spiritual entity is called upon, (i.e., invoked, declared, or given negative attention) that spirit is being treated hospitably, granting it dominion to be in the midst of that person's life; and, where these two have come to a mutual agreement, what has been agreed upon shall come to pass. That's a covenant. It's a legal contract with the enemy and he has every right to enforce it.

Mark 11:22-24, Matthew 21:22 and Prov. 18:21 are scriptures that remind us that when we place ourselves in agreement – either with faith or negativity – we are giving permission for the spirit realm to create what we say. Jesus said in Matthew 12:34-36 that out of the abundance of the heart the mouth speaks, whether we call forth evil things or good things. Whatever we have faith for will be done, but the principle of agreement works for the demonic realm, too. Every time we speak words laced with unbelief or negativity, we partner with the enemy and put him on the throne to reign and rule over our emotions, and create the circumstances we speak.

In an article entitled ***Prophecy: God is Raising up Temple Cleansers and Idol Smashers in This Hour***, Dawn Hill writes, "The Father is looking for those who are fearless and faithful, revolutionary reformers who will conquer the places surrendered to the devil. His heart is turned to those who will rend their hearts for His truth." [8] Sin has had its place on the altars of men's hearts long enough. It is time to tear down the thrones where spirits of darkness are glorified so that people can worship Jesus in purity.

---

[8] Hill, Dawn: Prophecy: God is Raising Up Temple Cleansers and Idol Smashers in this Hour, CharismaMagazine.com, accessed Feb. 22, 2018

Sometimes God allows people to feel frustrated, angry and disappointed for a while until they are ready to actually partner with God to defeat the enemy that's been robbing all their blessings. There is a story in the Bible in Judges chapter 6 about a man who was sick and tired of all his blessings being thieved away by the enemy. He was actually hiding out in the wine vats threshing wheat, but he finally asked the right question, "Why is this happening, and where are all the miracles we've heard about?" Gideon understood that there was a contradiction about the events happening in his life versus the stories he had heard about the miracles of God. What he was really asking was, "God, where are You in all this? How can we change what's happening to us?" While he was busy complaining about it, an angel showed up to answer his questions.

The first thing he was reminded about was God's faithfulness to His people. He was reminded of God delivering His people but the people had failed to honor God and stay faithful to Him. When the angel showed up to encourage the man named Gideon, the angel pointed out the root of the issue that had left the people vulnerable at the hands of their enemies. It was due to idolatry. The next thing that happened is that the angel encouraged Gideon by saying that he would deliver his nation by his obedience to destroy the altars of idolatry, to which Gideon essentially responded with the question, "Who, me?" Under protest, Gideon began to make excuses why he felt he was completely unsuitable and unfit for the task at hand. "Not me – I'm the smallest of my clan...the least in my father's house!" In other words, Gideon was saying, "You've got the wrong person – I'm a nobody!" He was asking the angel of the Lord, "Shouldn't you look for someone else?"

Gideon failed to see himself the way God saw him, as a mighty man of God, and his mind was full of unbelief that God would actually choose him for such an important assignment. Gideon was given instruction to tear down the idol of Baal that was on his father's land.

Now, that was not a small thing because people get very attached to their idols, but he did it by night so as not to be noticed. At the same time, Gideon built a proper altar to the Lord and offered his sacrifices on it. The altar that dishonored the Lord was torn down, and the proper altar was built – in the same 24 hours! When the men of the city woke up the next morning, they started asking questions and came to the conclusion that it was Gideon who had done all of this. They wanted him dead! Just about that time, the people realized that their enemies had gathered together in a nearby field and were preparing to ambush them yet again, to steal the blessings from their harvest. Suddenly, the Spirit of God came upon Gideon with boldness and caused such courage to rise up within him that the men of the city began to rally around him. They, too, had suffered defeat after defeat over the years. They were tired of it, but they were afraid it would happen again. They needed bold, courageous leadership and at the very moment they needed it, they found it in Gideon!

The angel of the Lord continued to inspire and encourage Gideon with signs that He was with Gideon and together they would win the victory. And so they did. The nation was delivered from idolatry and their obedience resulted in a very satisfying win against their enemies. Read the whole story in Judges 6 and 7.

Lance Wallnau makes an interesting point in an article titled, *"Alter the Altar and Break the Curse!"* Wallnau writes, "Once Gideon tore down the family stronghold and built an altar in its place, the older living generation got delivered and actually defended the son!" [9] So, while you may not have been the one to open the door to the thief, you can certainly be the one in your family that closes the door and allows the blessings to return to your family line.

"The reconstruction of life must begin at the point of its incipient overthrow. However tired the feet may be, and however painful the journey, men must retrace their steps along the sad way of their disobedience, until they stand at the point of their departure from the precepts of the Lord. They must confront the past with wide-open eyes, see every bit of its disloyalty and tragic failure; the erring of heart as well as of feet; its revolt against high heaven and dissonance with the spirit of goodness. Every bit of stable reconstruction either in personal or national life must go back and begin at the point of departure, it must build on the old foundation when every uncertain stone has been removed; so, and so only, can it hope to be secure." – G. Beesley Austin [10]

Another great portion of scripture that I won't go into now is the story of Elijah the prophet found in 1 Kings 18. Through this story we come to understand that idolatry and broken altars to the Lord resulted in agricultural loss, extreme drought, a lack of resources and extreme poverty. Where ever you find broken altars (or demonic altars), there is suffering and a loss of blessings. Broken altars are the source of a broken society, but repairing the

[9] Wallnau, Lance: Alter the Altar and Break the Curse, accessed Aug. 21, 2018, https://lancewallnau.com/alter-altar-break-curse/
[10] G. Beesley Austin, 1 Kings 18 Verse-by-Verse bible Commentary, Studylight.org, accessed Feb. 17, 2018, https://www.studylight.org/commentary/1-kings/18-30.html

altars becomes a strategy for healing our cities. Until we deal with the spiritually rooted issues that have affected the families that live in our cities we cannot change the culture. Every city is built upon the ancient ruins of another city or civilization. Those things are buried deep within the earth. Even in the United States, the whole western part of what is now the United States was once Mexico. So, many of those idolatrous practices from Mexico (and other nations) has defiled the land with the customs, traditions and religious practices that practice rebellion towards God. We cannot see the altars where human sacrifices or other agreements with dark powers were made, but the spirits connected to those idols and sins understand that they still have authority to reproduce the strongholds and curses in each generation. Remember, it takes obedience as well as the exercise of authority in order to evict the enemy.

Some might argue, what is all this emphasis on curses and witchcraft? Is it relevant to the modern church? Yes, it is. It is really only the Western church that fails to understand the significance of these matters because they have not chosen to understand the motivation and soul issues of those involved in it. People controlled by their fears slip into rebellion and witchcraft quite easily, because self is at the center of what motivates their actions. Everything is perceived as to what will make them feel better, restore their peace of mind or help them achieve a goal. If they want something, they are going to make it happen through their own self will, but actions apart from God is rebellion.. Witchcraft has at the root of it all, a fear of not being able to control certain people or events in the natural world, but once they partake of it they are even more afraid of displeasing their master for fear of punishment. Christianity has the answers to those fears that trouble their conscience *because* Jesus Christ has authority over every realm. Satan must bow to the name and authority of Jesus Christ! Many people have adopted an attitude of just trying to ignore the enemy but witchcraft doesn't just go away. The spirit realm is just as real as our natural realm, so we need to understand it. Other nations understand the supernatural realm far better because their world view includes the occult practices. They are quite familiar with it and often much more open about them. We will never defeat the presence of evil until we can understand the fears, insecurities and concerns of those that don't know God, because those are the things that drive people to partner with the occult realm. If churches and ministries will effectively address people's fears and help them get free from demonic entanglements, they will become healthy, life-giving organisms that continue to grow and have a kingdom influence.

The teaching and prophetic ministry is vital to empowering people with the knowledge of spiritual realities that can help them break free from demonic attachments and be set free in their heart and mind. A person that is not free will find it extremely difficult to fulfill their calling and destiny. A mind weighed down with negative thoughts becomes the enemy's playground. **We may not even realize that we are enthroning the enemy because it first takes place in our thought life.** Things such as fear, worry, insecurity, regret, doubt, pride, even vanity or our own ego can be 'enthroned' so that these wrong thought processes consume all our attention. Holding on to grudges, offense, shame, anger, infatuation, lust, rejection and self-hatred, self-pity – all these toxic emotions demand attention. Toxic emotions elicits worship from ourselves and others in the form of seeking attention, sympathy, and affirmation (a form of praise). All of these things are contrary to an abundant life in Christ. Yet, we undoubtedly make room for them to exalt themselves above the knowledge of God, even to the point where we enthrone the enemy in our mind and heart. We often don't realize that is what we are doing, and the enemy loves all the attention we give him. It becomes very important to recognize the origin of our thoughts. 'Renegade thoughts' must be cast down in obedience to Christ. When God takes His rightful place in our heart, He shifts us from a defeated, victim mentality to a victorious, "I-Can-Do-All-Things-In-Christ" winning attitude.

"For the weapons of our warfare are not carnal but mighty in God for pulling down strongholds, casting down arguments and every high thing that exalts itself against the knowledge of God, bringing every thought into captivity to the obedience of Christ, and being ready to punish all disobedience when your obedience is fulfilled." 2 Corinthians 10:4-6, NKJV

Ungodly actions build altars and thrones for the enemy that need to be torn down. These evil altars exist in the spirit realm until people take responsibility for them, tearing down thrones where satan has been worshipped and a new altar has been planted in its place. How do we do that? It starts with one family at a time recognizing their need for repentance and cleansing, then turning to worship Jesus Christ.

Now that we have established the importance of destroying ungodly altars, dethroning the enemy, repairing the altars of the Lord, and the matter of obedience, in the next chapter we will take a look at some long standing beliefs and traditions that affect the lives of many people.

CHAPTER FOUR

DANGEROUS DECEPTIONS

For what partnership can righteousness have with wickedness? Or what fellowship does light have with darkness?
2 Corinthians 6:14

This next section deals with doctrine and other dangerous deceptions, specifically concerning the teachings of the Catholic faith. The reason this is important is because there is a mixture of religious error, idolatry, witchcraft and the occult that is tied into Catholic practices. Catholicism is very prevalent in Mexican and native ancestry and many of the Catholic saints have been syncretized with other religious practices in other nations. These forbidden occult practices began with native tribes in various nations, but they didn't remain isolated to just a few nations. Today these practices affect those with ancestry from Mexico, Africa, Cuba, Puerto Rico, Haiti, Guatemala, Canada, the United States and many other nations. Many people do not realize that their ancestry is a very important factor in helping determine spiritually rooted issues and generational curses.

There have been many historical references that suggest there are irreconcilable differences between those of the Catholic faith and those who are Protestant. However, if we return to the truth as found in the word of God, it is possible for us to find that we can repair the great divide. It is not truth that divides us; it is man's interpretation of truth, false teaching and the man-made traditions of religion. Demonic spirits attached to idolatrous rituals and traditions have helped create misunderstanding and disunity. Those spirits have been in control a long, long time and they do not want to be sent away. They don't want people to side with the truth because then they would lose their hosts! When we stand with Christ for the truth we will find we are on the Lord's side. A person can become born again and Catholic; in fact, there are many people in the Catholic Church that have encountered a life changing relationship with Jesus Christ.

The Catholic Church believes in the Nicene Creed, which is a statement of beliefs widely accepted by the Christian Church. They also believe in the Holy Trinity and salvation by grace. These truths are in their official documents in the Catechism of the Catholic Church. The fact that there are people who have discovered an authentic relationship with Jesus Christ is proof. Many of the same foundational beliefs are shared by both Catholics and Protestants, however there are also some leaders that have clearly strayed from the truth. This has led to the teaching of a false, works based gospel, and though not all in the Catholic Church are guilty of it, it has definitely made room for confusion. The rest of this chapter is presented with the intention to help shed light on what is truth (as found in the whole counsel of scripture) and what has been taught in error. There has been a bitter division for hundreds of years over spiritual error. As fellow brothers and sisters in Christ, should we not labor to adhere to the truth of God's Word so that we can reform what has gone astray and come back to a place of love and unity?

Every church has a statement of official beliefs that define their doctrine. However, in the life of any true Christian, **scripture, not church doctrine, must be the ultimate authority in a believer's life**. It is God's Word, as the highest authoritative counsel of God Himself, that settles every debate and disagreement. There is no higher authority, and so we realize that it is not wisdom to defend church doctrine or religious traditions established by man if it is not supported by the truth of scripture.

There is a great deal of confusion due to the mixture of Christianity and the traditions of man that have been added to scripture, and then proclaimed as though they originated from God. Some use of scripture is accurate, but there are other portions that are clearly taken out of context and presented as truth when that was clearly not God's intention. People often accept the false teaching without question because it is mixed in with the truth, and they trust the person or the organization presenting it to them. You may wonder how you can discern between truth and error. Jesus said,

"My doctrine is not Mine, but His who sent Me. If anyone wills to do His will, he shall know concerning the doctrine, whether it is from God or whether I speak on My own authority."

Every person has a responsibility to search the Word of God for themselves. We should ask God to reveal the difference between truth and error. The world looks for credibility in religious institutions by the way the people generally define success: wealth, influence and longevity. While the Catholic Church has been around for thousands of years, that in itself has nothing to do with the way God defines credibility or success. Jesus was not wealthy and His ministry only lasted three years, but He was extremely successful. Not the way the world counts success; in fact, in the eyes of the world, it looked like the complete opposite. Jesus hanging on the cross, to many, looked like a life that ended in failure but the kingdom of God is one of opposites. Let us look with eyes of faith to see beyond the world's definition of a successful ministry. Let us look with eyes of the Spirit. Without the power and demonstration of the Holy Spirit, one cannot validate or have a credible message of the Cross of Jesus Christ. The message of the kingdom of God must be validated and made credible by the demonstration of God's power. Signs, wonders and miracles were always trademarks of Jesus' ministry because they validated His identity as the Son of God and the reality of God's kingdom. They still are.

If you or your family identify with the Catholic religion (even if it's in the past), there are some things you should be aware of connected to Catholic religious practices. And, while it is certainly not my intent to offend anyone, the need for teaching in order to clarify what is truth and what is error becomes necessary if people are to be set free from deceptive doctrines.

Some people just adopt the religion that's been in their family without any real sense of what they believe. Many assume that if they are a good person they will go to heaven. Others may think that if they were baptized as an infant they will go to heaven. These are erroneous assumptions. The Bible is very clear that unless we have a personal relationship with Jesus Christ we are not saved and our sins are not forgiven, therefore we cannot enter heaven. Each person has the personal responsibility of repentance and inviting Jesus to be their Lord and Savior. Where repentance has not occurred, there can be no genuine conversion to the faith. We must turn away from our old ways and turn to Jesus for the forgiveness of sins. Some people try to adhere to the traditions of religion without a personal relationship with Jesus Christ. Religion in itself is impersonal and superficial, and following religious traditions cannot save one's soul. Some people have only had a relationship with the traditions and practices of Catholicism but no life-saving connection with Jesus. They have not yet experienced a revelation of their heavenly Father's love, nor have they gained an understanding of their identity in Christ. They live outside of the Christian life as an outsider looking in, rather than participating in the rich fellowship available to them through a life-changing connection with our Creator and Father. God did not create us to have a relationship with religion. His purpose is to have sons and daughters that have relationship with Him. The following are some characteristics of an authentic relationship with Christ.

AUTHENTIC RELATIONSHIPS WITH CHRIST

1.   You have a deeply important, life giving relationship with the person of Jesus Christ.
2.   In an authentic relationship, you learn to trust God and worry less.
3.   You develop a love for the Word of God, because it is synonymous with Jesus Christ.
4.   You have a relationship through prayer.
5.   You learn of God's ways through experience, and thus gain a better understanding of His heart.
6.   You love what God loves and hate sin.
7.   God's desires become your desires.
8.   You consistently desire to yield to the Holy Spirit.
9.   You become transparent with God and others.
10. Truth is a trademark of your life and relationships.

One cannot have a relationship with Jesus without reading the Word of God because Jesus is the Word of God. God the Father is an invisible Spirit, who can be known through His acts of creation. Jesus the Son, who has always been with the Father, took a different form after creation, but He is referred to as the logos (word). The word logos is from the ancient Greek. "Λόγος is from the root λεγ, appearing in λεγω, the primitive meaning of which is to lay: then, to pick out, gather, pick up: hence to gather or put words together, and so, to speak. Hence λόγος is, first of all, a collecting or collection both of things in the mind, and of words by which they are expressed." Before Jesus came to earth to be born as a child, He also existed as a voice that helped create everything that exists. When God set about 'creating' the world in the Book of Genesis, the Son understood His Father's desires.

The Father's collection of thoughts and intent towards all He wanted to create became spoken words – and those words are filled with His power. The very words of God are just as much God as He is; it's His voice. The Father spoke and Jesus, taking the form of God's spoken Word, partnered with Holy Spirit to create what God had in mind.

The written word is also God's Word; His voice to us. John 1:3 tells us that everything that was created was done through God's spoken word. That is why Jesus is known as the Word of God. He is a person just as real as you or I. We cannot see Him, but we can know Him through the expression of His Word, and we can understand Him because of His Holy Spirit that comes to live within us. Holy Spirit helps us understand not just the word, but the intent of scripture. In the Bible, Jesus is synonymous with the Word because He is the voice of God that we hear.

We cannot know Jesus unless we study His word, because that is where He reveals Himself! Many people feel they can have a relationship with Jesus without interacting with Him personally, but that is not the case. What type of relationship could you have with your mother, or father, husband, wife, sister or brother if you did not have conversation with them? How strong would your relationship be if you rarely saw one another or spent any time together? Jesus is a person and loves to spend time with us. He wants us to know Him and enjoy spending time with Him!

A very religious person may confuse a sense of loving religious observances with having a relationship with Christ. The definition of religious piety is "a belief or point of view that is accepted with unthinking conventional reverence." It is the quality of being reverent to religious devotion, but the adherence to religious observances has no ability to cleanse a person from their sin. Unless the blood of Jesus atones for a person's sin, they cannot enter God's presence. Adhering to family customs or even religious practices without a true connection to God is simply going through the motions. It doesn't satisfy the longing of the human heart to connect with God, and it doesn't satisfy God's desire to be known by His creation. He wants relationship! Relationship between God and man is so important to Him that He gave His Son as payment for our redemption. Religion in itself cannot save anyone. Only the blood of Jesus Christ can impute righteousness and wash away our sin. In John 3:3 Jesus said,

"I tell you the truth, no one can see the kingdom of God unless he is born again."

Becoming 'born again' is a necessary requirement to salvation, but Jesus said that it was important to also have a relationship with His Holy Spirit, because it is Holy Spirit that renews us.

"He came to save us. It's not that we earned it by doing good works or righteous deeds; He came because He is merciful. He brought us out of our old ways of living to a new beginning through the washing of regeneration; and He made us completely new through the Holy Spirit..."

We must each endeavor to restore Christian beliefs and practices back towards Christ's original intention. That intention is found in scripture. It is placing our faith and trust in Jesus Christ, and laboring together to honor His truth. This isn't about what I believe or what you believe, or our differences in opinion but about what God has stated in His Word and the truth that Christ died for. Catholicism is a mixture of Christianity, religious works, idolatry and witchcraft. I understand that is a strong statement, but please keep reading and looking for the truth. Scripture teaches us that God gave us the ten commandments in which He commanded us to have no others gods before us. We are to worship only Him. Many of the doctrinal beliefs stated in the Catechism of the Catholic Church seem to agree with many Protestant Christian beliefs, however, there are other practices that compromise the validity of God's Word.

"I am the Lord your God, who brought you out of the land of Egypt, out of the house of slavery. You shall have no other gods before me. You shall not make for yourself a carved image, or any likeness of anything that is in heaven above, or that is in the earth beneath, or that is in the water under the earth. You shall not bow down to them or serve them, for I the Lord your God am a jealous God…"

Where there is mixture, a perverse spirit also comes to twist truth. It is the spirit behind false doctrine. There are also some very dark occult practices that are connected to the Catholic Church. Santeria and Lukemi are parallel religions hidden within the Catholic Church. They exist simultaneously, side by side. Some of the following excerpts are taken from my books, Healing the Heart of a Nation as well as Seduced into Shame.

The Catholic church does not openly admit to any association with Santeria, Lukumi and its sister religions; however, many of those who do practice these things consider themselves to be members of the Catholic church. Demons don't differentiate between whether a person identifies with Santeria, Lukumi or Catholicism. They simply look for whether or not someone has granted them legal grounds to access their life. Forbidden practices such as praying to anyone other than our heavenly Father through His Son Jesus Christ grants the enemy legal grounds to enforce a curse or inflict some sort of sickness, poverty or loss. The reason this is wrong is because ONLY Jesus Christ gave His life to be a mediator between God and man. Only Christ shed His sinless blood to redeem mankind from their sin. He is the only one who has a legitimate right to be the door to our Father. Jesus said that all those who attempted to go through a different door were considered a thief and a robber. [11]

Santeria and Lukumi are forms of voodoo that merge the spiritual practices of people from Cuba, Puerto Rico, the Dominican Republic (who were also Roman Catholics), Haiti and tribes from West Africa. Centuries ago, slave traders sold captured members of the Yoruba tribe to the Spaniards as slaves. The slave owners baptized the slaves into Catholicism as a forced

---

[11] Ref. John 10:1

religious conversion. "As a result of the fusion of Francophone culture and Voodoo in Louisiana, Creole African Americans associated many Voodoo spirits with the Christian saints known to preside over the same domain. Although some dominate leaders of each tradition believe Voodoo and Catholic practices are in conflict, in popular culture both saints and spirits are believed to act as mediators, with the Catholic priest or Voodoo Legba presiding over specific respective activities. Early followers of Voodoo in the United States adopted the image of the Catholic saints to represent their spirits.[12] "Other Catholic practices adopted into Louisiana Voodoo include reciting the Hail Mary and the Lord's Prayer."[13]

In earlier times when nations were being settled, missionaries were not necessarily evangelizing and leading people to Christ by sharing the gospel. The emphasis was more about bringing people, by force if necessary, into the culture of the church. In many cases it was not an authentic conversion to the faith so the culture that was actually being created was done so through resistance and rebellion. Forcing the will of one upon another without their permission is the essence of witchcraft, and it just bred more of it. Since the slaves could not worship their own gods openly, they pretended to be devoted to the Catholic saints, but they were actually worshiping their own gods. This led to parallel religions that exist side by side, hidden within the Catholic religion. Santeria is a Spanish word but originates in Cuba. It is estimated that somewhere between 75-100 million people are a part of this growing religion.

Everything in Satan's kingdom is a counterfeit of the kingdom of God. Santeria and Lukumi have many rituals and ceremonies that are held in a house temple, or what is called a 'House of Saints.' The meetings are conducted by Priests or Priestesses. There is a display of 'thrones' that represents the kings, queens and deified warriors who are invoked for guidance and blessing. The 'disciples' of Santeria are given prayer beads as a sacred point of contact with the spirits called upon in these witchcraft ceremonies. After many rituals are performed, the person is 'born again' into the faith. Not the faith of God, mind you, but of the occult. In many of these traditions, parents bring their children before an occult priest or priestess for initiation into the occult.

"The slaves simply renamed their gods using the saints' names and

[12] Jacobs, Claude F. & Andrew J. Kaslow (2001). The Spiritual Churches of New Orleans: Origins, Beliefs, and Rituals of an African-American Religion. University of Tennessee Press.
Nickell, Joe (2006). "Voodoo in New Orleans". The Skeptical Inquirer.[13]

continued with their old worship. The blending of these two religions became known as Voodoo in Haiti and the islands to the South and as Santería in Cuba and the islands to the North of Haiti."[14] Those that practice this religion identify as sons and daughters of their 'supreme being' known as Olodumare. They have a 'trinity' in their godhead also, but they are all demonic spirits in one form or another. The same false gods of Santeria and the Yoruba religions are known by various names of the Catholic saints. Listed below are the dual identities by which these pagan saints are known. [15]

Yemaya/Mary, Star of the Sea.

Yemaya is the African Mother Goddess. She rules over the oceans, the moon, women and children, fishermen and sailors, witches, and secrets. The belief is that all life comes from Yemaya the sea. She is associated with the Virgin Mary in two of her aspects: Our Lady of Rule and Mary, Star of the Sea. Mary is known and worshipped under many titles and is the corresponding saint for a number of African gods.

Obatala/Our Lady of Mercy

Obatala is another aspect of the pagan "Divine Trinity." Like Yemaya, he is associated with the Virgin Mary, this time in the aspect of Mercy. As the first-born of the gods, Obatala is regal and wise. He blows away negative energies and resolves ethical issues. As Yemaya is the patron of mothers, Obatala is the patron of fathers.

Chango/Saint Barbara

Chango is the third member of the pagan trinity. He is the god of transformations, the god of thunder and lightning. Chango is invoked when a person seeks revenge on his enemies, and Saint Barbara is patron of wrongful death. Lightning is a potent symbol for both the Catholic saint and the Santería god, and both Chango and Saint Barbara are prayed to for protection in storms.

Eleggua/Saint Anthony

---

[14] Gardener, Cult of the Saints: An Introduction to Santeria; The Llewellyn Journal.
[15] Gardener, Cult of the Saints: An Introduction to Santeria; The Llewellyn Journal.

Eleggua is known as Legba in the Haitian faith, and sometimes as Eshu. As patron of doorways, Eleggua's place in the home is by the door to protect the home from any negativity. Saint Anthony is also known to be a finder of lost things and a worker of miracles.

Osain/Saint Joseph

Osain is the god of the forest. He is the patron of all healers and herbalists. Some people bury statues of Saint Joseph on their properties to "leave a blessing" for the next occupant or property owner. (Obviously, this can leave a curse instead of a blessing).

Oshun/Our Lady of la Caridad del Cobre (Our Lady of Charity)

Oshun is another goddess worshipped under the umbrella of the Virgin Mary—in this instance, Our Lady of la Caridad del Cobre, patroness of Cuba. As the love goddess, Oshun rules pleasure and sexuality, marriage and the arts, but she also oversees all money matters.

Oggun/Saint Peter

As the god of war, Oggun is belligerent and combative, and the patron of human effort. Saint Peter is petitioned for success and employment.

There are many more 'saints' that are used in Catholic prayers as well. Please let me be clear that my intention is not about bad mouthing the Catholic Church or those that belong to the Catholic faith. It's about exposing spiritual practices that bring defilement and invite a demonic presence in people's lives. Idolatry could exist in a family for generations yet God continues to look for those that are hungry for truth and willing to carve out a new future for themselves. The pursuit of truth and holiness will return a people that have been lost to an authentic relationship with the living God; it will begin to heal their family's destiny. "Though generations in one's family may have chosen another god, all it takes is one to change the course of history." – Dawn Hill, Charisma Magazine [16]

---

[16] Hill, Dawn: "Prophecy: God is Raising Up Temple Cleansers and Idol Smashers in This Hour", Charisma Magazine.com, accessed Feb. 22, 2018, https://charismamag.com/blogs/prophetic-insight/35914-prophecy-god-is-raising-up-temple-cleansers-and-idol-smashers-in-this-hour

WHAT ABOUT MARY?

There is no doubt that Mary, the mother of Jesus, has a special place in heaven. When I think about Mary, I often reflect on what it was about her life that caught heaven's attention. The Heavenly Father hand-picked this lovely girl out from all the other young women of her day to be the mother of God's own Son. Obviously there was something that stood out to the Father about Mary's heart that qualified her to become the unsuspecting recipient of a miracle so astounding that it would never, ever be repeated.

I think how proud Mary was, and still is, of her beloved Son. I think Mary would say, "Don't put me on a pedestal, honor my Son. Think of all He did for you. He bore your sins on the cross. He deserves the glory. Pray to Jesus." What mother wouldn't want to direct the attention to her son instead of herself? Mary would defer to Jesus. She would not want people idolizing her and taking glory away from her Son.

Mary did not think of herself as someone worthy of being worshipped. Mary was a sinner just like everyone else, in need of a Savior like everyone else. The Catholic Church holds the viewpoint that Mary was preserved free from all stain of original sin, she kept her virginity, (even though she went on to birth other children), and when her earthly life was completed she was taken to heaven and exalted by the Lord as "Queen" over all things. The Catholic Church also teaches that through her prayers she has been granted power to deliver others from death, and is known as the Mother of the Church. This statement summarizes what is stated under the Vatican archives of the Catechism of the Catholic Church, paragraph 6, section 966. [17] The problem is, this is another viewpoint that usurps glory from God and does not agree with scripture. The Catholic Church, in the Catechism of the Catholic Church, goes on to say that Mary is invoked through the names of "Helper and Advocate" – names God has assigned to the Holy Spirit. To invoke means "to call on (a deity or spirit) in prayer, as a witness, or for inspiration."

"Queen of Heaven was a title given to a number of ancient sky goddesses worshipped throughout the ancient Mediterranean and Near East during ancient times. Goddesses known to have been referred to by the title include Inanna, Anat, Isis, Astarte, Hera, and possibly Asherah (by the

---

[17] Paragraph 6: Mary – Mother of the Church, taken from the Catechism of the Catholic Church, section 966, footnote 507:Byzantine Liturgy, Troparion, Feast of the Dormition, August 15th.
http://www.vatican.va/archive/ENG0015/__P2C.HTM accessed Feb. 22, 2018.

prophet Jeremiah). In Greco-Roman times Hera, and her Roman aspect Juno bore this title. Forms and content of worship varied. In modern times, the title "Queen of Heaven" is still used by contemporary pagans to refer to the Great Goddess, while Catholics, Orthodox, and some Anglican Christians now apply the ancient title to Mary, the mother of Jesus."[18]   The phrase "Queen of Heaven" has always been associated with ancient goddesses and idolatrous worship. Many variations of Mary's name are also associated with demonic water spirits and take on the appearance of either half human/half fish (or serpent), or the mermaid/merman. Ancient native tribes both in Mexico as well as Africa have a variety of names for water spirits. In Africa, for instance, a water spirit may be known as Mami Wata, River Goddess or River Maiden, but in the Yoruba and Africo-Cuban religions they have syncretized their water spirits with Our Lady of Regla as well as Mary, Star of the Sea and other names associated with the Virgin Mary.[19] This is a practice that took place during the era of African slave trade and allowed those religious practices to reproduce in America and many other nations.   In fact, in many areas of Mexico the mixture of Mayan traditions, Catholic idols and statues of Mary, and occult rituals are practiced even today with the use of a shaman. There is no evidence of Christianity, just the mixture of various pagan practices.

I do encourage anyone with questions to study the CCC for yourself, as well as some of the other details I have included. Compare it against scripture. Look into the Word of God and examine the context of particular scriptures that are used to support the beliefs of Catholicism. Then you can see for yourself what is true. The CCC can be found online.

Mary was definitely chosen by God to play a significant role in history but Mary took on the role of a humble servant. She never sought praise or adoration from others. And Mary said:

"My soul magnifies the Lord,
And my spirit has rejoiced in God my Savior.
For He has regarded the lowly state of His maidservant;
For behold, henceforth all generations will call me blessed." [20]

---

[18] "Queen of Heaven: Antiquity", Wikipedia.com accessed Feb. 24, 2018, https://en.wikipedia.org/wiki/Queen_of_heaven_(antiquity)
[19] "Yemoja," https://en.wikipedia.org/wiki/Yemoja, accessed August 3, 2018
[20] Luke 1:46-48, NKJV, Bible Gateway.com, accessed Feb. 19, 2018, Scripture taken from the New King James Version®. Copyright © 1982 by Thomas Nelson. Used by permission. All rights reserved.

Paul Tautges, in his article, "Was Jesus His Mother's Savior?" writes the following:

FOUR QUALITIES OF MARY'S SAVIOR

"Jesus is a glorious Savior – My soul magnifies the Lord. With these words, Mary lifted God up by lifting up her voice in praise. She did as Psalm 99:5 commands, Exalt the Lord our God; worship at his footstool! Holy is he! Jesus will one day receive worship from people from every tribe, tongue, and nation (Revelation 5:9).

He is a divine Savior – my spirit exalts the Lord; God my Savior. Mary recognized that her Savior not only had been provided by God, but He was God. Gabriel said the child would be "the Son of the Highest" (Luke 1:32), that is, son of the Most High God, i.e. God (see also 1:35). Jesus is the eternal Word made flesh to dwell among us, the glory of the Father (John 1:14).

He is a personal Savior – my Savior. Though she was a humble servant and a God-fearing woman, Mary was a sinner in need of redemption. Mary was not holy and sinless, as the Roman Catholic Church teaches. Instead, according to the Bible, Mary recognized the Lord as her Redeemer because she knew in her heart that she was a sinner. Yes, Gabriel told Mary to rejoice "highly favored one" (1:21), but that draws attention to the grace of God in choosing her, not to any inherent grace. Mary was a sinner in need of God's saving grace. The Scriptures always speak of salvation as being personal, i.e. for the individual person (see John 3:16-18, 36).

He is a gracious Savior – He has regard for the humble state of His bond slave. Jesus is the Savior who voluntarily lowered Himself to the level of man in order to redeem him. Mary recognized this about God, and she acknowledged that it was purely of His grace that she was chosen for this purpose. It is not unlike God to choose those whom man would never choose. The apostle Paul—who himself was an unimpressive man in the flesh—was chosen by God to be the apostle to the Gentiles. Though he was not easy to look at, and lacked public speaking skill, he was used by God to bring to us 13 books of the New Testament. He explains the reason God prefers to choose lowly people is so that "no man may boast before God" (1 Corinthians 1:26-29).

Because of the record of Scripture, Mary knew that all future generations would recognize the happy, fortunate state she found herself in. To be chosen to give birth to the promised Messiah was a privilege any Hebrew maiden would cherish. However, Mary does not even hint that she somehow deserves any praise or worship. She knew that God alone is to be praised (Ps 148:13)."[21]

The mixture of Catholicism, praying to Mary or other saints, and the parallel religions of Santeria and Lukemi hidden within the Catholic Church involves a great deal of false teaching and Voodoo practices that are also connected to the perverse spirit and lust. These spirits are responsible for sexual sins and sexual demons that oppress and harass their victims. Santeria and Lukumi are occult practices that involves invoking spirits by calling on the names of these pagan "saints." Prayer candles and statues of Mary or other saints are a common practice in constructing altars to summon these spirits. These 'agreements' with demonic spirits form covenants and contracts in the spirit realm that give the enemy legal rights to be in a person's life. These ungodly altars must be destroyed so that people can build an altar to the Lord in their life that is pleasing to Him. We cannot worship God on the same altars where spirits of darkness are worshipped.

Catholics do admit they pray to various saints. Many of these saints were real people who attained sainthood status after they died. However, it doesn't matter how good a person was; nowhere in scripture are we advised to pray to other people, living or dead, or to make our petitions to them. One explanation is that Catholics ask the saints to take their 'intentions' to Christ and pray with them that their prayers might be heard. The thought behind it is that the saints in heaven are closer to God than those here on earth. Again, this religious tradition redirects people away from God and directs them to enlist the aid of other spirits. Not only is this idolatry, it's also unbelief to think that prayers are disregarded simply because of proximity, or the thought that God won't hear a person's sincere prayer. Scripture says that whatever is not of faith is sin. God cannot answer prayer if the person is bound by idolatry, unbelief or doublemindedness. There are some valid reasons in scripture why prayers are not heard. This is not an exhaustive list, but these are some for your consideration.

- Willful blindness and rejecting truth. Jeremiah 14:10, Prov. 1:24-25, Prov. 28:9, Zech. 7:11-13
- Sin. Isaiah 59:2, Ps. 66:18, John 9:31
- Doublemindedness. James 1:6-7
- Unbelief. Romans 14:23
- Guilty of bloodshed. Isaiah 1:15, Is. 59:3

---

[21] Tautges, Paul: "Was Jesus His Mother's Savior?", Dec. 1, 2015, Counseling One Another, accessed Feb. 19, 2018, http://counselingoneanother.com/2015/12/01/was-jesus-his-mothers-savior/

- Pride, Job 35:11-13
- Unforgiveness, Matt. 6:14-15, Matt. 18:21-35

Scripture tells us to pray to our heavenly Father in Jesus name. When our hearts do not condemn us, we can come boldly to our Father and pray with confidence that our prayers are heard, according to 1 John 3:21,22. It is obedience to God's Word – the entirety of God's Word – that opens the door to answered prayer and confidence towards God.

Perhaps those who are in heaven do pray for us. Romans 8:34 tells us that Jesus is at the right hand of the Father interceding for His people. It is not a stretch of the imagination to think that those in heaven would be praying for those on earth; however, in God's Word we are never told to pray for people who have passed, or to the saints, and we are never advised to ask the saints that have passed on to the spiritual realm to pray for us. Even though Catholics may attempt to justify their reasons by saying they are not asking for the saints to intervene for them, the practice suggests otherwise and invokes demonic spirits. We are to pray to the Father through His Son, Jesus Christ.

Jesus said, "In this manner, therefore, pray:

> Our Father in heaven,
> Hallowed be Your name.
> Your kingdom come.
> Your will be done
> On earth as it is in heaven.
> Give us this day our daily bread.
> And forgive us our debts,
> As we forgive our debtors.
> And do not lead us into temptation,
> But deliver us from the evil one.
> For Yours is the kingdom and the power and the glory forever. Amen."

Jesus himself told His disciples how to pray in the Lord's prayer. There is only one mediator between God and man, and that is Jesus Christ.

"For there is one God, and there is one mediator between God and men, the man Christ Jesus."

For those that may not know scripture, the Catholic explanation may seem quite believable. The use of scripture to justify religious traditions implies that many of the Catholic traditions are acceptable practices. It is suggested that it is no different than asking our Christian friends and loved ones here on earth to intercede for us, and that those that have passed on offer prayers and incense to God on our behalf. However, this is an improper use of scripture. Consulting with the dead has always been associated with sorcery, conjuring and divination in scripture. Let me reiterate that nowhere in scripture are we instructed to pray this way. Furthermore, scripture advises us to 'test the spirits' in 1 John 4:1, to see whether they are from God, because many false prophets have gone out into the world. In John 14:13-14, Jesus said:

"And whatever you ask in My name, that I will do, that the Father may be glorified in the Son. If you ask anything in My name, I will do it."

"But because Jesus lives forever, He has a permanent priesthood. Therefore He is able to save completely those who draw near to God through Him, since He always lives to intercede for them. Such a high priest truly befits us—One who is holy, innocent, undefiled, set apart from sinners, and exalted above the heavens...." Hebrews 7:24-26

Additional scriptures on praying in Jesus name are: John 16:24, John 15:16, John 15:7, Col. 3:17, 1 Cor. 1:2, John 14:6, Jer. 33:3, Phil. 4:6, 2 Tim. 4:3-4, Acts 4:12. There are NO scriptures that indicate we should ever call on anyone else's name or petition those who have passed away for assistance, even to pray with us or for us. This is idolatry and forbidden by God.

Now that we have settled the issue of what name to pray in as confirmed through scripture, let us return to the subject of the mixture of religious practices. African and Cuban cultures hid their true worship behind the faces of the Catholic saints, but even those that do not necessarily practice Santeria or Lukemi are committing the same sins if they pray to various saints. When praying to any other name instead of Jesus, the face of that 'saint', idol or deity is a demonic spirit. Regardless of a person's intention, even if it is innocent because they simply did not know any better, demons understand spiritual laws. If people participate with forbidden acts and idolatrous practices, demons will gladly impersonate whatever person, saint or idol someone is praying to; all demons are liars and deceivers. They know when they have been granted legal grounds.

Earlier in the chapter I mentioned the need for discernment, and to 'test the spirits.' The problem with these practices and traditions is that Catholicism teaches a different message that includes religious witchcraft. Yes, the church's official teaching on salvation lines up with truth, but many of the other accepted practices do not and the result is a perverse mixture that does not honor the Lord Jesus. The Bible says 'what does light have to do with darkness?'

"It's clear that our flesh entices us into practicing some of its most heinous acts: participating in corrupt sexual relationships, impurity, unbridled lust, idolatry, witchcraft, hatred, arguing, jealousy, anger, selfishness, contentiousness, division, envy of others' good fortune, drunkenness, drunken revelry, and other shameful vices that plague humankind. I told you this clearly before, and I only tell you again so there is no room for confusion: those who give in to these ways will not inherit the kingdom of God." Gal. 5:19 The Voice Translation

"What agreement can exist between the temple of God and idols? For we are the temple of the living God. As God has said: "I will live with them and walk among them, and I will be their God, and they will be My people. Therefore come out from among them and be separate, says the Lord. Touch no unclean thing, and I will receive you. And: "I will be a Father to you, and you will be My sons and daughters, says the Lord Almighty." 2 Cor. 6:16-18 Berean Study Bible

Many people are unaware of the fact that the doctrines of the Catholic church are compromised. Due to the longstanding existence of the Catholic church, many things have been accepted without question, but God does not want His people destroyed for lack of knowledge. The mixture of forbidden practices such as praying to the saints, praying ritualistic prayers, or looking for absolution through a priest are not Biblical. The Catholic Church teaches that Christ's ministers act "in His person" or as a representation of Jesus ministering to others. This much is true; all of God's servants are to do the works of ministry. Jesus gave His followers the mandate of ministering to others in Matthew 10:8.

"Heal the sick, bring the dead back to life, heal those who suffer from dreaded skin diseases, and drive out demons. You have received without paying, so give without being paid." Matt. 10:8 Good News Translation

However, this does not extend to the matter of a priest absolving others of their sins. This is proven by the scripture in Luke 5:17-26:

"Now on one of those days, while he was teaching, there were Pharisees and teachers of the law sitting nearby (who had come from every village of Galilee and Judea and from Jerusalem), and the power of the Lord was with him to heal. Just then some men showed up, carrying a paralyzed man on a stretcher. They were trying to bring him in and place him before Jesus. But since they found no way to carry him in because of the crowd, they went up on the roof and let him down on the stretcher through the roof tiles right in front of Jesus. When Jesus saw their faith he said, "Friend, your sins are forgiven." Then the experts in the law and the Pharisees began to think to themselves, "Who is this man who is uttering blasphemies? Who can forgive sins but God alone?" When Jesus perceived their hostile thoughts, he said to them, "Why are you raising objections within yourselves? Which is easier, to say, 'Your sins are forgiven,' or to say, 'Stand up and walk'? But so that you may know that the Son of Man has authority on earth to forgive sins" – he said to the paralyzed man – "I tell you, stand up, take your stretcher and go home." Immediately he stood up before them, picked up the stretcher he had been lying on, and went home, glorifying God. Then astonishment seized them all, and they glorified God. They were filled with awe, saying, "We have seen incredible things today." Luke 5:17-26 NET

Matthew Henry's Commentary on John 20:22,23 has this to say: "...Christ directed the apostles to declare the only method by which sin would be forgiven. This power did not exist at all in the apostles as a power to give judgment, but only as a power to declare the character of those whom God would accept or reject in the day of judgment. They have clearly laid down the marks whereby a child of God may be discerned and be distinguished from a false professor; and according to what they have declared shall every case be decided in the day of judgment." The power to forgive sin was not granted to the original apostles in a universal sense; meaning, it was not a blanket of authority to be applied to every situation regardless of circumstances; neither is it granted to priests today.

Let me further clarify. If you commit a sin against me, I can forgive you and your debt is cancelled. But, if you commit a sin against another person or against God, I am in no place to forgive those sins. I have no authority or power to do so. Only God can do that. In John 20:23 when Jesus said, "If you forgive the sins of any they are forgiven, but if you retain the sins of any, they are not forgiven," I believe what He was really saying is that if we forgive someone, the sin is forgiven; it's wiped off the books. But, if we choose not to forgive someone's sin, who retains it? We do. We hold on to the offense, the anger, bitterness and mental torment that comes with the refusal to forgive. Not only that, but our refusal to forgive someone else stays with us as a judgment against us, according to Matthew 7:1. "Judge not lest we be judged." The judgment by which we judge others (or the failure to show mercy) is retained against us, and then becomes a measuring rod by which we must then be judged. James 2:13 declares that judgment without mercy will be shown to anyone that has withheld mercy from others. In Matthew 6:14-15 Jesus stated that if we forgive others for their trespasses then we are forgiven, but if we do not, then neither can our Father in heaven forgive us of our sins. Forgiveness is a two-way street. If we want to be forgiven, then we must extend forgiveness to others. Freely we have received from God; freely we must release that same grace. The person that did wrong is responsible to seek forgiveness from God, but the act of forgiving is for us so that we are not imprisoned by bitterness and torment. It restores us to right relationship with God. Cleansing from sin can only be through confession of sin with a sincere heart, and it's the blood of Christ that offers atonement. Jesus, not a priest and not even the pope can forgive sin because Christ is the One who gave His life in exchange for our sins.

"If we confess our sins, He is faithful and just to forgive us our sins and to cleanse us from all unrighteousness." 1 John 1:9 Berean Study Bible

PAPAL INFALLIBILITY

Much of this subject matter does not have a simple answer. As I stated earlier in this chapter, it is my goal to help reform some of the incorrect assumptions and teaching that could lead people astray from biblical truth. Please, don't take my word for it. Do your own research. Ask Holy Spirit to show you anything contrary to the way He intended scripture to be understood.

Another position held by the Roman Catholic Church that should be questioned is the subject of papal infallibility. The definition of infallible, as defined by Miriam Webster Dictionary is:

Infallible:

1. Incapable of erring, unerring
2. Not liable to mislead, deceive or disappoint
3. Incapable of error in defining doctrines touching faith or morals.

"Papal infallibility, in Roman Catholic theology, is the doctrine that the pope, acting as supreme teacher and under certain conditions, cannot err when he teaches in matters of faith or morals. As an element of the broader understanding of the infallibility of the church, this doctrine is based on the belief that the church has been entrusted with the teaching mission of Jesus Christ and that, in view of its mandate from Christ, it will remain faithful to that teaching through the assistance of the Holy Spirit." [22] There is a portion

---

[22]The Editors of Encyclopaedia Brittanica: "Papal Infallibility," Encyclopaedia Brittanica, July 20, 1998, accessed Feb. 19, 2018

of the Catechism of the Catholic Church that reads, "When the Church through its supreme Magisterium proposes a doctrine "for belief as being divinely revealed," and as the teaching of Christ, the definitions "must be adhered to with the obedience of faith." [23]This infallibility extends as far as the deposit of divine Revelation itself." (paragraph 4, section 891, footnote 421). The Catholic Church does seem to hold the view that Papal infallibility is rarely exercised, yet there are some other erroneous teachings on spiritual authority that are connected to it, so we will examine those official statements.

While we all need the assistance of the Holy Spirit, and certainly any minister genuine in their faith would never want to make a mistake, I don't know anyone that would go so far as to declare that they cannot err. Even the best Bible teachers can be prone to making a mistake. Scripture says in 1 Cor. 3:9,

"Our knowledge is incomplete and our ability to speak what God has revealed is incomplete." And, in 1 Cor. 8:2 it says: "Anyone who claims to know all the answers doesn't really know very much."

These scriptures make a great case for not getting carried away with oneself or thinking anyone has all the answers! The authors at Catholic Faith and Reason explain papal infallibility like this: "Infallibility belongs to the Pope in a special way since Christ gave him primacy (Mt. 16:17-10 "you are Peter, and on this rock, I will build my church, and the powers of death [gates of hell] shall not prevail against it.") Only Peter is given the keys to the kingdom of heaven (see Isaiah 22) and only Peter is declared the rock (see Jn. 1:42 where the Aramaic term Cephas or rock is given to him by Jesus). This primacy is seen in John 21: 15-17, where Jesus instructs Peter as chief shepherd of the flock, his Church, to "feed my lambs...tend my sheep. Together with the apostles he enjoys the power to "bind and loose" on earth and in heaven. Vatican II puts it this way: " [Infallibility] is something he enjoys in virtue of his office, when, as the supreme shepherd and teacher of all the faithful, who confirms his brethren in their faith. (Luke 22:32 "...but I have prayed that your own faith may not fail; and once you have turned back, you must strengthen your brothers."), he proclaims by a definitive act some doctrine of faith or morals. Therefore his definitions, of themselves, and not from the consent of the Church, are justly held irreformable, for they

https://www.britannica.com/topic/papal-infallibility
[23]The Authors at Catholic Faith and Reason: "Papal Infallibility", Catholic Faith and Reason.com accessed Feb. 19, 2018,
http://www.catholicfaithandreason.org/papal-infallibility.html

are pronounced with the assistance of the Holy Spirit, an assistance promised to him in blessed Peter."

The Catechism of the Catholic Church, as taken from the Vatican archives, makes this statement: 'The Pope, Bishop of Rome and Peter's successor, "is the perpetual and visible source and foundation of the unity both of the bishops and of the whole company of the faithful." "For the Roman Pontiff, by reason of his office as Vicar of Christ, and as pastor of the entire Church has full, supreme, and universal power over the whole Church, a power which he can always exercise unhindered." Authority without restraint is subject to abuse of power and position. The only One who has supreme, universal power over the entire church is God Himself.

I don't want to get lost in the various arguments on Papal Infallibility, (I have written in more detail in the book Unmasking the Culture),. There are many contradictory statements by various previous popes that brings confusion to those trying to understand the church's official position. There is a mixture of truth combined with religious works.

Authority is used to imply fear of losing one's salvation if certain Catholic teachings are questioned or rejected. These perspectives undermine the teaching of salvation by grace alone. Galatians 2:21 declares,

"I do not set aside the grace of God; for if righteousness comes through the law, then Christ died in vain."

Though it is true that Christ died for 'the church,' which are those that profess Him as Lord and Savior, and without calling on the name of the Lord Jesus Christ none can be saved; in this sense those that are truly His belong to the universal Christian church. It is true that if we are a part of God's family, through being 'born again,' then we are subject to the authority of His Holy Spirit. However, salvation is not conditional to being subject to the pope, the bishops or those the Catholic Church deems Peter's successors.

Let's compare this thought to scripture. The Bible tells us that we must be born again in order to be saved.

Jesus answered and said to him, "Truly, truly, I say to you, unless one is born again he cannot see the kingdom of God." And, Jesus answered, "Truly, truly, I say to you, unless one is born of water and the Spirit he cannot enter into the kingdom of God." John 3:3-5

"Who then overcomes the world? Only he who believes that Jesus is the

Son of God. This is the One who came by water and blood, Jesus Christ—not by water alone, but by water and blood. And it is the Spirit who testifies to this, because the Spirit is the truth. For there are three that testify: the Spirit, the water, and the blood--and these three are in agreement. Even if we accept human testimony, the testimony of God is greater. For this is the testimony that God has given about His Son. Whoever believes in the Son of God has this testimony within him; whoever does not believe God has made Him out to be a liar, because he has not believed in the testimony God has given about His Son...."1 John 5:5-10

While submission to authority is a very important biblical teaching, we can only submit to the authority of man in as much as it does not cause us to walk contrary to our own conscience (engaging in sin), or deny the Lordship of Christ. Scripture advises us to beware of the fear of man because it brings a snare. Nowhere, ever, is it stated in the Bible that salvation is conditional upon subjecting oneself to any man. It was never stated about Peter, so how then can it be stated about the pope? Salvation is conditional upon calling on the name of Jesus Christ and placing oneself under the authority of His Holy Spirit. Peter preached the gospel of Jesus Christ and men were convicted in their heart, leading them to repent of their sins and be saved. These are Peter's words in Acts 4:10-12:

"...let it be known to you all, and to all the people of Israel, that by the name of Jesus Christ of Nazareth, whom you crucified, whom God raised from the dead, by Him this man stands here before you whole. This is the 'stone which was rejected by you builders, which has become the chief cornerstone.'[a] Nor is there salvation in any other, for there is no other name under heaven given among men by which we must be saved."

Another verse concerning the requirements of salvation is found in Romans 10:8-10:

"But what does it say? "The word is near you, in your mouth and in your heart"[a] (that is, the word of faith which we preach): that if you confess with your mouth the Lord Jesus and believe in your heart that God has raised Him from the dead, you will be saved. For with the heart one believes unto righteousness, and with the mouth confession is made unto salvation."

"Is the Catholic Church's assertion about Peter true? If it is, then we should see such a supremacy in the person of Peter as revealed in the New Testament--the place where spiritual truth must be verified. Unfortunately, we find no such supremacy of Peter in the Scriptures." [24]

The Catholic Church has consistently used scripture out of context to justify many things that are not Biblical. This communicates to others that certain religious practices are approved by God when they are simply made up by men. First of all, when Jesus told Peter that upon him (Peter) He would build the church, Jesus was referring to the revelation that Peter had when Peter understood Jesus to be the Son of God. In Matthew 16:15-16, Jesus had asked Peter a direct question: "Who do you say I am?" Peter said, "You are the Anointed One; You are the Son of the living God. "He had found at last the clear, unshaken, unwavering faith which was the indispensable condition for the manifestation of His kingdom as a visible society upon earth. The disciple had received the faith which he now professed, not through popular rumors, not through the teaching of scribes, but by a revelation from the Father." [25] This revelation of Jesus as the Anointed Son of God is the solid foundation of the gospel.

Jesus is referred to 'the Rock' in scripture. Christ, not Peter, is the 'rock' that is referred to in 1 Corinthians 10:4. In the parable about the wise builder and the foolish builder in Matthew 7:24-27, the rock represents the principles of Christ and His teaching. In Matthew 21:42, Mark 12:10, Luke 20:17 and 1 Peter 2:7 Christ is the 'rock' – the chief cornerstone. The cornerstone is the principle stone upon which the rest of the foundation is built. Scripture is clear in the intent that JESUS, not Peter (a man), is the rock upon which His church is built. Old Testament references associated the steadfastness and greatness of God being likened to a rock. Those thoughts were never indicated to reference a mere man. It is the revelation of Jesus Christ that comes as a spiritual awakening – that is the cornerstone of truth. Once a person has the revelation that the gospel story is actual truth and Jesus is real, something within them comes alive. It is the blessed hope that is found in Jesus Christ. The individual also understands the desire of their own soul to connect with God in a real way. Then and only then can a foundation be laid in a person's life. Salvation is entered into by faith in the person of Jesus Christ, accepting that He is the Son of God. Line by line, precept upon precept, truth is established in a person's life, and that truth brings stability. It is the bedrock of faith that anchors the hope of Christ deep in the heart. This is the foundation that we build upon!

---

[24]Slick, Matt: "Is Peter Supreme Among the Apostles?", accessed Feb. 18, 2018, https://carm.org/peter-supreme-among-apostles
[25] Matthew 16:17, Ellicott's Commentary for English Readers, accessed Feb. 24, 2018; http://biblehub.com/commentaries/matthew/16-17.htm

DISTRIBUTION OF SPIRITUAL AUTHORITY

The statement made by the Catholic Church indicating that only Peter was given authority to bind and loose, or exercise dominion on earth is another contradiction of scripture. Jesus told ALL His disciples that He had given them authority in Matthew 18:18. If Peter was supreme among the apostles, then why did Jesus extend the same authority to the rest of His disciples? In Luke chapter 10, Jesus sent out 70 men to do the work of the ministry. In verse 9, they were given the commission to 'heal the sick and say to them, 'the kingdom of God has come near you.' In Luke 10: 16-19 the men returned from ministering to others. They were excited to report the events of their day. Jesus said,

"Whoever listens to you listens to Me; whoever rejects you rejects Me; and whoever rejects Me rejects the One who sent Me." The seventy-two returned with joy and said, "Lord, even the demons submit to us in Your name." So He said to them, "I saw Satan fall like lightning from heaven." "Behold, I give you the authority to tread upon serpents and scorpions, and upon all the power of the enemy, and nothing will injure you."

It has always been God's plan for mankind to walk in dominion. We have always been appointed as His ambassadors to exercise authority, bringing God's kingdom 'on earth as it is in heaven.' The statement that only Peter was given the keys to the kingdom of heaven, referencing Isiah 22:22 to support this point is an incorrect statement. This teaching promotes elitism, a thought that only a few special select individuals can know the truth and be endowed with power and authority. This is not what the Bible teaches. Jesus distributed authority to every believer.

"For the Son of Man is as a man taking a far journey, who left his house, and gave authority to his servants, and to every man his work, and commanded the porter to watch." Mark 13:34 KJV

"Then He called His twelve disciples together and gave them power and authority over all demons, and to cure diseases. He sent them to preach the kingdom of God and to heal the sick.... So they departed and went through the towns, preaching the gospel and healing everywhere." Luke 9:1,2,6

"The key of the house of David I will lay on his shoulder;
So he shall open, and no one shall shut; And he shall shut, and no one shall open." Is. 22:22 KJV

In the above scripture (Isaiah 22:22), God was speaking to Eliakim (not

Peter), but it is a reference to the authority given to believers because of their position as God's children and heirs to the kingdom of God.

"But when the fullness of the time had come, God sent forth His Son, born[a] of a woman, born under the law, to redeem those who were under the law, that we might receive the adoption as sons. And because you are sons, God has sent forth the Spirit of His Son into your hearts, crying out, "Abba, Father!" Therefore you are no longer a slave but a son, and if a son, then an heir of[b] God through Christ." Gal.4:4-7 NKJV

An heir has full rights of inheritance to whatever belongs to their Father. As heirs to the kingdom, we have been given authority to bind and loose, to forbid the enemy from wreaking havoc on earth, and to loose people from bondage, sin, sickness and disease. We can release people from spiritual shackles and set the captives free. As heirs, we are seated in heavenly places with Christ. How do you feel, knowing that God has given you authority over spiritual darkness and forces of evil? Are you ready to use the power God gave you to change the world? God distributed His authority to all that would call on His name and be saved, not just a few. He has empowered all those that are born-again to become children of God, and the right to exercise dominion over the works of the enemy. [26]

Perhaps not all authority figures in the Roman Catholic Church have taught the wrong use of scripture, but there has been widespread miscommunication of certain truths that has essentially placed man in the position as a substitute 'voice of God' to those in the Catholic faith. Placing man above God is idolatry. This leaves anyone that practices these religious traditions at risk of being under a curse.

Another side effect of being under a false religious system is that people tend to feel like they have an orphan spirit. This is because they have looked to man or religious observances to fill that void rather than forming an authentic relationship with their heavenly Father. God longs to pour out His Spirit upon those that are His, and give them the revelation that they truly do have a Father that loves and adores them! Although many people look to the pope as the father of the Catholic faith, they have no legitimate relationship with him. In as much as the president of a nation may be considered the father of that country, and that person may have concern for those they

---

[26]Ref. Gal. 4:4-6; Mark 3:27, Is. 22:22, Is. 61:1, Luke 4:18 ,NKJV, BibleGateway.com, accessed Feb. 20, 2018, Scripture taken from the New King James Version®. Copyright © 1982 by Thomas Nelson. Used by permission. All rights reserved.

govern, there is no actual personal relationship with the majority of citizens. It is the same type of relationship with the pope. People cannot find healing for their souls through a replica of a father-child relationship. Religion leaves people spiritually weak, hungry for authentic relationship and empty. Healing and wholeness can only be achieved through authentic relationship with Jesus Christ whereby the love of God, poured out through His Holy Spirit, fills the empty, longing places in our hearts.

"And because you are sons, God has sent forth the Spirit of His Son into your hearts, crying out, "Abba, Father!" Gal. 4:8 NKJV

"And this hope will not lead to disappointment. For we know how dearly God loves us, because he has given us the Holy Spirit to fill our hearts with his love." Rom. 5:5 NLT

If people are aligned with an idolatrous religious structure then there will always be some sort of negative effect. Whatever spirits people submit themselves to has authority over them and their household. Religious legalism (a spirit of control), the perverse spirit, the voodoo of Santeria, Lukemi and other witchcraft spirits will affect people's lives because they have directly or indirectly associated themselves with those things. As a result, demonic spirits become attached to families with assignments to perpetuate things like poverty, addictions, divorce, adultery, gambling and other things intent on causing ruin.

A person doesn't have to actively practice witchcraft for it to exist as an unbroken curse, and those things can still be affecting families even today. People who can be quite sincere in their desire to worship God can be sincerely wrong in what they've been taught and accepted as truth. They may be in a religious system that has altered truth and they never realize that they are partaking of a doctrine that carries a curse. Demons are not interested in our excuses. Either they have legal grounds to be there or they don't. Demons count on people being ignorant of how they work, but it's my hope that I can help shed light on some of these things so that people can avoid those pitfalls.

"I testify to anyone that adds to the prophecy in this book: if anyone adds to them, God will add to them the plagues that are written in this book; and if anyone takes away from the words of the book of this prophecy, God will take away his part from the tree of life and from the holy city, which are written in this book..." Rev. 22:18,19

Father Dimitri Sala, OFM, in his book *The Stained Glass Curtain* writes, "Does the Catholic Church teach its adherents to worship statues? Is it a tenant of Evangelicalism to disrespect Catholics? Is it true that there are no saved people in the Catholic Church? Do Evangelicals believe that real Christianity basically stopped after the apostles, and only picked up again with Martin Luther? These questions articulate pre-judgments Catholics and Evangelicals have toward one another – judgments for which either group might find what it considers to be ample supporting evidence today. For there are Catholics who have idolatrous relationships with religious art, Evangelicals who do "Catholic bash," people in the Catholic Church who are not in a saving relationship with Jesus Christ, and Evangelicals who are ignorant of the fifteen centuries of Catholic history between biblical times and the Reformation. But a non-prejudiced heart will carefully weigh in the fact that his or her experience with such people is qualified: it is subjective, and it is limited. To the extent we draw conclusions through the lenses of present prejudice fashioned by the conditioning of history, we will surely not attain the unity our spiritual instincts prompt in our hearts." Sala writes on the importance of both Catholics and Evangelicals admitting they may have prejudices and filters that may need to be laid aside in order to listen to one another and develop trust in our relationships. This is how we learn from one another so that we can build a bridge of healing between both groups. It won't come by compromising the truth, however. Unity in the faith will come as a result of pursuing the truth of God's Word.

MEXICAN CUSTOMS AND HOLIDAYS

As we come to the end of this chapter, I feel it's important to bring up the subject of certain holidays that are also questionable and forbidden practices. We are still exploring truth about recognizing and tearing down ungodly altars. I realize this is another one of those things that some people may find difficult to accept because of long-standing accepted traditions but it cannot be ignored.

Christians should not celebrate the dead or built altars to the deceased because it provides legal grounds for the enemy to enforce a curse. In order for a spirit to find a place to work in someone's life, they must first have their cooperation. Sometimes witchcraft spirits will even appear in dreams as faces of deceased loved ones in order to gain the person's trust. It isn't really the deceased person; the spirit is simply appearing as someone familiar. In this way, they are able to enlist the person's cooperation. A spirit that is not resisted is one that ends up staying and establishing a covert covenant. This enables them to manifest whatever it is that particular spirit represents. People cannot worship Jesus Christ on one altar and worship the dead on another.

"The Day of the Dead (Spanish: Día de Muertos) is a Mexican holiday celebrated throughout Mexico, in particular the Central and South regions, and by people of Mexican ancestry living in other places, especially the United States. It is acknowledged internationally in many other cultures. Traditions connected with the holiday include building private altars called ofrendas, honoring the deceased using calaveras, aztec marigolds, and the favorite foods and beverages of the departed, and visiting graves with these as gifts." [27] Visitors also leave possessions of the deceased at the graves.

"Scholars trace the origins of the modern Mexican holiday to indigenous observances dating back hundreds of years and to an Aztec festival dedicated to the goddess Mictecacihuatl. The holiday has spread throughout the world, being absorbed into other deep traditions in honor of the dead. It has become a national symbol and as such is taught in the nation's schools. Many families celebrate a traditional "All Saints' Day" associated with the Catholic Church. The festivities were dedicated to the goddess known as the "Lady of the Dead", corresponding to the modern La Calavera Catrina."[28]

Frances Ann Day summarizes the three-day celebration, the Day of the Dead: "On October 31, All Hallows Eve, the children make a children's altar to invite the angelitos (spirits of dead children) to come back for a visit. November 1 is All Saints Day, and the adult spirits will come to visit. November 2 is All Souls Day, when families go to the cemetery to decorate the graves and tombs of their relatives. The three-day fiesta is filled with marigolds, the flowers of the dead; muertos (the bread of the dead); sugar skulls; cardboard skeletons; tissue paper decorations; fruit and nuts; incense, and other traditional foods and decorations."[29]

But scripture says, "And when they say to you, "Inquire of the mediums and the necromancers who chirp and mutter," should not a people inquire

---

[27] "Dia de los Muertos". National Geographic Society. "Day of the Dead", Wikipedia, accessed Feb. 13, 2018,
https://en.wikipedia.org/wiki/Day_of_the_Dead
[28]Salvador, R. J. (2003). John D. Morgan and Pittu Laungani, ed. Death and Bereavement Around the World: Death and Bereavement in the Americas. Death, Value and Meaning Series, Vol. II. Amityville, New York: Baywood Publishing Company. pp. 75–76. ISBN 0-89503-232-5. "Day of the Dead," Wikipedia, accessed Feb. 14, 2018.
https://en.wikipedia.org/wiki/Day_of_the_Dead
[29] Day, Frances Ann (2003). Latina and Latino Voices in Literature. Greenwood Publishing Group. p. 72. ISBN 978-0313323942. "Day of the Dead," Wikipedia, accessed Feb. 14, 2018. https://en.wikipedia.org/wiki/Day_of_the_Dead

of their God? Should they inquire of the dead on behalf of the living?" Isaiah 8:19

Building altars to the dead is a form of idolatry and forms soul ties, which is a bond in the soul. They are another form of an ungodly covenant in the spirit realm that needs to be broken. While it is understandable that people want to remember their deceased loved ones with positive memories, it can be done without building ungodly altars or inviting the spirits of the dead to visit those families. Sometimes there are soul ties with the deceased that need to be broken. The loss of a child or another loved one can cause overwhelming grief, but if the grief and mourning continues long after a normal period of grieving and healing then it becomes necessary to break the spirit of grief as well as the soul tie to the person that died. It is not dishonoring to the person that passed. On the contrary, it sets the person that has been captive free. The spirit goes back to the spirit realm and the living individual is set free from continual grief and loss. If soul ties are not broken, the person can stay stuck in grief indefinitely.

Christian symbols such as the cross at the site of these altars do not make this a Christian holiday. The festivities surrounding the celebration of the dead serve to disguise the evil spirits that are a part of these holidays. The reality is people that invite spirits of the dead are actually invoking demonic spirits to inhabit their families, and because they are invited in, they have every right to stay, bringing curses in with them.

As children of God, we have been given dominion to exercise authority over the enemy and command demons to leave; however, people cannot exercise authority over things they willingly invite in unless they recognize the error of their ways, repent, and ask God to help them get the enemy out. Only when a person is truly submitted to God can they resist the enemy and then the enemy must obey. Submission to God, through our repentance and obedience, allows us to effectively exercise authority over the works of darkness.

"So submit yourselves to the one true God and fight against the devil and his schemes. If you do, he will run away in failure." James 4:6,7 The Voice

Jesus warned us in His word that the traditions of man have the power to nullify the word of God in our lives. Traditions can be many things, not just religious observances. The Day of the Dead, All Saints Day and All Souls Day are traditions that have existed for many, many generations, but they glorify Satan and death. They do not bring glory to God, and inviting devils into one's life in the name of deceased loved ones certainly does not honor the memory of those that have passed. These traditions and celebrations of death also do not honor the Lord. Christians celebrate testimonies of salvation, healing, resurrection, miracles and the wonderful works of the Holy Spirit. These are the things that bring glory to God.

When the traditions of man obscure truth and the right ways of God, it leaves people vulnerable to the enemy. People's faith will be severely constricted and compromised producing doublemindedness. God's word tells us that He is pleased by faith. Real faith is not settling for the form of religion, but seeking the person of Jesus Christ. It is getting to know our Heavenly Father through His Son and Holy Spirit. Each person of the trinity wants to be deeply connected to us in personal relationship. Religion is just a form that has no power to produce intimacy with God. It is a counterfeit and a substitute for actual relationship with the Lord and his Holy Spirit. When outward religious practices serve as a replacement for intimacy and authentic relationship with God, it grieves the Holy Spirit. If we will seek His presence through thanksgiving, praise and worship, we will encounter Him. Authentic encounters with the Holy Spirit guide us into the truth that can make us free. It's not just the acknowledgement of truth, it's embracing it and allowing it to have it's perfect work in our life. That is what sets us free.

It was "Martin Luther, who on All Saints' Eve in 1517, publicly objected to the way preacher Johann Tetzel sold indulgences. These were documents prepared by the church and bought by individuals either for themselves or on behalf of the dead that would release them from punishment due to their sins. As Tetzel preached, "Once the coin into the coffer clings, a soul from purgatory heavenward springs!" Luther questioned the validity of this practice and challenged the Catholic Church to a public debate of the 95 Theses he had written." [30]

Luther recognized then, as I hope many others do now, that there is a constant need to abide in the truth and encourage church reformation. "The mainstream Reformation was not concerned with establishing a new Christian tradition, but with the renewal and correction of an existing tradition. On the basis of their assertion that Christian theology was ultimately grounded in Scripture, reformers such as Luther and Calvin argued for the need to return to Scripture as the primary and critical source of Christian theology." — Robert Kennerson, author, "The theological agenda

---

[30] "Martin Luther," http://www.christianitytoday.com/history/people/theologians/martin-luther.html, accessed Mar. 17, 2018.

of the Reformation" [31]

There are those in the Catholic religion that would say, "I am Catholic and I will always be Catholic." They seem to view it the same as being born Irish, Hispanic or like their race that cannot be changed. They think their identity is tied into a label associated with their religious affiliation. That is not true. Anyone can leave a religion if they choose. It may not be easy, but it's not impossible. Anyone involved in an idolatrous religious structure should seek the Lord about whether or not they should remain there. The Bible tells us to come out and be separate from unclean things.

If we fail to renew our minds with the Word of God, we will become susceptible to deception and destructive doctrines. Truth is the person of the Holy Spirit. Without a vital, life-giving relationship with the Word of God and the Holy Spirit, we are vulnerable to temptation and deception. While we cannot afford to make excuses for wrong teaching or forbidden religious practices, neither can we forsake those that have yet to find their way out of darkness. Our job is to love others, share truth and lead people into the light. God has not called us to compromise with the very things that destroy the grace of God. While we should always seek opportunities to exercise love, grace and understanding towards others, we must not compromise with idolatrous practices or think that we must ignore them for the sake of peace and unity. God always warned His people not to mix the idolatrous worship of other nations with the way they were instructed to worship Him. He alone is the One true God. Our responsibility is to pursue purity, forsaking our old ways and allowing our minds to be renewed by the Word of God. The gospel we preach and the gospel we live from should be pure. Whatever is truly from Christ is where we find our common ground.

---

[31] Robert Kennerson, author, "The theological agenda of the Reformation", Living Lutheran: Reformation 500. Accessed Mar. 18, 2018, https://www.livinglutheran.org/2017/01/reformation-500/

CHAPTER FIVE

THE COURTS OF HEAVEN

Therefore the Lord will wait, that He may be gracious to you;
And therefore He will be exalted, that He may have mercy on you.
For the Lord is a God of justice;
Blessed are all those who wait for Him.
Isaiah 30:18

Many years ago my husband and I were ministering to a woman who had come to the altar for prayer. She had been struggling with bone cancer for 7 years. As we were praying, my husband heard the Lord say, "This is not just a health issue, this is a legal issue in the court of heaven!" At that point, something definitely shifted in the atmosphere and we began to listen intently for more leading by the Holy Spirit. We took authority over some things and also made the declaration over this woman that the matter had been settled in the court of heaven. Afterwards the Lord told me to write out some scriptures for healing and send it to her, with the instructions that she was to make those declarations of healing over her body. Her faith was elevated after the prayer and she obediently spoke the scriptures over her body. It was about 6 months to a year later when I saw her again and asked her about her health. Praise the Lord, she said she had just gotten a doctor's report that the cancer was in remission!

There have been a few times when I have gone into the courts of heaven on my own, seeking a favorable judgment from God. Each time it was when I was struggling over an issue and my emotions were getting the better of me. I remember one day when I was very broken over someone's hurtful words. I felt completely betrayed by their actions and it really wounded me. Those words were demonically empowered to release poison. My husband literally dragged me into the court of heaven through his insistence to pray that thing out! I was so hurt and angry I did not want to participate. How's that for being a woman of God? Don't laugh – I bet you have some bad days too!

Thank goodness for Norm, he did not let me stay in that pit. He took me step by step into the court of heaven, and he told me I needed to forgive the offenders, which I did. That part was more difficult than I'd like to admit, but I know enough by now not to let that sort of thing stick in my heart! Next, he told me to tell the judge what the accuser said and the charges that had been brought against me. Finally, he told me to envision myself standing next to Jesus, my attorney. Jesus told the judge that He had paid my debt with His blood. I was crying and all the hurt was pouring out, but Norm told me the judge had something to say and I needed to hear it from His mouth. The verdict was being read. He asked me, "What do you hear?" The first 5-10 minutes I could not hear anything outside of my own brokenness, but my husband would not surrender the ground we were taking in the Spirit. He insisted I listen until I heard the words out of the Judge's mouth. Finally, I heard the words, "NOT GUILTY!" My husband knew I needed to hear it for myself so that I could feel the release of that heavy burden caused by the accuser, and it worked. Sometimes we just need a revelation from God to help us get the breakthrough, and that's what this teaching is about. Other people can tell us certain things about what scripture says and they can even tell us what to say if they lead us in a prayer, but there are times when that does not do the trick. People need to hear from God for themselves. It's a game changer when they hear truth out of the mouth of God. Going into the court of heaven teaches us to listen intently for the voice of our Father.

The court most people are familiar with is the court of accusation. Rev. 12:10 states that the adversary seeks to accuse us before God day and night, but he has been cast down. Those who question the validity of this particular teaching on the courts of heaven may view it as unbiblical because 'the accuser has been cast down.' Christ has indeed won the victory for us but it doesn't stop the accuser from constantly looking for the opportunity to inflict some sort of demonic attack.

A minister known as "Praying Medic" writes, "Sin and how it's dealt with in the courts has nothing to do with our relationship with God. The issue being addressed is the opportunity it provides for evil spirits to attack us. The apostle Paul, writing after the death and resurrection of Jesus, teaching a new covenant reality wrote:

"Do not let the sun go down on your anger, and do not give the devil an opportunity." Eph 4:26-27

Paul taught that being angry creates an opportunity for the devil. If we choose to sin, it doesn't make us less righteous in God's eyes, but it does make us a target for demonic attack. The apostle John, again, teaching a new covenant reality, prescribed the remedy:

My dear children, I am writing this to you so that you will not sin. But if anyone does sin, we have an advocate who pleads our case before the Father. He is Jesus Christ, the one who is truly righteous. 1 Jn 2:1

The word "advocate" in this verse can be translated, attorney. John taught that when we sin, we should let Jesus, our attorney, plead our case before the Father. And that is exactly what we do in the court of accusation. Demons can torment us until we face them in court and have the Judge pass sentence on them and clear us of the accusation." [32] - Praying Medic, from *The Courts of Heaven: Answering Critics.*

I understand what he meant, but I do believe that our ability to enter the courts of heaven has everything to do with our relationship with Him. We can come with confidence before God because of the blood of Christ on our behalf. It's just that our relationship with God is not what is at stake. This isn't about our salvation or our relational position as God's child; it's about freedom. This is not teaching about coming under the law or leaving people with a sense of condemnation. That is not the case at all. Romans 8:2 tells us, There is therefore now no condemnation to those who are in Christ Jesus, *who do not walk according to the flesh*, but according to the Spirit." (Emphasis mine). Sometimes people tend to forget that part about our flesh. When we get into carnal behavior we provide Satan opportunity to release condemnation to our conscience, but even then, God has provided for our cleansing, freedom and healing. I think it is important to understand something about the law vs. grace. A Christian does not keep the law because he must, but gratitude for what Christ has done for us should result in changed behavior. Christians serve God with their obedience not out of fear of punishment but because they love God and are thankful for all He has done on our behalf. We don't have to live under guilt and condemnation if we sin, but we should be motivated by a desire to conduct ourselves as one that identifies with Christ. Changed behavior is a sign that our conversion is authentic.

The devil has only one job description: to kill, steal and destroy. He is constantly on the prowl to see whom he may devour. 1 Peter 5:8 says, "Be sober, be vigilant; because your **adversary**, the devil, walks about like a roaring lion seeking whom he may devour."

---

[32] Praying Medic: The Courts of Heaven, Answering Critics, accessed Aug. 19, 2018, https://prayingmedic.com/2017/01/12/courts-heaven-answering-critics/

The word adversary in the above scripture comes from the Greek word 'antidikos,' which means an opponent (in a lawsuit); specially, Satan (as the arch-enemy) -- adversary. Antidikos is a technical legal term used to refer to a prosecuting attorney in a courtroom; someone seeking official (formal, binding) damages. [33]

Matthew 5:25-26 is another scripture that references the adversary. In this portion of scripture, Jesus is talking about anger, slander and offense. He tells us to forgive others lest the adversary deliver us over to the judge, so as to avoid the possibility of being thrown into jail.

"Therefore if you bring your gift to the altar and there remember that your brother has something against you, leave your gift there before the altar and go your way – First be reconciled to your brother and then come and offer your gift. Agree with your adversary quickly, while you are on the way with him, **lest your adversary deliver you to the judge, and the judge hand you over to the officer, and you be thrown into prison.** Assuredly, I say to you, you will by no means get out of there till you have paid the last penny."

Luke 12:58 reiterates this principle. We have an adversary that is looking for legal grounds to inflict suffering and the right to withhold what is ours. Unforgiveness will definitely block our ability to have prayers answered. It will block finances, is a cause for deterioration in emotional health and well-being, and it is a spiritual root for infirmity, disease and death. People often overlook unforgiveness as a reason why they cannot seem to prosper, but it is a very common door the enemy uses to his advantage. Unforgiveness can cause things to come to halt until it is dealt with properly. A prosecuting attorney must follow the law. In a similar fashion, Satan, otherwise known as the accuser, seeks ways to bring charges against us. When we sin, we become a target for demonic attack.

"When you go with your adversary to the magistrate, make every effort along the way to settle with him, lest he drag you to the **judge,** the judge deliver you to the officer, and the officer throw you into prison. I tell you, you shall not depart from there till you have paid the very last mite." Luke 12:58

---

[33] Strong's Concordance, "antidikos," from Biblehub.com accessed Mar. 7, 2018, http://biblehub.com/greek/476.htm, HAYER'S GREEK LEXICON, Electronic Database. Copyright © 2002, 2003, 2006, 2011 by Biblesoft, Inc. All rights reserved. Used by permission. BibleSoft.com

Here we see evidence that **heavenly courts do exist**. Isaiah 43:26 in The Voice translation says, "Now help Me remember. Let's get this settled. **State your case and prove to Me that you are in the right.**"

Isaiah 33:22 states, "For the Lord is our **judge**, the Lord is our lawgiver, the Lord is our king." It is He that we serve.

Of course there is another reference to a courtroom setting in Daniel chapter 7 where it states that the 'court was seated,' and the enemy was prevailing until the Ancient of Days came and rendered a judgment on behalf of the saints.[34] This is another scripture that proves heavenly realities. In the spirit realm exist kings and kingdoms, thrones and councils, courts and courtrooms.

The next scripture reference proves that Jesus is our advocate and attorney. 1 Timothy 2:5 states, "For there is one God and one **mediator** between God and man[kind], [and that is] Christ Jesus."

The Holy Spirit is our **witness**. Romans 8:16 says, "The Spirit himself **testifies** with our spirit that we are children of God." Do you see a courtroom portrayed in scripture? I do.

Satan, of course, is the **prosecutor**. He is known as the accuser of the brethren in Rev. 12:10.

While we must do our part to be diligent and walk in obedience to God, the good news is that when we sin, we have an advocate – **an attorney** – that will speak on our behalf.

"My dear children, I am writing this to you so that you do not sin. But if anyone does sin, **we have an advocate who pleads our case** before the Father. He is Jesus Christ, the one who is truly righteous." 1 John 2:1. If there was no courtroom, why would we need an attorney?

There are spiritual concepts and images that are portrayed by certain scriptures, and there are many references in the word of God that create visual imagery for the reader. Jesus frequently spoke in parables to illustrate a point and He did so for a reason. He spoke in language that was familiar to those around him. Certain scriptures definitely reference things you would find in a courtroom.

---

[34] Ref. Daniel 7:22-28

The word for advocate in this scripture is the Greek word 'parakletos,' which means a legal advocate who makes the right judgment because he is close enough to the situation to know what is going on. **It is the New Testament term for attorney (lawyer); in other words, someone that gives testimony that stands up in a court of law**. Parakletos also references a helper, an advocate, an intercessor, a consoler and comforter. [35] It is the same word Jesus used to describe the Holy Spirit.

There are different levels of the heavenly realms. We know this is true because the Apostle Paul spoke about visiting the third heaven. Ephesians 6:12 tells us,

"For we do not wrestle against flesh and blood, but against principalities, against powers, against the rulers of the darkness of this age, against spiritual hosts of wickedness in the **heavenly places**."

Through this we understand that even though Satan was cast down from the highest heavens (where God dwells), he still has access to different levels of the heavenly realms. One of the names for the enemy is also called the Prince of the Power of the Air. So, even though Satan cannot necessarily go before the throne of God anymore, it would appear that he still has the ability to enter the courtroom and act as an accuser. Rev. 12:10 says that the accuser of the brethren accuses us before God day and night. This means Satan is constantly looking for any opportunity to act as a prosecuting attorney. Depriving others of justice is exactly what Satan does. His whole purpose of bringing a lawsuit against us in the court of heaven is to deny us what is rightfully ours. The good news is that we overcome by the blood of the Lamb and the word of our testimony!

There are courts other than just the court of accusation, but in order to find them you must search principles of scripture. Pay attention to certain words and look them up in the Lexicon. You will discover that many New Testament words actually have legal definitions. This is the key information that most critics fail to understand and that is why they claim the courts of heaven is either not biblical or they don't see it in scripture. You have to dig it out! (Study Daniel 7:9-10, Psalm 89:7, Ezekiel 1:14-28, Psalm 149:5-9 for some additional references.) "In the court of war, we learn the strategies of heaven. In the court of kings, we learn to make decrees that establish heaven's

---

[35] Parakletos," Biblehub.com accessed Mar. 7, 2018, NAS Exhaustive Concordance of the Bible with Hebrew-Aramaic and Greek Dictionaries. Copyright © 1981, 1998 by The Lockman Foundation. All rights reserved Lockman.org

rule. We receive angelic help in the court of angels. In the divine council, the Lord meets with angels and saints to decide the affairs of heaven and earth. There are many other courts and councils in heaven. In time, and with experience, we'll gain access to all of them. As we explore them and meet with the Lord in person, we're transformed into sons and kings who fully reflect the glorious image of God."[36]

When we are faced with trials, temptations, frustrations and difficulties they can definitely take their toll on our emotions. However, we cannot approach God in our pride, anger or self-righteousness. The only proper response, when approaching the just Judge of all heaven and earth, is one of humility. He resists the proud but gives grace to the humble. We have access to His throne at any time. We can come boldly to the throne of grace and find help in the time of our need!

In Luke 18:1-8 there is a story about a woman who continued to approach an unjust judge in her city to petition him for justice. Jesus gave a parable about this woman.

Then He spoke a parable to them, that men always ought to pray and not lose heart, saying: "There was in a certain city a judge who did not fear God nor regard man. Now there was a widow in that city; and she came to him, saying, 'Get justice for me from my adversary.' And he would not for a while; but afterward he said within himself, 'Though I do not fear God nor regard man, yet because this widow troubles me I will avenge her, lest by her continual coming she weary me.' "

Then the Lord said, "Hear what the unjust judge said. And shall God not avenge His own elect who cry out day and night to Him, though He bears long with them? I tell you that He will avenge them speedily. Nevertheless, when the Son of Man comes, will He really find faith on the earth?"

This example illustrates a court situation with God as our judge, as well as the need to persist in prayer and not give up until an answer comes. There are times when it seems as though our prayers are just stuck and we don't know why. It is not because God doesn't want to answer, but He is teaching us persistence and patience. There are times when God wants us to seek Him for a particular answer that comes by revelation and He knows the breakthrough isn't going to happen without prophetic insight or a word of

---

[36] Praying Medic, The Courts of Heaven: Answering the Critics, dated Jan. 12, 2017; accessed Aug. 19, 2018, https://prayingmedic.com/2017/01/12/courts-heaven-answering-critics/

knowledge. This is the whole essence behind this type of teaching. Again, it teaches us to listen for spiritual keys that will unlock something in the spirit realm.

We already covered the issue of how generational curses and unconfessed sin can hinder prayers from being answered. We know that the enemy always examines us for places where we have made some agreement with him and unintentionally surrendered our dominion or authority. I used to think that Satan could only operate if we had given him legal grounds to do so, but then another thing occurred to me. The enemy is known as a thief, and thieves are law breakers. Satan was thrown out of heaven because he broke the rules and acted in rebellion to God. He has never changed, and the enemy is still a law breaker. That means that there will be times when he does something that is completely against the law, but it's our job to catch him doing something illegally, take the situation to the court room and ask the judge to grant us a legal judgment in our favor. That is why the scripture says,

"But **if** he is caught, he must pay back seven times what he stole, even if he has to sell everything in his house." Prov. 6:31 (Emphasis mine)

Do you notice that the scripture says, "IF he is caught?" You have to catch him, before you can make him repay! How are you going to catch a thief? Through revelatory knowledge!

Doug Addison, in a blog post titled, **"*How to Reclaim What's Yours in the Court of Heaven,*"** had a guest host by the name of Elizabeth Nixon. Ms. Nixon is also an attorney and has some incredibly powerful insights that I would like to share.

There are times when we do all that we know how to do to put ourselves in right alignment with God and we still can't seem to get a break. We pray, we declare the blood of Jesus, we renounce generational sins and still the breakthrough resists us. I do believe that sometimes God allows this sort of resistance because He wants to teach us something new or reveal a new strategy. Doug had suffered with a debilitating illness for four years without a significant breakthrough in his health. As Elizabeth began to pray for him, she asked the Lord what she should pray. She began to share how the Lord spoke to her and gave her the words, 'squatter's rights.' The following is a portion of the transcript from the blog post.

Elizabeth: "He showed me that sin is not the only way that the enemy gets access to our life…in the natural, you can have somebody who trespasses onto somebody else's land. They don't own it, but they trespass on it. And they sit there, and they try to establish ownership by occupation.

And so, for people who have gone to the courts, and they've gone through repentance, and they've gone through bloodline issues and probably had breakthrough in a lot of different ways— but still feel like they can't quite break through the next area in their life—it's very possible that what's happening is the enemy actually has taken illegal access into your territory. And I would define "territory" in two ways: It is physical land, because there are physical, geographic places and people groups the we're called to, to serve God. But it's also our own personal and spiritual territories. And by that, I mean our physical state, our mental, emotional, and spiritual selves, that the enemy has just basically come in and said, "I want this."

So, in the law in the natural, if you were to define what a squatter's rights are, it's simply when somebody occupies territory that does not belong to them, but they have the gall of securing occupation and even title."

Now in the natural, somebody who is trespassing like a squatter—which means they're occupying territory that does not actually belong to them, but their goal is to have it become theirs—they have to meet two things. They have to occupy the land in an open way so that it's not hidden, and they also have to pay off any debt associated with the property, and that was usually like a property tax. Because under the natural laws, if you don't pay property tax on your property, that's considered abandoning your property.

So here's how it would relate in the spirit: If the enemy is trying to squat on a part of your territory—I mean, if that's a physical territory—that means you have a city or a region or a people group that you are called to and you cannot get breakthrough in that city. The enemy is just absolutely strong against you. Or if in your own self ... If you have chronic illness. If you have chronic poverty. If you deal with mental health issues and spiritually, just always this torment of the enemy. And you've gone through bloodline cleansing, you've gone through repentance and you've applied the blood to those things so that there's no legal access anymore, this is a way that we can identify that, more likely than not, the enemy is actually trespassing in that place.

Here's a great thing. In Luke 10:19 we're told that we have power over the enemy. I'm going to tell you what that verse sounds like in most translations of the Bible.

Luke 10:19 (KJV) says, "Behold," this is Jesus speaking, "I give unto you power to tread on serpents and scorpions, and over all power of the enemy: and nothing shall by any means hurt you." Sometimes that's a difficult verse when we're living in a place where we're like, "It feels like the enemy's completely in my face. He's completely up against me. I'm suffering and I actually am being hurt." And so, we have to reconcile this contradiction.

So, in that verse where it says, "I give you power over the enemy," this is what that word means. It means, "Liberty and power of choice." It means, "Power to influence and change a situation." It means, "Governmental rulership power, judicial decision-making power, and royal authority. That is way more impactful than just what we would say, "I have power over the enemy." That's describing the extent and the kind of power. And then when it says at the end that, "Nothing by any means shall hurt you," that word 'hurt' is a legal word. It means that, "Nothing shall by any means be able to criminally violate the law against you or engage in unjust action or to offend you." That doesn't mean my feelings are hurt. It means as in a legal defender, a perpetrator who has committed a crime against you. So I took all those meanings and I rewrote Luke 10:19. And I want to read it to everybody now, because this is the mentality that we have to have. Because sometimes when we're dealing with the enemy, we begin to see our own situation and our ability to combat him as futile. And we need to shift that. and come to the place where we see his position is futile, not ours.

So let me read you Luke 10:19 the way that Jesus would have fully said it, and how it would have been understood by those who were listening to Him.

He says, "Behold, I give you liberty to do as you please. I give you the power of choice and the power to influence and change all situations, even to the level of a governmental rulership power, including judicial decision-making power like that of a judge. And you are to use this power and operate in it over any and all power and authority of the enemy. And given this power and authority that I invest in you, the enemy will not have any ability to violate you or to cause unjust consequences against you. He will have no power to perpetrate crimes against you." [37]

Do you see how powerful this is? I want to allow you to get the full impact of what she's saying, so let's continue.

Elizabeth: Well, I think I said briefly ways that you can identify if the

_____

[37] "How to Reclaim What Belongs to You in the Courts of Heaven," Addison, Doug and Nixon, Elizabeth; podcast transcription. Episode 61, accessed Aug. 10, 2018, © Copyright 2018 Doug Addison and InLight Connection. All Rights Reserved.

enemy is trespassing or squatting on your territories. And I just want to hit that again, so that you can say, "All right, here's how I can identify areas where I need to bring this kind of power and authority over the enemy."

So, because one of the elements of a squatter trying to change his position from just possessing or occupying to actually owning, he has to be there in the open and what they call a "notorious or obvious way." One of those ways would be to have trauma or chronic illness. They fit this category because, if it's open and obvious, then people around you will be easily able to tell that something's wrong. So, something is hidden in you. And you don't have to worry, "Oh, the enemy's hiding and I can't find this trespasser." No, it will be open and obvious.

Trauma and chronic illness fit that. Chronic poverty fits that. In business, if you're always suffering losses—if you can't get ahead, opportunities are lost, everything comes in to pay off debt or to fix things instead of actually moving forward—those are good signs that there's an enemy trespassing in your territory." "…there are two things that a trespasser needs to do to stop just being somebody who is trespassing, to somebody who actually has a legal right to possess that property and maybe even get ownership of it. The first part is he gets access to those unoccupied areas. We have talked about how acknowledging them and being willing to take a stand in those areas is our first step.

The second step is actually the easiest step of all. And this is so remarkable, because the second thing that a trespasser has to do is pay off the debt. Remember, I said he has to pay off the debt to the property, and in the natural that means pay off the property taxes. Well, the Word tells us that Jesus is the one who has paid the debt that was on our territories.

In Galatians 3:13, it says Jesus' blood paid off the debt. And see, we know that this is both physical, geographical territories, because the Earth is the Lord's and all it contains, the Earth and the fullness thereof. That's Psalm 24. We also know that His blood has redeemed us. That's the whole Book of Galatians. That's the whole message of salvation. That is our mind, our will, our emotions, our physical health, our spiritual health, our mental health, our emotional health. Both of those territories have been covered with the blood. 1 Corinthians 6:20 and 1 Peter 1:18 also confirm we have been bought with a price. So, here's what that means. Even though this squatter, this enemy, may be able to occupy areas of your life—territories of your life that don't involve any sin on your part—it's a complete trespass and an illegal move on his part. He has no grounds that will give him any rights over those territories, because there is no longer any debt existing on that territory. And also, Jesus' blood is the only payment that satisfies that debt." [38]– Elizabeth Nixon.

Elizabeth has written a very powerful prayer that I've included in chapter nine, which I highly recommend people take the time to do, but let's continue learning some more on the courts of heaven.

There are many great teachings on the courts of heaven by various teachers. Some people may not choose to believe this is a valid teaching because they claim they cannot find it in scripture. However, these teachings were given by revelation from the Holy Spirit, and revelation is a powerful teacher. If we were to discount other people's revelations, experiences and testimonies simply because we didn't find the exact words in the Bible, we would miss out on a lot. Everything I've shared both from my own experience as well as what Elizabeth Nixon and Doug Addison shared line up with principles of scripture.

Robert Henderson is another prophetic minister who has teachings on this subject, and his teachings are also a direct result of revelation and an encounter with God. One of the things he pointed out is that we can approach God on three different dimensions. The first one is as our Father, the second is as a friend, but the third way to approach God is as a judge. Judges rule over judicial systems, and we know that our God is a God of justice. Henderson makes a lot of great points but allow me to sum up a testimony he shared in a meeting at Catch the Fire Toronto.

Robert explained how his son had gone through a very difficult time in his life after getting a divorce. His son was terribly depressed for two years. Robert prayed and did everything he knew how to do, but there was no change. Then one day, after praying for two years, Robert went to pray again for his son, but that time he heard the Lord tell him, "Bring your son to my courtroom." He said that he wasn't sure what to do, but he began by repenting on his son's behalf. As he explained, he could do so as an intercessor because intercessors pray for others until they are able to do it for themselves. Then he began to repent for any mistakes he had made as a father. The Lord told Robert to repent for negative words he had spoken about his son out of his frustration. He didn't speak them to his son, but he spoke out of his frustration to his mother, and the Lord told him that the enemy had used those negative words as an assignment against the son. The Bible does say the power of life and death reside in the words we speak. I

---

[38] Doug Addison and Elizabeth Nixon, "How to Get Back What's Yours in the Courts of Heaven" podcast transcription. Episode 61, accessed Aug. 10, 2018, © Copyright 2018 Doug Addison and InLight Connection. All Rights Reserved.

believe the enemy found legal grounds to carry out certain assignments because he found someone to agree with a negative report. The Lord told Robert to repent for speaking negative words over his son's future and to begin to declare that his son would fulfill his destiny. Then the judge of heaven issued a judgment against the enemy. As Henderson testified, a short time later his son remarkably turned a corner and came out of the depression that had been holding him captive. [39]

Protocol to Enter the Courtroom

1. **Humility**. Scripture tells us that God resists the proud but gives grace to the humble.1 Peter 5:5,6
2. **Thanksgiving and praise.** Psalm 100:4
3. **Blood covenant.** We do not come before God claiming to have any righteousness of our own. We approach God on the basis of what Jesus' shed blood has afforded to us. Heb. 10:19; Rom. 5:2, Eph. 3:12.
4. **Confession & Repentance**. 1 John 1:9

When we bring the sins of our ancestors before God, we identify with them as well. We have inherited everything that's been a part of our past, whether or not we wanted it. Identificational repentance takes responsibility for sin that never had the blood of Jesus applied to it, and asks God to remove the enemy's inroad into our lives.

Part of the reason I find this effective is that it causes a person to earnestly seek God for His intervention and to listen to what is being communicated in the spirit. The voice of the enemy is always waiting, ready to launch a fiery dart when he sees an opportunity or present some sort of accusation. The enemy loves to bombard people's minds with accusation, toxic shame, fear, and dread. He wants people to feel insecure, inferior, and intimidated because if they do, they spend all their time battling negative emotions rather than taking authority over the voice of the accuser and getting the victory. When the enemy comes to remind you of your past — however he chooses to do it — enlist this visual aid as a form of help.

See yourself walking into a courtroom. On one side, you are sitting behind a desk with your attorney. Who is your attorney? Jesus, of course!

He is standing right beside you. On the other side of the room, there are all your accusers. Say them out loud, one by one.

---

[39]"Introduction to the Courts of Heaven," Robert Henderson, July 29, 2016, https://www.youtube.com/watch?v=4Xk2UChVsB0

The Judge has been seated. The Court is now in session.

Out loud, say,
"Your honor, these are my accusers. They are accusing me of _____.
(Say each name and what each person lists as charges against you. Or, you can ask God to make the enemy list the charges brought against you because he has found some legal grounds.")

Jesus: "Excuse me, Your Honor, but I shed My blood for my client. I became sin for my client. Everything that the accusers list as charges against my client, I became for (_____insert your name.) when I took his/ her sin upon the cross.

Jesus: "I became a bad parent. I took on the role of the rebellious, disrespectful child. I became an alcoholic, a gambler, a pedophile, a thief, an adulterer, a rapist, a drug dealer, a murderer.

I became a failure. I became a source of pain to others. I became every one of their weaknesses, failures, and sins.

I became the curse on behalf of those for which I died. I was called every foul, shameful name people could muster up.

I was accused of every sordid, wicked thing that people did in secret. I became despised, rejected and an outcast – for them.

I willingly took it all upon myself, and every sin and sick, evil deed was absorbed into the power of My cross.

I paid the price for them with My life and My blood. I insist that You must acquit my client!"

Judge:

"Granted. Defendant is acquitted of all charges. Case dismissed!"

I love what Jesus said in John 3:16-18. This is from the Message Translation:

"This is how much God loved the world: He gave His son, His one and only Son. And this is why: so that no one need be destroyed; by believing in Him, anyone can have a whole and lasting life.

God didn't go to all the trouble of sending His Son merely to point an accusing finger, telling the world how bad it was. He came to help, to put the world right again.

Anyone who trusts in Him is acquitted; anyone who refuses to trust Him has long since been under the death sentence without knowing it.

And why? Because of that person's failure to believe in the One-of-a-kind Son of God when they were introduced to Him."

When the enemy comes to remind a person of their past, it's not a reflection on the individual as much as it is an accusation against the cross of Christ. Verses 19,21 say this:

"This is the crisis we're in: God-light streamed into the world but men and women everywhere ran to the darkness. They ran for the darkness because they were not really interested in pleasing God. Everyone who makes a practice of doing evil, addicted to denial and illusion, hates God-light and won't come near it, fearing a painful exposure. But anyone working and living in truth and reality welcomes God-light so that God-work can be seen for what it is."

We either live in the light and the truth of God's word, or we reject it, embracing lies and self-deception. Sometimes those lies come from others that have not yet worked through their own ability to process things that we may have done that affected them.

Everyone has the ability to take whatever time they need, but delayed obedience to the word of God can also have consequences. A failure to fully forgive others, entertaining self-pity, blaming others and other negative behaviors can put people in a spiritual prison. When someone's pride gets offended, the first thing they do is form a negative judgment. Pride will cause a person to sit in the place of prosecuting attorney, judge, jury and executioner towards others. That puts them in alignment with the accuser instead of God. That is why none of us should step into the place of the accuser towards another person If someone is going to hold another person accountable to the law rather than extending grace, the law of reciprocation demands that they also be placed under penalty of the law. Is that what any of us want?

Absolutely not! When someone brings up your past, it is usually because there is something that is still offended in them. Retaining judgments against others places those who are guilty of them under judgment themselves, according to Matthew 6:15 and 7:1.

When a person carries a grudge against someone else, they too stand guilty before God because they fail to exercise mercy. Matthew 7:1 and James 2:13 are key to understanding this principle.

Therefore, the Father must judge them according to His word. Perhaps someone else feels you are not truly forgiven until you jump through their hoops or pay some form of penance that makes them feel better. Perhaps they are trying to avoid conviction concerning other matters of their life. Many times it is because they fail to recognize their own need for God's mercy or forgiveness.

On the other hand, sometimes we simply need to believe God's word and take it by faith that we truly are forgiven, then move forward. We have just as much a responsibility to take authority over the voice of the enemy when it attempts to work through a spirit of guilt, condemnation, discouragement, and unbelief towards the promises of God.

It's our responsibility to BELIEVE GOD and put our trust in Him. We must put on the helmet of salvation and trust the blood of Jesus to cleanse our thoughts and renew our mind of constantly thinking we're under condemnation.

If we are around others that place us under a false burden of guilt, then that too, is something we need to deal with and cut off. Discern what spirit is at work! Don't let the enemy feed you with lies, because he is coming against your identity in Christ. God doesn't point accusing fingers, telling people how bad they are. He doesn't remind them of their painful past. He doesn't continue to place negative labels on people or cover them with toxic shame. He reminds people who they are in Christ. He shifts their focus into the present because the past has been dealt with. Jesus became every sin, every failure mankind would experience. The scripture in James 2:12-14 reminds us,

"Speak and act as those who are going to be judged by the law that gives freedom. For judgment without mercy will be shown to anyone who has not been merciful. Mercy triumphs over judgment. What good is it, my brethren, if someone claims to have faith but has no deeds? Can such faith save him?"

Take the shield of faith and the sword of the Spirit, which is the word of God. Hammer away at the lies. If the enemy is using someone to accuse you, even if it's in your own heart accusing you to yourself, stop and take authority over those lies. Throw the spear of truth into the heart of the enemy. Remember that you have an advocate and an attorney that stands with you – and for you – against every accusation.

It doesn't belong to you; Jesus paid for it all! Let the cross of Christ absorb the pain, the wounding, the word curses, the negative labels that you've worn. He paid the price for your emotional healing as well as your physical healing.

Every person has the right to experience genuine forgiveness and wholeness. Every person should be able to live free from the labels that others try to force them to wear. Every person should be able to live out from under toxic shame and other debilitating emotions. Jesus Christ can do that for each and every one of us. His blood and His love are that powerful!

Let God renew your mind and remind you that you are not what others tell you. Your identity is not tied to the past. God doesn't need the approval of those that have rejected or disowned you, those that can't see your value – in order to give you a blessed future. You are made in the image of God and the blood of Jesus acquits you.

Just remember, freely you have received; freely extend the grace of God to others as well. May His grace empower you to free those ensnared by their own judgments and set the captives free!

OBTAINING A FAVORABLE JUDGMENT

After we confess our sin, we have removed the legal rights to the accuser. The prosecuting attorney (Satan) no longer has access. That is the time to ask the just Judge of heaven for a judgment granting restitution. The enemy must comply with the law. It is always necessary to utilize God's Word in our petitions, declarations and decrees because when we return it to God, He dispatches angels to work on our behalf. God's Word always has an assignment!

Let me share another story. Some friends of mine are missionaries. Before they went to Mexico they read the book *Unmasking the Culture* and decided they would put the teaching and the prayers to the test. They shared messages on forgiveness and the gospel, but they also spoke about how generational curses keep people in bondage. They led an entire church through the prayers that are in the book, and they also demonstrated how to take someone into the courts of heaven. They witnessed God do many miraculous encounters with His people!

One man, who had been abusive to his wife and family repented in front of the entire church and asked his wife's forgiveness.

Another young man got set free from demonic bondage, including sexual spirits.

The missions team demonstrated taking a person into the courts of heaven by doing it publicly with the pastor. The congregation was encouraged to listen and call out accusations they felt Satan was using against this dear woman of God. Many were generational sins that she knew she had personally never committed. One such accusation was human sacrifice, and there were other things that were equally shocking, but each time she acknowledged the accusation and applied the blood of Jesus over that sin. Finally, when no one heard any more accusations, they asked the Judge to read His verdict. He declared His daughter NOT GUILTY! It was at that point that the woman pastor was able to ask the Judge for a favorable judgment on her behalf and to make the enemy restore her losses.

An interesting part of this story is that this woman's teenage daughter had been yelling out some of the accusations - and feeling pretty good about it, too. She had been very angry and wanted to see her mother publicly embarrassed. The relationship between her and her mother had been strained and broken for quite some time. Later that evening, after the service was over, the girl heard the voice of the Lord clearly for the first time in her life. Suddenly, the Lord interrupted her and asked, "How can I forgive you of your sin if you refuse to forgive your mother?" Instantly, the girl broke into tears and ran to her mother and repented. This is evidence of God turning a situation once the legal grounds were removed. A relationship that had previously been unable to be healed, He did in a matter of moments.

Another testimony from this church family had to do with finances. This church had barely been able to bring in a weekly offering because the families were in such financial hardship. They typically raised less than $100 a week, but that weekend they raised an offering of almost ten times as much! The faith level so accelerated after witnessing God move that the congregation gave over and above what they were used to giving! This truly was miraculous in light of the fact that many of those families were struggling to feed their families. There were many other testimonies as well.

Effective spiritual warfare can have many components. Praise and worship are one component. Prayers of renouncement are another. Decreeing God's Word and reminding Him of His promises is another. Sacrificial giving is also a way to move God's heart and open His hand towards us. These are things that capture heaven's attention and move the blessings of the Lord towards us.

When it comes to unlocking the blessings of God, He has some strategies to help us get there. Bless others and be generous to those that cannot repay you. When you lend to the poor, you lend to the Lord and He will repay you. The principle found in Isaiah 58 is also a good reminder that when we bless those that are in need and practice loving others as we love ourselves, it releases breakthrough. I know from experience this is a principle that works! The laws of sowing and reaping are always in effect, so if we want to reap a harvest of blessings, then we must first sow into others.

Prayers that serve to remove the legal grounds from the enemy can shift things in our lives and in the lives of our entire family. These are strategic prayers that unlock destiny, restoration, finances and much more.

CHAPTER SIX

COMMISSIONED FOR HIS GLORY

*Declare His glory among the nations, His wonderful deeds
among all peoples.*
Psalm 96:3

God pursues us because He wants intimate relationship with us. Every wound we receive in some spiritual battle is inflicted by the enemy as vengeance towards God, hurting the Father by taking away His children.

Andy Glover, in his book, **Double Portion: Our Inheritance** writes, "Many are searching and seeking for intimacy in all the wrong places, only to miss the one source of intimacy they need most: an encounter with God the Father. They search for love and acceptance from frivolous sexual encounters or from a host of so-called friends, only to find themselves more alone and dejected than before. Soon an orphan spirit emerges within their hearts. As these fatherless children grow and reproduce, the orphan spirit they carry is reproduced in turn. Orphans reproduce orphans. Only Fathers can reproduce sons." [40] Indeed, Glover also makes the point that only sons receive an inheritance from their father. Orphans do not know what it is to have a father. If we seek only purpose to our life we will miss the most important thing: *relationship*. We cannot know what our inheritance is or what our purpose details outside of relationship with our Father. If we seek the Father's heart, we would experience Him picking us up, pulling us up on His lap, and holding us close enough for us to hear His heart beat. We would find comfort, assurance and rest for our souls, and as we do, hear our Father impart important truths that direct us into His plans and purpose for our life.

For years I missed this important reality. I never had much of a father

---

[40] Glover, Andy; Double Portion: Our Inheritance – Entering into the Father's Promise, Revival to the Nations, pg.66.

growing up because he was mentally ill and quite incapacitated. He was alive, but not engaged in any sort of a relationship with me as his daughter. He couldn't connect with any of us emotionally because the voices in his head demanded all his attention. Because of this I grew up with a sense of rejection, unworthiness and shame. I was deeply sorrowful that other kids had normal dads and I did not. I was ashamed at my father's odd behavior and wanted to distance myself from him, but that caused me to feel enormous guilt. He was a hurting person that deserved to feel loved and I could not give him love. He couldn't give it to us and we (my mom and my siblings) could not give it to him, either. It was like each one of us lived on autopilot, somewhat robotically. We functioned through school and work but with emotional disconnect because we got good at stuffing our emotions deep in the well. I realized that mental illness was a living hell for him, but it was for us, too. I felt so awkward and uncomfortable around him that I wanted nothing to do with him. His instability led to instability in the family. Shame, fear, rejection and anger cloaked my family with an oppressive weight of hopelessness. None of us knew what it was to have a healthy sense of identity because we were all emotionally and spiritually bankrupt. Because of the emotional disconnect, it became very difficult to learn how to connect with my Heavenly Father.

This caused me to overlook the intimacy factor for many years. I sought God for my prayer burdens, purpose, and direction, yet I still carried the feelings of an orphan. My lack of a healthy parental role model left a void in my life and I had no idea how to relate to a father. Over time, God healed that void. I will never forget the day when I read through a commentary on a certain portion of scripture, and it referred to the Father as loving us like a pregnant mother loves her child in the womb. Although I had a disconnect with a father figure, I was a mother and could clearly relate to loving my children. I remembered how I would speak to them while they were in my womb. I loved them before they could ever love me, simply because they were mine. I wanted the best for them, and spoke loving words over their destiny. When they were born, I couldn't wait to hold them, cuddle them and watch over them as they grew up. Suddenly, the Holy Spirit connected the dots. This is the same heart our Father has for us. At that moment of revelation, I knew without a doubt I had a Father that loved me and would do anything for me!

Every Believer needs to understand their identity in Christ. When a person understands who they are as a child of God, they can then enter the works of God. We are all called to the ministry of reconciliation, but we are also called to release healing and deliverance to others. This is a kingdom mandate. You are commissioned as an ambassador of His kingdom to bring

Him glory.

God does not define you by your past. He does not define you by things you've done, your work or what others say about you. He defines you as His child, and as such, you have all the rewards and blessings of a child of God. A child of God also becomes an heir to the kingdom of God. It is vital to your growth to understand who you are in Christ, and feel secure in that knowledge. God set His seal of ownership on you and put His Spirit in you as the security deposit and guarantee of the fulfillment of His promise. In Romans 8:11, scripture reminds us that the same Spirit that raised Christ from the dead lives in us! Therefore, the Spirit of God that defeated the enemy at the cross dwells in us, enabling us to have overcoming power against any enemy that stands before us. The Spirit also empowers us to help others, and He has given us the gifts of the Holy Spirit to help others live free and healed. This is why Jesus commissioned every believer to go do the same works as He did, and to accept by faith that what God has said about us is true. When we accept who we are in Christ, then we understand how precious the Holy Spirit is. We cannot accomplish anything in our own power or authority, but we have been graciously granted the use of Jesus' name to accomplish all His purpose.

The following is a list of statements about your identity in Christ. [41]

WHO YOU ARE IN CHRIST

Because you are in Christ, EVERY ONE of these statements is true of you.

- I am loved. 1 John 3:3
- I am accepted. Ephesians 1:6
- I am a child of God. John 1:12
- I am Jesus' friend. John 15:14
- I am a joint heir with Jesus, sharing His inheritance with Him. Romans 8:17
- I am united with God and one spirit with Him. 1 Corinthians 6:17
- I am a temple of God. His Spirit and his life lives in me. 1 Corinthians 6:19
- I am a member of Christ's body. 1 Corinthians 12:27
- I am a Saint. Ephesians 1:1
- I am redeemed and forgiven. Colossians 1:14

---

[41] "Who You Are in Christ," Christian Life Coaching UK, accessed Mar. 21, 2018, https://www.christianlifecoaching.co.uk/who-you-are-in-Christ.html

- I am complete in Jesus Christ. Colossians 2:10
- I am free from condemnation. Romans 8:1
- I am a new creation because I am in Christ. 2 Corinthians 5:17
- I am chosen of God, holy and dearly loved. Colossians 3:12
- I am established, anointed, and sealed by God. 2 Corinthians 1:21
- I do not have a spirit of fear, but of love, power, and a sound mind. 2 Timothy 1:7
- I am God's co-worker. 2 Corinthians 6:1
- I am seated in heavenly places with Christ. Eph 2:6
- I have direct access to God Ephesians. 2:18
- I am chosen to bear fruit John. 15:16
- I am one of God's living stones, being built up in Christ as a spiritual house. 1 Peter 2:5
- I have been given exceedingly great and precious promises by God by which I share His nature. 2 Peter 1:4
- I can always know the presence of God because He never leaves me Hebrews. 13:5
- God works in me to help me do the things He wants me to do Philippians 2:13
- I can ask God for wisdom and He will give me what I need. James 1:5

As you remain in God's presence you will bear much fruit! Perhaps the most important thing to remember is that the anointing and the gifts of the Holy Spirit flow from a place of love and compassion for others. 1 Corinthians 13 reminds us that we can do many things in the name of the Lord but the greatest virtue is love. When love is our motivation miraculous things can happen.

HOW DOES FAITH WORK?

- Faith works through love, Gal. 5:6
- We have been given a measure of faith, Rom. 12:3
- We 'build ourselves up in our most holy faith.' Jude 1:20
- Faith comes by hearing the word. Rom. 10:17
- Faith increases through our obedience. John 15:14, 2 John 1:6, 1 John 3:21,22
- Faith rests in the finished work of the cross. Heb. 4:3

Ephesians 2:8 tells us, "For by grace you are saved through faith; and that not of yourselves: it is the gift of God." Everything we receive from God is a gift, even the measure of faith that we needed for salvation. Faith comes as a seed but we must cooperate with God in order for our faith to grow. Obedience grows our faith. Fellowship with God, learning to listen for His voice and resting in what He has already done for us is also an expression of our faith. Everyone has been given the same seed (measure) of faith, but not everyone has grown their faith at the same rate. Faith grows with practice. That means we must act – take a risk in obedience to what we've heard – and do what God is leading us to do. The more we are obedient to act on what we hear, God will trust us with more. Matthew 17:20 states that even faith the size of a tiny mustard seed is enough to move a mountain! Isn't that amazing?

Jesus lives in us as Healer, Deliverer, and our Teacher. Holy Spirit is the Spirit of Truth, the Spirit of Prophecy, and the dynamic power of God that raised Jesus from the dead. He lives in us, and because He does, we are carriers of God's glory. As we pray for others, the power of Jesus Christ is released through us to touch, heal, minister and restore others.

RELEASING HEALING

When we pray, we don't ask or beg God to do something. He has put His Spirit in us and given us authority to declare His will 'on earth as it is in heaven.' We can be bold in prayer! The Greek word for authority is **'exousia.'** The definition below is from the NAS New Testament Greek Lexicon found online:

Definition:

1.power of choice, liberty of doing as one pleases
a. leave or permission
2. physical and mental power
a. the ability or strength with which one is endued, which he either possesses or exercises
3. the power of authority (influence) and of right (privilege)
4. the power of rule or government (the power of him whose will and commands must be submitted to by others and obeyed)
a. universally
1. authority over mankind
b. specifically
1. the power of judicial decisions
2. of authority to manage domestic affairs
c. metonymically
1. a thing subject to authority or rule
d. jurisdiction
1. one who possesses authority
e. a ruler, a human magistrate

f. the leading and more powerful among created beings superior to man, spiritual potentates

g. a sign of the husband's authority over his wife

1. the veil with which propriety required a women to cover herself

h. the sign of regal authority, a crown

This is your true identity in Christ! That is why scripture tells us in 1 John 4:4, "Greater is He that lives within us than he that is in the world." You've been given power and authority to reign and rule with Jesus. Jesus gave us power and authority over every sickness, disease, and all kinds of spirits. He expects us to go do the work of the ministry! Allow me to put this in a more clear explanation. If Jesus were speaking to you, this is what He would say:

"I trust you to do the works of the ministry. Even though you may feel inadequate or unsure of yourself at times, I have chosen to trust YOU with My delegated authority to do the works I've called you to! Therefore, go do them knowing that I've commissioned you to a mighty work of God. I trust you to do what's right. You have the liberty to take decisive action. You are endued with supernatural strength by My Holy Spirit to accomplish My will and purpose. You have the right to exercise authority in My name because I have given you the right to rule with governmental authority. This means that the enemy must submit to MY NAME and he must obey. You have the right to make judicial decisions that will restore justice to the oppressed and to manage domestic affairs. You have jurisdiction where I've placed you and you have spiritual potency to bind the enemy and make him inoperable. I have set this seal of My ownership over you because you are a child of God. You have royal authority – use it well!"

"And when He had called His twelve disciples to Him, He gave them power over unclean spirits, to cast them out, and to heal all kinds of sickness and all kinds of disease…And as you go, preach, saying, 'The kingdom of heaven is at hand.' Heal the sick, cleanse the lepers, raise the dead, cast out demons. Freely you have received, freely give." Matt. 10:1,7,8 NJKV

We have dominion and jurisdiction over evil spirits, sickness and disease. Those things are subject to the authority of Christ in us. Luke 10:19 declares, "Behold, I give you power to tread on serpents and scorpions, and over all the power of the enemy; and nothing shall by any means hurt you."

"So Jesus answered and said to them, "Have faith in God. For assuredly, I say to you, whoever says to this mountain, 'Be removed and be cast into the sea,' and does not doubt in his heart, but believes that those things he says will be done, he will have whatever he says. Therefore I say to you, whatever things you ask when you pray, believe that you receive them, and you will have them." Mark 11:22-24 NKJV

God's will is to heal. He is sovereign in how He chooses to work in each person's life, but it is always His will to heal. Healings can be progressive, but miracles are instantaneous. Speak to every detail of the problem. Command the enemy to leave in Jesus name. God has given us His favor and we know according to Isaiah 55:11 that His word does not return to Him void. It is not an empty promise! God's word will accomplish much good and do exactly what it is designed to do, therefore we can have confidence in knowing that it is impossible to pray and nothing happen! Everything is possible to those that believe.

God has made a covenant of healing with His people. In Mark 16:18 we are commissioned to lay hands on the sick and they will recover. Sometimes healing comes by the person confessing their sin first, then anointing them with oil and praying for them. We find this principle in James 5:14-15. At other times, healing may be released through some act of obedience, or the person exercising their faith to bend, move, stand, sit or attempt to do what they had not been able to do previously. John 9:6-7 and 2 Kings 5:10-14 are examples of people receiving their healing when they acted in obedience to the Word from the Lord.

Another way that people can receive their healing is through taking communion. 1 Corinthians 11:25-31. There is power in taking communion because we partake of Jesus' death and resurrection. We acknowledge the price that He paid for us to be able to receive that blessing. We can command every sin, sickness, disease and form of torment to be absorbed into the cross of Christ. As we declare our faith in what Jesus did for us, and take communion with Him and others, we are meeting at **His altar**. We are exalting the Lord. We can have what we decide upon based on the promises found in His word. Job 22:28 tells us that what we decide upon (and declare out of our mouth) is what shall be established, so that light will shine on our ways. It is once again applying the principle of agreement: (where two or more agree on touching anything) – Jesus is there to answer our prayer, (Matthew 18:20).

God's desire is to heal and restore His people. Scripture tells us it is the kindness of God that leads men to repentance. Christians can pray for those who are saved and unsaved and often they will receive a touch from God. We have the authority to cast out devils, but sometimes it is not wisdom to do so if the individual is not ready to commit to Christ and make a change in direction for their life. This is what genuine repentance is, and without repentance, then the person is really just looking for a quick fix. They want relief from whatever pain or torment they may have in their life, but without a commitment to Christ, they will lose their healing. The devils that caused the problems will come right back, and often times leave the person in a worse state than before. This is an example of an ungodly covenant with the enemy that would need to be broken. Negative covenants are often those things that cause a person to agree with a lie – either about themselves, God or in their belief system.

God is incredibly gracious. It is His desire to heal, restore and lead people into freedom. John 10:10b tells us that Jesus came to give us abundant life, and the gospels are full of other scriptures that confirm this. However, the method He chooses to accomplish this is up to Him. There are times when God will heal someone without requiring anything more than faith to be healed. There are also times when He knows that the person requesting prayer may need to cooperate with Him in some matters in order to receive their healing.

For instance, there was a woman I prayed for who had suffered with various health issues for a very long time, and debilitating back pain for over 20 years. Her ability to walk was severely crippled. She had gone to many ministers to be prayed for, but she had not been healed. Now, this woman was a Christian and had been for a long time. I watched as a team of people prayed over her and periodically they would ask her if she felt any better. This went on for about 20 minutes without any progress. Finally, I walked up and whispered in her ear, "Is there anyone you need to forgive?" Immediately, tears welled up in her eyes and she nodded yes. I said, "Your unforgiveness is blocking your ability to receive your healing. In light of this, are you willing to forgive the person that hurt you?" She nodded yes, so I asked her to verbalize her prayer of forgiveness. The team continued to pray, but this time healing began to manifest quickly. She began to smile as the pain left her body. She left quite different than when she walked in! In this situation, God required her to obey His word before she could receive her healing. It wasn't that she didn't know she needed to forgive someone, but she was trying to obtain her healing by bypassing the requirement of obedience. That rarely works because the enemy knows when he has legal rights to enforce the curse. Healing ministry is dependent upon the One who is doing the healing. We must listen for the Holy Spirit, and listen to the words of the person we are ministering to. Often times they will reveal key information that can unlock their healing if dealt with properly. Whenever possible, it is always more productive to have the person you are praying for break any agreements with the enemy so that prayer can be effective.

In another situation, I was praying for a woman with cancer. She was at the end of chemo treatments and surgery had gone well. As I listened to this woman speak, my spiritual radar pickup up on a few things. First, she referred to the health crisis as 'her cancer.' That indicated that she had taken ownership of it, and I began to instruct her that it was not her cancer at all; Jesus had paid the full price for it! The second thing I noticed is that she felt responsible for having a powerful testimony of healing because she acknowledged there were so many people watching her life. I told her that it was not her responsibility but God's, for only He could heal. Then I asked her if she was afraid of letting people down and she burst into tears. She admitted that she did, and also felt the sickness and all that came with it put a tremendous burden on her family. So much so, she often felt it was better for her to die and go home to be with the Lord. That was such a revelation that was key to her healing! It was certainly understandable for her to feel the way she did, and certainly, no one would condemn her for not wanting to be a burden to her family, but her words conveyed that she was full of fear and double-mindedness. She had not yet made up her mind whether she wanted to live or die. I told her she had to make a decision, because scripture says a double-minded man receives nothing from the Lord. She decided she wanted to live, and I had her renounce agreements she had made with fear, doubt, and ultimately, death. Her words had given the enemy a legal entry point to act upon her confession, and she would have lost any healing she had gained up to that point. She also broke agreements with bearing a false sense of responsibility and the fear of man (being afraid to let people down). There is so much we can learn by listening to people that can help us be more effective ministers.

Devils know when the person has given them authority to stay – and they will! You can end up wasting your time trying to get spirits to leave if the individual is not ready to commit to a different way of life. They may not be ready to give up some area of sin, or refuse to forgive someone they are offended with. You may not feel a freedom to pray for healing but you can pray that God would touch them and remove the blocks that hinder the person from surrendering those things to God. Jesus himself could only work where He saw His Father at work. It is wisdom to discern where a person is at before you attempt to pray for them. Even Jesus asked the man in John chapter 5 if he wanted to be healed. Sometimes we need to ask a few questions and see where the individual is at in their beliefs. God responds to faith. Jesus discerned that he really did want to be made well and healed him.

Allow me to share another brief story. I was preparing to minister to a man who said he had a particular disease. As he began to speak about his condition he revealed that it ran in his family. The Lord had also told me that there was witchcraft in his family line, but I felt a bit timid in sharing that because I wasn't sure if he would receive it. I knew there was a generational curse because of the disease but when I mentioned witchcraft he said his parents were Christians. Then I asked him the origin of his ancestry. It was Puerto Rico, and suddenly the word the Lord gave me about witchcraft in the family made sense, even if it didn't make sense to him. Puerto Rico is known for a mixture of religions that include Catholicism, African voodoo, Muslim beliefs and many other things. I had him pray to renounce witchcraft and broke generational curses, then prayed for healing of his physical body. Before he left, the Lord showed me that this man had his guard up. I sensed it and the Lord confirmed it. This is important for two reasons. First, many people that may ask for prayer may not know if the person they are approaching can be trusted, and so they remain guarded. A guarded person does not feel comfortable revealing too much information, which means you are going to have very limited information. It is very important to minister out of love and grace, and just let Holy Spirit lead the session because it may help them to become more comfortable and come back for additional prayer. The second important thing to remember is that you cannot be effective if you approach ministry to others by what you think you already know. You can't carry pre-conceived ideas; it's important to listen to Holy Spirit to reveal information. It's not always the time or place at an altar call to get into a lengthy counseling session, but you can certainly have the person make an appointment or refer them to trained Christian counselors and prayer ministers to help finish the job.

Please bear with me as I share one last story. One man, whose reputation preceded him, came for prayer. I had been informed that this person had previously manifested demons and was difficult to work with. It took a lot for this person to finally commit to allowing anyone to pray for him because the demons would keep him away. I had all these thoughts in my mind, such as "Oh, it's pride. He's just toying with God. He's not serious about wanting deliverance." He had addictions, anger and a lot of demons resisting him getting help. So I had all this in my mind, but as I stood in front of him, I asked Holy Spirit to show me the root of the issue. Instantly, I heard 'Grief.' I was shocked because that had not occurred to me, but after I heard the word everything else made perfect sense. I asked this young man (who looked very tough and macho), if there was an event or a memory in his life connected to grief, and I explained that God wanted to heal it. He said, "Yes. It was the day my daughter was born."

My heart grieved with him. I had no idea what I was about to hear next, but he explained that he had only held his daughter a few times and she was taken out of his life by the mother. He had not seen her since. That is indeed a pain that will cause enormous grief, and it can also cause anger and many other emotions to the point where people will try to self-medicate to escape their emotions. That is what was going on with this person. This man also carried a lot of regret, because it was his actions that had caused the mother to take the child and move out of state.

This man had to first forgive himself and renounce the spirit of regret, because regret kept him bound to the past. I told him that he did not have to live under self-condemnation because when a person was 'in Christ,' God made all things new. I encouraged him to believe for a miracle that would restore the child back into his life. I also began to prophesy that God saw him different than he saw himself and speak into his future. It is so important to reveal a new future and a new destiny than how people currently see themselves or their situation. Releasing God's words to an individual has the ability to act as a divine steering wheel, redirecting people away from a path of destruction, into making choices that will align them with God's path and plan for their lives.

As you pray for others, it is important to remember that other individuals may not have the same level of faith that you do. We need to meet them at the point of their faith. Ask them what they would like Jesus to do for them before you pray, because Jesus will meet them at their level of faith. Then you can agree together and expect God to answer.

"Again, I tell you truly that if two of you on the earth agree about anything you ask for, it will be done for you by My Father in heaven. For where two or three gather together in My name, there am I with them." Matthew 18:19,20

In John 10:25, Jesus said that the works that He did testified on His behalf. In John 16:23 He said that whatever we asked the Father in His name, He would do. These are our assurances that when we pray in Jesus' name we act in His authority. The burden is not on us to perform. It's not our job to answer prayer; it's His! Our responsibility is to come into agreement with what He has already said in His word. When we act on His behalf for the sake of helping others and give Him praise for answered prayer, we bring Him glory.

In every place on the globe people can gather, pray, seek His face, give Him praise – and Jesus is in the midst of us all. We get to experience the truth of His promise, that He is with us. God is always present, keeping a watchful eye on those that would come into agreement with one another. It is gathering in His name that draws Him into our midst. Jesus is attracted to faith, unity, love and compassion. If we agree on touching anything, He is there to respond by sending an answer down to earth. What a premium we should put on unified prayer!

Sin brings people into captivity, but repentance and obedience will bring them out of it. Agreements with the enemy can bring about sickness and disease, but breaking those agreements (through prayers of renouncements) can reverse and restore health issues. Many of God's prophets have made declarations in faith that His people will be set free, healed and delivered from their captivity – but, God will not violate His own principles simply because people want an easier way. He has prerequisites to revival and restoration that He will not disregard. Without repentance, there can be no restoration. That is why prayer is such a vital component and a necessary prerequisite to spiritual breakthrough. He longs to pour out His blessing and restoration to those that call upon His name!

Scripture is full of references when God's people humbled themselves, prayed, and turned back to God. He responded by sending deliverers to lead them out of their captivity.

"God heard their groaning, and God remembered His covenant with Abraham, Isaac, and Jacob. God looked on the children of Israel, and God had concern for them" Exodus 2:24-25, NIV

"Then they cried out to the LORD in their trouble; He saved them out of their distresses. He brought them out of darkness and the shadow of death And broke their bands apart. Let them give thanks to the LORD for His lovingkindness, And for His wonders to the sons of men!" Psalm 107:13-15 NASB

There are many other scriptures as well that affirm God's plan for His people is to give them a future and a hope (Jer. 29:11). Prayer precedes every spiritual breakthrough and every revival. Prayer is the catalyst that drives men to repentance, to humble themselves before a mighty God, so that they can experience the goodness of their Father.

CHAPTER SEVEN

POWER IN THE BLOOD OF JESUS

In the same way after supper He took the cup saying, "This cup is
the New Covenant of my blood, which is poured out for you."
Luke 22:20

Every drop of blood that Jesus shed for mankind was divine. 100% holy; 100% God. Mary was overshadowed by the Holy Spirit and became pregnant supernaturally. There was **no mixture**, none of man's blood that flowed through Jesus Christ. The supernatural impregnation of Mary is proof that the word of God is his sperm. God spoke into Mary's womb and the Holy Spirit created new life within her. No part of the child growing within her was contaminated by the sin inherited by the first Adam. Jesus became the divine expression of His Father's seed, which was His spoken word.

God's word is potent and so is the blood of His Son. There is no impotency in God, no weakness whatsoever. It is because Jesus' blood is 100% pure, holy and divine that it makes it so powerful. It has the power to heal our bodies and deliver our soul from eternal damnation. It has the power to make us completely whole in every way!

The problem does not lie in the potency of the blood to deliver on God's promises. The problem is that many people overlook its significance. The salvation message has been so contemporized that it omits the pain, suffering, and sacrifice that Jesus experienced on our behalf. In many churches, and in many lives the gospel has been made into just another feel good message. The message of the cross has been watered down to make it more appealing, without people having the conviction of the price that was paid for our freedom. When is the last time you heard about the power of the blood to save and deliver you?

When Peter preached on the day of Pentecost he fearlessly dove right in and didn't mince words. First the bad news.

"All of you Israelites, listen to my message: it's about Jesus of Nazareth, a man whom God authenticated for you by performing in your presence powerful deeds, wonders, and signs through Him, just as you yourselves know. **This man, Jesus, who came into your hands by God's sure plan and advanced knowledge, you nailed to a cross and killed in collaboration with lawless outsiders.** But God raised Jesus and unleashed Him from the agonizing birth pangs of death, for death could not possibly keep Jesus in its power." Acts 2:22-24 The Voice

Can you just imagine what's going through Peter's mind? How long had he rehearsed what he might say if he was given a chance? "Yes, folks, you made a grievous error in judgment. You killed the long awaited Messiah. You know the one we've been waiting for all these years? Yeah, *that* One. You nailed the darling of heaven to a cross by conspiring to commit murder. What are you going to do about that?" Those aren't exactly Peter's words, but Peter spoke with such power and authority that the crowd was moved with conviction. By the time Peter wraps up his message in verses 36-37, take a look at what takes place.

"Everyone in Israel should now realize with certainty what God has done: God has made Jesus both Lord and Anointed King—this same Jesus whom you crucified. When the people heard this, **their hearts were pierced**; and they said to Peter and his fellow apostles, " Our brothers, what should we do?"(Emphasis mine)

The realization that they had killed not just an innocent man, but **the Christ** who had been prophesied about for hundreds of years – well, that revelation compelled them to take action. They had to do what was called for in that moment, and that meant acknowledging their crime. They also realized they could not escape the penalty for their actions.

Peter presented the message so effectively that it elicited the right response to those that heard him. *"What should we do now?"* Peter then announced the good news: a lifeline of hope awaited them so that their souls would be spared from eternal damnation.

"Reconsider your lives; change your direction. Participate in the ceremonial washing of baptism in the name of Jesus God's Anointed, the Liberating King. Then your sins will be forgiven, and the gift of the Holy Spirit will be yours. For the promise of the Spirit is for you, for your children, for all people—even those considered outsiders and outcasts—the Lord our

God invites everyone to come to Him."

Just as God raised Jesus from a decaying body, Peter holds out hope for God to liberate those who follow Him from their decaying culture.

Peter was pleading and offering many logical reasons to believe. Whoever made a place for his message in their hearts received the baptism; in fact, that day alone, about 3,000 people joined the disciples." Acts 2:38-41 The Voice

Many people hear the gospel told to them, but until someone has a personal revelation of how it applies to them, the power of that message is obscured. Jesus gave himself up for us all. He didn't hold anything back! He surrendered His life in the most sacrificial gift He could ever give us, all so that we would have an opportunity to live free and healed. Now *that's* love.

In a similar fashion, I believe that people have also heard about the power of the blood, they've received it as truth and they say they believe it, but they haven't yet received the full revelation of it. If a person hasn't had a revelation of a truth, they can't fully walk into it. It's one thing to know something because you've heard it so frequently that you've accepted it as truth. It's another thing altogether when the Holy Spirit illuminates it and it is birthed in your heart as a profound revelation. It's like being born again. There are some things that can only come by His Spirit.

The Bible teaches us that the life is in the blood according to Leviticus 17:11"For the life of the flesh is in the blood and I have given it to you upon the altar to make an atonement for your souls: for it is the blood that makes an atonement for the soul."

"For it is the life of all flesh, the blood of it is for the life thereof." Lev. 17:14. The Old Testament gives us an illustration of the power of the sacrificial blood. In Exodus 12, God was preparing to deliver the Israelites out of Egypt. The last of the ten plagues was about to occur, in which all the firstborn males – both humans and animals – would die. This was a miraculous sign to Pharaoh and all of Egypt that God would bestow judgment upon those that had hardened their hearts towards Him and in contrast all of Egypt would see His hand of protection over His people.

In Leviticus 12:7, the children of God were to sacrifice a lamb and put some of the blood on their door posts. When God passed over the land, those with the blood upon their house would be spared the judgment that came upon Egypt. "The blood on the houses where you are staying will distinguish them; when I see the blood, I will pass over you. No plague will fall on you to destroy you when I strike the land of Egypt...." Exodus 12:13

In the New Testament, Romans 5:9 tells us that we are spared from God's wrath. "Much more then, having now been justified by His blood, we shall be saved from wrath through Him."

It was Adam's sin that was transferred down the bloodlines to humanity, that is why it took the blood of a pure and holy God, who was also fully man, to redeem mankind. Not one drop of Jesus' blood was contaminated by inherited sin *because* the blood of the mother and the blood of the developing fetus never mixed. This is important because it took sinless blood to redeem mankind from the curse of death.

The late Martin DeHaan, M.D, in his book *The Chemistry of the Blood.* writes, "It is now definitely known that the blood which flows in an unborn babies arteries and veins is not derived from the mother but is produced within the body of the fetus itself only after the introduction of the male sperm. An unfertilized ovum can never develop blood since the female egg does not by itself contain the elements essential for the production of this blood. It is only after the male element has entered the ovum that blood can develop." [42]

This is confirmed by science. "The fetal blood in the vessels of the chorionic villae at no time gains access to the maternal blood in the intervillous space, BEING SEPARATED FROM ONE ANOTHER by the double layer of chorionic epithelium."- Williams' Practice of Obstetrics, Third Edition, page 133 [43]

"One of the placenta's jobs is to make sure blood from the mother and fetus never mixes. The placenta acts as an exchange surface between the mother and the fetus. Nutrients and oxygen are passed over by diffusion only. If the mother's and fetus's blood mixed, it could be deadly for both of them. If the mother and the fetus had different blood types, they might both die if their blood mixed."[44]

The significance of this information is that it provides proof that Jesus'

---

[42] DeHaan, Martin, M.D.,The Chemistry of the Blood, from http://www.jesus-is-savior.com/BTP/Dr_MR_DeHaan/Chemistry/04.htm , accessed Aug. 12, 2018
[43] DeHaan, Martin, M.D.,The Chemistry of the Blood, from http://www.jesus-is-savior.com/BTP/Dr_MR_DeHaan/Chemistry/04.htm , accessed Aug. 12, 2018
[44] "Placenta", Wikipedia.com , https://simple.wikipedia.org/wiki/Placenta , accessed Aug. 12, 2018

blood was 100% pure, incorruptible and divine. The blood of a holy God was shed for us as Jesus died our death on the cross. The blood of a holy God was sufficient to purge the stain of sin from those that would receive Him as their Lord and Savior, and it's the blood of a holy God that has the power to heal us completely. Meditate on this thought until it fully convinces you of the truth: The blood of Jesus Christ is powerful and effective. The revelation of this truth has the ability to elevate your faith and make it incredibly potent!.

"… from Jesus Christ, who is the faithful witness, the firstborn from the dead, and the ruler of the kings of the earth. To him who loves us and has freed us from our sins by his blood…" Rev. 1:5

- The blood of Jesus has paid our debt, once and for all. (Heb. 9:28)
- The blood of Jesus offers us redemption through the forgiveness of sins. Eph. 1:7
- Partaking of Jesus' blood through taking communion has the power to make us spiritually alive. John 6:53
- The blood of Jesus heals us. 1 Peter 2:24
- The blood of Jesus purifies us from all sin. 1 John 1:7
- We are no longer alienated as strangers, but the blood of Jesus allows us to draw near to God. Eph. 2:12-13
- The blood of Jesus takes my sin and exchanges it for the righteousness of God. 2 Cor. 5:21
- The blood of Jesus cleanses my conscience from guilt. Heb. 10:22
- The blood of Jesus allows Christ to live in me, through His Holy Spirit. Gal. 2:20
- The blood of Jesus gives me victory. Rev. 12:11

Jesus took all of mankind's suspicion, distrust, hostility and pride, and through His blood, destroyed the wall of separation to bring reconciliation. Through offering His body upon the cross, Jesus demonstrated His willingness to let love kill all the hostility and build a bridge back to His Father. This act of humility and love allowed us to become family. By His blood, He redeemed us, bought us back from the wicked one, and made every tribe and language. He took people from every race and every nation and gave us a kingdom. He has appointed us priests and kings to serve God and rule upon the earth.[45] Meditate upon this until you sense the essence of His pure devotion and love towards you. If your desire is to partake of the potency of His blood, then you must ask Holy Spirit to reveal it in your heart.

---

[45] Ref. Rev.5:9,10

If the blood of Christ is so potent, why then do so many people not walk in divine health? I do not have all the answers to that, but I do believe it is often a combination of factors. While it is not my intention to put anyone under condemnation, I do want to encourage people to examine themselves in light of what scripture says, because most people rationalize certain behaviors and beliefs and think it doesn't matter. The standard we are held accountable to is scripture, not our own opinions of ourselves. Let us take a look at something I believe is often overlooked in scripture.

The Bible tells us in 1 Cor.11:26-30 that many people do not rightly discern the significance of the Lord's body, especially when taking communion, and that this is a cause of spiritual weakness, sickness and even death. This is also another significant reminder about the body that He gave for us and the blood that was shed on our behalf. Let's read this in the scripture.

"Every time you taste this bread and every time you place the cup to your mouths and drink, you are declaring the Lord's death, which is the ultimate expression of His faithfulness and love, until He comes again.

So if someone takes of this bread and drinks from the Lord's cup improperly—as you are doing—he is guilty of violating the body and blood of our Lord. Examine yourselves first. Then you can properly approach the table to eat the bread and drink from the cup; because otherwise, if you eat and drink without properly discerning the significance of the Lord's body, then you eat and drink a mouthful of judgment upon yourself. Because of this violation, many in your community are now sick and weak; some have even died." [46]

Paul addressed some problematic behaviors with God's people. Corinth was known as a place where there was a lot of sinful, immoral behavior, and the people in the church were having their fair share of difficulties in growing up in Christ. The Corinthian church was troubled with divisiveness, scandal, and carnal, immature, unbecoming behavior. Their behavior towards the poor was selfish and rude. And While God doesn't demand perfection to partake at the Lord's table, He looked for humble, contrite hearts that appreciated His sacrifice and treated others in the same family of God with mutual love and respect. Instead, their gatherings were being counterproductive because their conduct was polarizing the community. Their self-centeredness included mistreating others, which didn't honor the Lord at all.

---

[46] 1 Cor. 11:26-30 The Voice

The whole act of taking communion is to remember the suffering Christ too upon His own body as He laid down His life for us. As we partake of the bread, which symbolizes the body of Christ that was broken for us, we must acknowledge that there is something within us that must also be broken before we can be restored to our true identity in Christ. There are things we must let go of and be willing to surrender in order to be more fully conformed to the image of Christ. Matthew 5:23,24 tells us that if we have something against another believer (or if someone has something against us), we are to leave our gift in front of the altar and go reconcile with them first, then we can come back and give our offering. This demonstrates the importance of dealing with offenses before we give to the Lord. Should we not do the same before taking communion? Communion is done in remembrance of God's forgiveness and mercy towards us when we were most undeserving. Taking communion is not to be done with the familiarity of a religious practice, but with the understanding that you were once the one that was hostile and resistance towards God. You were once the one in need of mercy and forgiveness. Jesus took all the sins you committed and died your death. Do you remember the things that once brought you shame? He took every one of them so that you would not live under a burden of guilt that you could not carry. When we partake of the juice, which represents His blood, we partake of the cleansing He made available, and the power of the blood to heal. "You know that a price was paid to redeem you from following the empty ways handed on to you by your ancestors. It was not paid with things that perish (like silver and gold), but with the precious blood of the Anointed, who was like a perfect and unblemished sacrificial lamb." 1 Peter 1:18,19.

"Now that you have taken care to purify your souls through your submission to the truth, you can experience real love for each other. So love each other deeply from a pure heart. You have been reborn – not from seed that eventually dies but from seed that is eternal – through the word of God that lives and endures forever." 1 Peter 1:22,23

The word of God was given to us to separate our flesh from our spirit, so that we could become more like Christ. "For the word of God is alive and active. Sharper than any double-edged sword, it penetrates even to dividing soul and spirit, joints and marrow; it judges the thoughts and attitudes of the heart" Hebrews 4:12 NIV.

There is a warning in Paul's words about familiarity. One cannot read 1 Cor. 11:26-30 and just apply a blanket of grace over every careless word and action, thinking that how we treat others has no relationship to our health and spiritual condition. The blood of Christ is deserving of honor and respect. Matthew Henry's Commentary has this to say about this portion of scripture:

(In reference to communion), "It is to be done in remembrance of Christ, to keep fresh in our minds his dying for us, as well as to remember Christ pleading for us, in virtue of his death, at God's right hand. It is not merely in remembrance of Christ, of what he has done and suffered; but to celebrate his grace in our redemption. We declare his death to be our life, the spring of all our comforts and hopes. And we glory in such a declaration; we show forth his death, and plead it as our accepted sacrifice and ransom. The Lord's supper is not an ordinance to be observed merely for a time, but to be continued. The apostle lays before the Corinthians the danger of receiving it with an unsuitable temper of mind; or keeping up the covenant with sin and death, while professing to renew and confirm the covenant with God. No doubt such incur great guilt, and so render themselves liable to spiritual judgements. But fearful believers should not be discouraged from attending at this holy ordinance. The Holy Spirit never caused this scripture to be written to deter serious Christians from their duty, though the devil has often made this use of it. The apostle was addressing Christians, and warning them to beware of the temporal judgements with which God chastised his offending servants. And in the midst of judgement, God remembers mercy: He many times punishes those whom he loves. It is better to bear trouble in this world, than to be miserable for ever. The apostle points out the duty of those who come to the Lord's table. Self-examination is necessary to right attendance at this holy ordinance. If we would thoroughly search ourselves, to condemn and set right what we find wrong, we should stop Divine judgements. The apostle closes all with a caution against the irregularities of which the Corinthians were guilty at the Lord's table. Let all look to it, that they do not come together to God's worship, so as to provoke him, and bring down vengeance on themselves." [47]

Vengeance is a strong word, and I'm not sure I entirely agree with Matthew Henry's choice of wording, because God's wrath was spent upon Jesus when He took all of our sin upon Himself. However, we also cannot ignore the warning of scripture that reminds us to examine ourselves.

Allow me to revisit a thought I briefly touched on in the beginning of the chapter. We know that through Jesus' death and resurrection His Holy Spirit lives within each person that receives Him as Lord and Savior. It's the same Spirit that raised Christ from the dead, and the same Spirit that acted

---

[47] 1 Cor. 11:26-30, Matthew Henry's Concise Commentary, https://biblehub.com/commentaries/1_corinthians/11-26.htm, accessed Aug. 12, 2018

on the spoken word of God to create new life. We have the power and presence of God living within us, which is an exciting thought. However, the words of God are known as seed. The Strong's Concordance #4690 is the word *sperma*, or that which is sown, i.e. seed. God's word is His seed. As He speaks, Holy Spirit captures the seed and causes it to spring up into new life.

"The tongue can bring death or life; those who love to talk will reap the consequences." Prov. 18:21

"When words are many, sin is unavoidable, but he who restrains his lips is wise." Prov. 10:19

He who guards his mouth protects his life, but the one who opens his lips invites his own ruin." Prov. 13:3

A good person produces good things from the treasury of a good heart, and an evil person produces evil things from the treasury of an evil heart." Matt. 12:35.

There are many more scriptures about the power of our words, but the point is, whatever we plant (scattering seeds) is going to reap a harvest. Our words are backed by the spirit of God living within us that are literally like sperm, releasing the power to create what we speak. We can either speak life, and be acquitted by our words, or speak critical, judgmental, unloving words and discover that our own words condemn us. Don't tear down your own house with the wrong use of your words. We are given a promise in Isaiah 54:17 which tells us, "No weapon formed against us shall prosper and every tongue that rises up against us in judgment we shall condemn." Who is to condemn unprofitable words? We are. We are to break the power of our own negative confessions just as much as the critical word curses of others so that the enemy cannot use them to form an assignment. Put the blood of Jesus over those words! If we don't want to walk in condemnation, then we must take responsibility for what comes out of our mouth.

"For by your words you will be acquitted, and by your words you will be condemned." Matt.21:37.

Sins of the mouth were part of the problem that Apostle Paul addressed in the Corinthian church. He started out in chapter one warning them to stop acting divisively and to respond to one another in love and humility, pursuing peace and unity with one another. He warned them to stop acting judgmentally and reminded them what it meant to walk in love. We must each remember the principle found in Matt. 25:40. The King's Spirit lives in us. How we treat others is how we treat Him. "The King will answer and say to them, 'Truly I say to you, to the extent that you did it to one of these brothers of Mine, even the least of them, you did it to Me.'

These people were not honoring one another, and because they dishonored each other, they also did it unto Him. I think this has a lot to do with Paul's comments in 1 Cor. 11, where he told them that it was the way they treated one another as well as the way they dishonored the practice of taking communion that caused them to drink judgment to themselves. I've said all of this as a reminder that the seeds you plant by the words of your mouth act as sperm to produce things in your life and in the lives of others. If you're spiritually weak, sick, or worse – examine yourself. Ask Holy Spirit to refresh your memory and bring to your remembrance anything you need to repent of and put under the blood of Jesus. Don't give the enemy seeds for his new assignment. Cancel it and condemn those words to bear no bad fruit!. Instead, declare all that the blood affords you!

There is POWER to FORGIVE SINS:

Jesus Christ conquered Satan on his own ground, and after Satan had taken his best effort to destroy the Son of God, after Jesus was crucified, He went into Satan's domain to strip him of all authority and power. He took the keys of Death and Hades away from him, forever putting the enemy of our souls to an open shame - in front of all his co-partners in the works of evil and destruction.

"For this is My blood of the new covenant, which is shed for many for the remission of sins." Matthew 26:28

"In Him we have redemption through His blood, the forgiveness of sins, according to the riches of His grace." Ephesians 1:7

"But now in Christ Jesus you who once were far off have been made near by the blood of Christ." Ephesians 2:13

"For the life of the flesh is in the blood ... for it is the blood that makes atonement for the soul." Leviticus 17:11

There is POWER for DELIVERANCE:

He obtained eternal redemption because of the shed blood, because He offered Himself without spot to God - and is able to cleanse our conscience from dead works. He does this so that we can serve the living God. Jesus

Christ is the Mediator of the New Covenant, by which we are saved by His grace and our faith in the Son of God. [48]

... that through death He might destroy him who had the power of death, that is, the devil, and release those who through fear of death were all their lifetime subject to bondage." Hebrews 2:14

"He has delivered us from the power of darkness and translated us into the kingdom of the Son of His love, in whom we have redemption through His blood, the forgiveness of sins." Colossians 1:13

"Having disarmed principalities and powers, He made a public spectacle of them, triumphing over them in it." Colossians 2:15

"For this purpose the Son of God was manifested, that He might destroy the works of the devil." 1 John 3:8

"And they overcame him by the blood of the Lamb and by the word of their testimony, and they did not love their lives to the death." Revelation 12:11

There is POWER and AUTHORITY:

Jesus' blood makes it possible for us to enjoy communion with the Father and bring the needs of others to Him through our prayers and intercession. It gives us the ability to release blessing into the lives of others

"Behold, I give you the authority to trample on serpents and scorpions, and over all the power of the enemy, and nothing shall by any means hurt you." Luke 10:19

"Then He called His twelve disciples together and gave them power and authority over all demons, and to cure diseases. He sent them to preach the kingdom of God and to heal the sick." Luke 9:1

There is POWER for PROTECTION.

It was the shed blood of Jesus that won the victory on the cross and defeated all the power of the enemy. What was true then is still true today. I suggest to you that you pray for the blood of Jesus to cover, guard, protect, save, redeem and restore every aspect of your life, family, home, vehicle, job

---

[48] Read Heb. 9:12-14

or business, finances, health, etc. Only God knows what is in the future. Only He can save, deliver and protect you from harm. Cut the enemy's plans off before they can be carried out. Declare the power of Jesus' blood over every aspect of your life and watch it change!

I Declare:

- The power of Jesus' blood heals my broken relationships, for the ministry of reconciliation is the ministry of Jesus Christ.
- The power of Jesus' blood over offense, unforgiveness and bitterness of past to heal every emotional wound.
- The power of Jesus' blood cleanses my heart and mind from toxic thoughts and emotions.
- The power of Jesus' blood destroys strongholds and areas of unbelief. I command every stronghold to collapse and yield to the Spirit of Truth.
- The power of Jesus' blood sanctifies my thoughts, removing all unclean thoughts and desires. I apply the blood of Jesus to every wrong desire that tempts me (or those you are praying for) into sin.
- The blood of Jesus cleanses my conscience from dead works and gives me power to live with honesty and integrity.
- The blood of Jesus destroys the spirit of lust and soulish ambitions.
- The blood of Jesus cleanses me from pride, rebellion, and allows my heart to yield in submission to God.
- The blood of Jesus heals my heart and soul from lies stemming from rejection, emotional brokenness, and feelings of being unwanted.
- The blood of Jesus is applied to ungodly covenants, contracts and agreements to sever them and pronounce them unenforceable. .
- The blood of Jesus protects myself, my home and family.
- The blood of Jesus grants me favor, which releases blessing over my income, job and finances, and rebukes the devourer.
- The blood of Jesus destroys the yoke of oppression, depression, hopelessness and grief.
- The blood of Jesus heals all my sickness and disease.
- The blood of Jesus forgives the iniquity of my ancestors and closes the doors to the enemy.
- The blood of Jesus protects the doors to my future, and guards my destiny.
- The blood of Jesus heals my body, mind and soul.
- The blood of Jesus has paid the debt for my land and property, whether in the spiritual or natural realm. The debt has been paid by

the Lord Jesus Christ. The earth and all it contains belongs to Him, and He guards the lines of my inheritance. I declare that what God has paid for the enemy must surrender and remove himself from that which is mine.

- The blood of Jesus destroys ungodly yokes of poverty, bondage, and labor that prevents me from getting ahead.
- The blood of Jesus has intervened in my situation and the power of God has brought my victory.

When the enemy tries to flood your life with trouble, there is a promise for you in Isaiah 59:19. **The Spirit of the Lord will raise up a standard against him.** What is that standard? The power of the blood of Jesus! There is nothing more powerful than what Jesus did by shedding His innocent blood on our behalf. Satan cannot penetrate the blood. Jesus died to redeem us from the power of every curse that we might receive the promise of His Spirit through faith. The only thing Satan can do is to lie, deceive and entice us to live in compromise because it provides the open door he needs to gain access to your life.

Whatever your need, it has already been provided for through the shed power of Jesus' blood. THERE IS POWER IN THE BLOOD! Jesus gave His life so that we could enter into His rest and enter into His promises. Everything in the kingdom of God is entered into THROUGH FAITH in what Jesus did for us. It is the same FAITH that BELIEVES there is power in His blood to provide everything we need. We overcome by HIS BLOOD, and by the WORDS which we speak. Declare His promise and you can stand on the fact that the power of Jesus' blood has made this promise real and available to you -TODAY! This is real faith. Faith is a substance, which means it is something you can stand on.

"Now faith is the assurance that what we hope for will come about and the certainty that what we cannot see exists." Hebrews 11:1 International Standard Version

It is because of the power of Jesus' blood that we stand before God loved, accepted and forgiven. We have no reason to fear punishment, rejection or condemnation. This is what it means to have God's perfect love cast out all fear. This revelation acts as a divine reset that changes the way we think. We are then able to walk into the abundant life promised to us in John 10:10.

CHAPTER EIGHT

SECRET ROOMS

When the unclean spirit has gone out of a person, it passes through waterless places seeking rest, and finding none it says, "I will return to my house from which I came." Luke 11:24

The Old Testament makes reference to both a tabernacle and a temple, which were to be made as a dwelling place for God. Moses received instructions how to build the tabernacle, and he made it according to the pattern God gave him. It was a portable tent also known as the tent of meeting where Moses would meet with God.

"Let them construct a sanctuary for Me, that I may dwell among them." Exodus 25:8

"For there was a tabernacle prepared, the outer one, in which were the lampstand and the table and the sacred bread; this is called the holy place." Hebrews 9:2

The Old Testament tabernacle contained an inner shrine known as the Holy of Holies. Inside the Holy of Holies was the Ark of the Covenant. It was a wooden chest overlaid with gold and inside were the two stone tablets containing the Ten Commandments, Aaron's rod, which was symbolic of God's authority, and a pot of manna, which symbolized the daily bread Yahweh provided to sustain His people in the wilderness. The lid of the Ark contained two cherubim, also overlaid with gold. It was said that Moses met with God 'between the two cherubim' in front of the Ark of the Covenant.

All of these things represented the relationship between Yahweh and the Israelites, and pointed us to a truth in the New Testament. The outer court of the temple would signify our flesh. The inner court represents our soul, but the Holy of Holies represents our heart. That is where we are containers for the ark of God, which represents His Holy Spirit. Within the heart of the individual where the presence of God dwells, we find God's authority; His commandments are written on the tablets of our heart and the manna represents the word of God. The gold represents the redemption and purifying work of the Holy Spirit that takes place on the inside of us. In John chapter one, Jesus came and lived among us, or shall we say He tabernacled among us. Jesus referenced his body as the temple in John 2:19 and the Apostle Paul stated that we are the temple of the living God in 2 Corinthians 6:16.

"...**For we are the temple of the living God**. As God has said: "I will live with them and walk among them, and I will be their God, and they will be my people."

"Do you not know that **your body is a temple of the Holy Spirit** who is in you, whom you have received from God? You are not your own;" 1 Cor. 6:19

2 Cor. 5:1 also references our earthly **house**, or our body, so we see that in the New Testament, the temple where God dwells (the human body) is known as a house.

What are houses made up of? Rooms.

This brings us to the question of whether or not the Spirit of God can co-exist with spirits of darkness. (Alexander Pagani's book, Secrets to Deliverance has helped tremendously to answer some of these questions). I believe the answer to that question is yes. .Let me give you a few examples. I do believe evil spirits can take up residence in any part of the body that is not sanctified to the Lord.

For instance, if a person has committed sexual sins and cannot get free from certain sinful behaviors, it could very well be due to the fact that a demon of lust or a perverse spirit has been given legal rights to that particular body part.

"I have the right to do anything," you say—but not everything is beneficial. "I have the right to do anything"—but I will not be mastered by anything. You say, "Food for the stomach and the stomach for food, and God will destroy them both." The body, however, is not meant for sexual immorality but for the Lord, and the Lord for the body. By his power God raised the Lord from the dead, and he will raise us also. Do you not know that your bodies are members of Christ himself? Shall I then take the members of Christ and unite them with a prostitute? Never! Do you not know that he who unites himself with a prostitute is one with her in body? For it is said, "The two will become one flesh." But whoever is united with the Lord is one with him in spirit. Flee from sexual immorality. All other sins a person commits are outside the body, but whoever sins sexually, sins against their own body. Do you not know that your bodies are temples of the Holy Spirit, who is in you, whom you have received from God? You are not your own; you were bought at a price. Therefore honor God with your bodies." 1 Cor. 6:12-20. NIV

This scriptures proves a point. A spirit of prostitution (or the spirit of adultery) can become one with the flesh. Lust can reside in the soul or even the eyes, because the eye gate is where lust is birthed.

"For all that is in the world—the desires of the flesh, the desires of the **eyes**, and the pride of life—is not from the Father but from the world." 1 John 2:16

"Sheol and Abaddon are never satisfied; so the **eyes** of man are never satisfied." Prov. 27:20

"But I tell you that anyone who **looks** at a woman lustfully has already committed adultery with her in his heart." Matt. 5:28

"The lamp of the body is the **eye**. Therefore, when your eye is good, your whole body also is full of light. **But when your eye is bad, your body also is full of darkness.** Therefore take heed that the light which is in you is not darkness." Luke 11:34-35 (Emphasis mine)

Luke 11:34-35 reminds us that we need to continually allow the word of God to illuminate our darkness and cleanse our heart. If we do not, the windows of our soul may become darkened, giving the enemy a place to influence how we 'see.' What we see and how we see it determines whether or not we will act upon certain impulses. The government of God is among us because He has written His laws on our heart, but a person must submit to it. They must submit themselves to God and yield to His authority, through humility and repentance before they can resist the devil and expect him to leave.

If a person has used their hands, for instance, for dishonorable purposes and sin against themselves or others, they have yielded that particular part of their body to evil, not God.

If a person has allowed their tongue to be used for gossip, strife, division, anger, vengeance or slander then they have yielded that body part to be used by the devil for his purposes. They have not brought their mouth under submission to God's authority.

The hands, the sexual organs, the mouth are all examples of how evil spirits can take up residence in various rooms of our house. The body has many rooms, but so does our soul.

Unhealed wounds, offenses, negative memories of traumatic events, bitter root judgments, internal vows, shame, agreements with negative words, twisted perceptions of God, feelings of abandonment or rejection, and lies in a person's belief system are all examples of various 'rooms' in the soul. These are places where the enemy can take up residence and create a stronghold in a person's belief system.

Alexander Pagani, in his book *The Secrets to Deliverance* writes, "Deliverance is not a power encounter, but a truth encounter! The more truth you understand, the freer you become and the more any areas (rooms) in your life where demons are hiding become exposed and resolved." [49] It is also important to understand that once demonic spirits have been identified, the individual has a responsibility (confession and repentance) and then there is the responsibility to command the spirit to leave. If it is not commanded out it will remain.

Our words can either give devils access to us or our words can help close the doors to the enemy. When deliverance is effective it results in people becoming free and healed. It is very important not to leave that space where darkness once resided empty. Invite the Holy Spirit to fill that place, to reveal light and truth. Speak blessing over that room in the soul. If it is a body part that has been delivered from an evil spirit and sanctified to the Lord, bless it. Speak what is pure, right and declare that it will no longer be used as an instrument of unrighteousness, but for God's intended purpose.

There is another way that demonic spirits can take up residence in body parts that causes sickness and disease. As in the case of inherited disease, there is physical weakness in the genes or DNA of a family towards certain health issues. Sometimes that is a result of an unbroken curse. I am not saying that every physical disease is spiritually rooted, however, I do believe that many times the spiritual roots are overlooked. If you examine the function

---

[49] Pagani, Alexander. The Secrets to Deliverance, Charisma House Publisher, pg.29.

of the affected body part and its purpose in the body sometimes you can figure out what type of questions to ask.

For instance, gall bladder and liver issues may have a spiritual root of bitterness, either towards oneself or another person. It is tied into unforgiveness, rejection (including self-rejection and self-hatred.),and sometimes even shame. The gall bladder produces bile, which is very bitter, but it is used to produce the necessary enzymes to break down food during the process of digestion. Any problems with the gall bladder usually first reside in the liver, because the liver dumps into the gall bladder. Therefore, the presence of gall stones is often evidence of a poorly functioning liver, and the liver's purpose is to eliminate toxins from the body. It's a filtering system.

What toxic thoughts, beliefs or negative self-talk is the person dwelling on?

Andy Glover, in his book *Double Portion: Our Inheritance* writes, "There have been a number of times in my life when I have harbored unforgiveness in my heart in relation to different individuals. These people have then become prominent in my thinking and feelings, and have ultimately influenced my decision making. I can't get them off my mind and when their names are brought up all the negative thoughts and emotions rise to the surface. My heart starts to suffer and I go through an emotional torture." "When your heart is connected to someone in unforgiveness, then it is not free to fully connect with your heavenly Father."[50]

Getting down to the root of emotional issues often reveals someone that needs to be forgiven. It can also reveal ungodly agreements the person has made about themselves. So much of what we carry with us on a daily basis is retained in painful memories and the trauma of past events. Those wounds become open doors to the enemy which grant him access. These things take up residence in the very cells of our bodies, creating room for illness, disease, infirmity and a whole host of other physical, emotional and spiritual problems. We know this is true because certain emotions can trigger hormonal responses, and hormones trigger physical responses. The issues between what is going on in our soul are often connected to what's going on in our bodies. Sometimes the issue in our physical body points right back to a spiritual reality. God wants to heal us so deep it touches the very core of our being and regenerates healing from the inside out.

Some years ago, I struggled with horrible gall bladder pain. The pain was

---

[50] Glover, Andy: Double Portion, Our Inheritance, pg.60

so constant and debilitating that it was unbearable. No matter what I prayed, I continued to suffer for about 4 years. During that time I also developed ulcers. It got so bad that I was forced to fast because every time I ate anything I was in terrible pain. Even water was painful to drink. My body was in total torment!

One evening we went to a worship service, and I was crying out to God for healing. One woman, who was part of the worship team, began to speak about the adulterous woman in the Bible who was dragged to the feet of Jesus. She had been accused by the religious crowd and the enemy used her as bait to try to entrap Jesus with his words. This woman had been publicly shamed and the religious crowd just wanted to see her stoned. They didn't care about her soul and they didn't care about her as a person. The religious crowd treated this woman as expendable, nothing more than a means to entrapping Jesus, and they were quite willing to stone her to achieve their objective. Everything that was being spoken during worship about the adulterous woman felt like it was telling my story. It was incredibly personal and a painful reminder of a past event. Then the lady speaking began to speak about forgiveness and how Jesus had forgiven our sin. She ended by saying, "Jesus forgave your sin and didn't condemn you, when you were like that adulterous woman. Shouldn't you also let others off the hook?

During the time when I had struggled with digestive issues, I had sought the Lord on many occasions and repeatedly prayed to release and forgive those that had hurt me. I thought I had done everything that was necessary because I had gone through the motions of speaking it out of my mouth that I forgave particular individuals – and I had done so for 10 years! I sincerely wanted my heart to be in the right place, and I prayed for certain people that despised me, believing that if they could just be set free they would also be able to see me in a different light. That is wrong motivation for prayer, right there! I had made it all about me, but I could not recognize it at the time. I could not get over the past, and then I discovered that 'Past,' 'Regret' and Perfectionism are the names of demonic spirits that needed to be renounced. One of the people I needed to forgive was myself. Because others had rejected me, I turned it inward and rejected myself. I never felt 'good enough.' The negative self-talk in my own head was critical and harsh towards myself. What I had not realized is that those things actually formed agreements in the spirit realm. I had gotten good at abusing myself, and by my agreements, I had allowed the enemy to influence my thoughts as though they were my own. It was no wonder I could not get free – I was the evil enforcer of my own negative thoughts! I was continuously looking back at the past until I renounced those spirits and broke all agreements I had made with them.

If you had asked me, I would have told you that I was not guilty of holding unforgiveness towards anyone, because that is what I believed – up until that moment. That night, however, as the woman said those words about letting others off of the hook, the Holy Spirit began to minister to my heart. He showed me that forgiveness was not complete until my heart testified that forgiveness was genuine. He brought a name to mind and encouraged me to forgive and hold nothing back. There was no place in my heart where I could hold on to a secret desire that she would get a taste of her own medicine. I had to let go completely and trust God to be my God of justice. Motivated by a sincere desire to be out of constant pain, I agreed to forgive this person who I felt was responsible for causing a lot of emotional pain. It was difficult because this person had absolutely no remorse whatsoever about things that she had done. Thankfully though, at that moment my heart agreed that we were both sinners in need of mercy and I surrendered the last of my judgments. I realized what I was really surrendering was my fear that God would just completely let her off the hook. I didn't feel that was justice, and yet, there I was being confronted with the fact that Jesus had let *me* off the hook. **Many times**. So how could I justify holding on to unforgiveness towards someone else?

Sometimes we need to be in the right atmosphere where we our hearts can become saturated by the presence of God in worship. The added component of fasting, even though I hadn't done it from a willing heart to seek God, served to humble my flesh and stomp on my pride. It was pride that had resisted my full compliance with the stipulations of God's word. Until the situation with my health got that bad, I couldn't recognize that about myself. Fasting helped to remove the blind spot. That night, I felt my heart soften towards that individual, and I knew the root of bitterness had been dissolved. It was finished! The whole ordeal also taught me that there are some spirits that only come out by prayer and fasting. Jesus told us so in Mark 9:29. Some translations omit the fasting part, but others include it. I learned a very painful, difficult lesson about deliverance through that situation. I also learned that God is not interested in mere lip service. He wants genuine forgiveness to register in our hearts, not just from our mouth. Matthew 18: reminds us of this truth in the parable of the unforgiving servant.

" In his anger, his master turned him over to the jailers to be tortured, until he should repay all that he owed. That is how My Heavenly Father will treat each of you, unless you forgive your brother from your heart." Matt. 18:34,35

It's important to understand things from a spiritual perspective. That root of bitterness had been in my life a long, long time, even before I was wounded by the person in question. It had been a generational root of bitterness. My grandmother, mother, and my sister all had it too.

Generational Rebellion is Tied to Witchcraft

"Rebellion is as sinful as witchcraft, and stubbornness as bad as worshiping idols. So because you have rejected the command of the LORD, he has rejected you as king." 1 Sam. 15:23 NLT

There is a relationship between bitterness, rebellion and witchcraft. Examine the scripture in Acts 8:23. Apostle Peter was rebuking Simon the Sorcerer for wanting to purchase the gift of the Holy Spirit with money. The sorcerer did not have the right heart towards the gifts of the Holy Spirit. He understood the supernatural because He had been involved in the occult prior to his salvation, but what he was attracted to was the power, not the person of the Holy Spirit. He wasn't interested in relationship with God; he wanted supernatural power to serve his own interests. So Peter rebuked him saying,

"Therefore repent of this wickedness of yours, and pray the Lord that if possible the intention of your heart may be forgiven you. For I see that you are in the **gall** of bitterness and in the bondage of iniquity." Acts 8:22,23

The word 'gall' in the Lexicon is #5521 which comes from the Greek word chole. It means gall or bile, i.e. (by analogy) poison or an anodyne (wormwood, poppy, etc.) -- gall.

Bitterness is #4088 in the Lexicon, or the word 'pikrias' which literally means 'poison.' [51]

Iniquity is #93, the word 'adikias,' which means (legal) injustice (properly, the quality, by implication, the act); morally, wrongfulness (of character, life or act) -- iniquity, unjust, unrighteousness, wrong."

So, in these verses we can see the relationship between gall, or bitterness that poisons the soul, as well as iniquity which is long term sin. Iniquity is rebellion towards God, which is the root of all witchcraft. Rebellion is stubbornness in doing what the flesh wants rather than submitting to God. It is self-will, which is idolatry. And, because of that, if these things are left

---

[51] Greek Lexicon, https://biblehub.com/lexicon/acts/8-23.htm, accessed Aug. 16, 2018

in an individual it will disqualify them for future works of ministry. Look at King Saul. He never dealt with his disobedience and it was his rebellion that caused God to reject him from being king. Just as Saul was disqualified from reigning and ruling as king, so can we be disqualified from the greater works of ministry. Bitterness and rebellion ARE the root of all witchcraft, and these are spirits that will defile others. The definition of **iniquity means to act towards other with 'legal injustice.'** Wow. Who wants to be guilty of having that on their record? Not me! That sort of sin warrants a corresponding disciplinary action from God. These spirits are anointed to produce hurt, offense, bitterness and poison in others. These spirits will shame and destroy others through slander. The spirit of rejection that comes from these things can also cause anger. A spirit of anger can cause abuse (another spirit) to take up residence in a person's life. These things deliberately rob people of justice, because the abused (if not healed and delivered) will turn right around to become the perpetuators of injustice towards others. It is a vicious cycle. Do you see how the root of bitterness creates a ripple effect? Scripture tells us 'a root of bitterness defiles many.'[52] That is why it is so important to stop the cycle through deliverance.

There have been people in my life that I have had to work very hard to forgive because those things were produced in me. A root of bitterness carries an evil anointing that seeks to defile and destroy others, and that is why God will go to great lengths to fully release the healing and deliverance we need. Our loving Father is very persistent in digging deep into our souls to heal any residual hurt. Although we may not like the process, ultimately it is because He wants us to live free and healed. Father also doesn't promote prematurely. He does not want us to retain any sort of corruption within our souls because all of that corruption is driven by selfish ambition. Selfish ambition comes from trying to prove to oneself and others that we are not inadequate or rejected. It is striving to prove one's worth, a crying out from the deepest part of the soul for others to validate our personal value. But, truly only God can impart that to us through revelation of our identity. We must learn to be at rest and trust God to work through us by His Spirit. His desire is for his ministers to have a pure heart.

All of that was a very lengthy explanation of how physical issues dealing with the gall bladder and liver can actually have a spiritual root of bitterness attached to them, so do your investigative homework. Find out if there is anyone that needs to be forgiven. That is always a good starting point. The individual must break the agreement of false judgment, offense and unforgiveness, and may need to incorporate fasting and prayer before the

---

[52] Hebrews 12:15

root will come all the way out. God insists that forgiveness is <u>genuine.</u>

Another example of a spiritually rooted health condition is auto-immune disorders. Auto immune disease can often be rooted in self-hatred, self-rejection, father issues, a sense of parental abandonment, and an orphan spirit. When the person rejects themselves, the body comes into agreement and the white blood cells begin to attack the body. That's not to say this is always the case, however. Vaccinations also work to slowly destroy the immune system, through the introduction of heavy metals and other adjuvants. Regardless of the cause, however, we still serve a God that works miraculously to reverse physical situations to heal and restore our bodies.

The bones are another example of things that can contribute to spiritually rooted sickness and disease.. The bones are used to create bone marrow. It's where our body produces red blood cells. So, if there is an issue with the blood or the bones, then we ought to examine what the scriptures tell us about the bones.

UNCONFESSED SIN REMOVES THE HEALTH: "There is no soundness in my flesh because of thine anger; neither is there any rest in my bones because of my sin" Psalm 38:3. KJV

UNCONFESSED SIN DRIES THE BONES: "When I kept silence, my bones waxed old through my roaring all the day long" Psalm 32:3. KJV

SIN FILLS THE BONES: "His bones are full of the sin of his youth, which shall lie down with him in the dust" Job 20:11 KJV

SHAME CAN ROT THE BONES: "A virtuous woman is a crown to her husband: but she that maketh ashamed is as rottenness in his bones" Proverbs 12:4. KJV

CURSING MAKES THE BONES UNSOUND: "As he clothed himself with cursing like as with his garment, so let it come into his bowels like water, and like oil into his bones". Psalm 109:18 KJV

FEAR & ROTTENNESS CAN CAUSE AN ENEMY TO TAKE UP RESIDENCE IN THE BONES:: "When I heard, my belly trembled; my lips quivered at the voice: rottenness entered into my bones, and I trembled in myself, that I might rest in the day of trouble: when he cometh up unto the people, he will invade them with his troops" Habakkuk 3:16 KJV

A BROKEN SPIRIT DRIES THE BONES: "A merry heart doeth

good like a medicine: but a broken spirit drieth the bones" Proverbs 17:22 KJV

GRIEF FROM INIQUITY CAUSES THE BONES TO BE CONSUMED. "For my life is spent with grief, and my years with sighing: my strength faileth because of mine iniquity, and my bones are consumed" Psalm 31:10. KJV

BUT, THE FEAR OF THE LORD PRODUCES BONE MARROW: "Be not wise in thine own eyes: fear the LORD, and depart from evil. It shall be health to thy navel, and marrow to thy bones" Proverbs 3:7-8 KJV

A GOOD REPORT MAKES THE BONES FAT: (PRODUCES BONE MARROW): "The light of the eyes rejoiceth the heart: and a good report maketh the bones fat" Proverbs 15:30. KJV

A CLEAR CONSCIENCE REJOICES THE BONES: "Behold, thou desirest truth in the inward parts: and in the hidden part thou shalt make me to know wisdom. Purge me with hyssop, and I shall be clean: wash me, and I shall be whiter than snow. Make me to hear joy and gladness; that the bones which thou hast broken may rejoice" Psalm 51:6-8. KJV

HEALTH COMES FROM SOUND BONES: "His breasts are full of milk, and his bones are moistened with marrow" Job 21:24. KJV

PLEASANT WORDS RESTORES BONE MARROW: "Pleasant words are as an honeycomb, sweet to the soul, and health to the bones" Proverbs 16:24. KJV

DELIVERANCE REJOICES THE BONES: "All my bones shall say, LORD, who is like unto thee, which deliverest the poor from him that is too strong for him, yea, the poor and the needy from him that spoileth him?" Psalm 35:10. KJV

ENVY ROTS THE BONES. "A sound heart is the life of the flesh but envy is rottenness to the bones." Prov. 14:30 KJV [53]

We know that the life is in the blood; therefore, if the blood is being attacked, or the bones that are responsible for creating the marrow and blood cells are sick and diseased, then we need to explore the possibility of a curse that needs to be broken. The previous scriptures are not an exhaustive list

---

[53] The Bones Cry Out, http://www.wholeperson-counseling.org/health/bones.html, accessed Aug. 22, 2018.

but they do offer proof that the bones are just another 'room' where spirits of infirmity that cause disease can hide. It becomes very important to consider family history that could be contributing factors to disease or issues that originate in the bones. Some things to consider might be some of the following: Many, many people are involved in the abortion industry or have had an abortion, and they may not stop to consider that taking a life can release a curse into the family. Cursing yourself or others can release a curse back into the family and it affects the bones. When people don't depart from their evil ways, the built up iniquity in the bloodline releases death to the bones. But, as with auto-immune issues, we realize that when the part of the body that is supposed to contribute to the body's health and defense begins to shut down, there can be a spiritually rooted issue that is contributing to the problem. Not always, but enough that one definitely does not want to disregard the possibility. The poetic language in scripture is not just figurative, it contains a spiritual truth. Many of the things mentioned in the scriptures are actually demonic spirits. Shame, cursing, fear, envy, pride (that causes silence, or a lack of repentance) is another demonic spirit. The spirit of infirmity is another one. These spirits can occupy one of the rooms of our spiritual house.

Psalm 91 gives us a blessing and a promise to those that seek their refuge in the Lord Jesus Christ. In verse 10, the word 'plague' is from the Hebrew word 'nega.' It is translated as: 1) a stroke or a blow, figuratively or inflicted {inflicted by man on man}; 2) also a second meaning, {stroke, metaphor, especially of a disease, regarded as sent by a divine chastisement}; 3) plague or a mark {regarded as the heavy touch or stroke of a disease}. The Strong's Concordance translates it like this: affliction, assault, infection, mark {regarded as the heavy touch or stroke of a disease, such as leprosy}, plague, plagues, stripes, stroke, strokes, wounds. [54]

What an amazing promise! Regardless of where the wound originated, God has made a provision to be free and healed from it! Do you remember the promise of Passover? The Israelites were spared from the death of the firstborn because of the blood of the lamb on the doorposts. They were spared from the **plague** because of the blood - just as you are spared from the plague because of Jesus' blood! Whatever you are struggling with, whatever the enemy has aimed against you - place it into one of the stripes Jesus took for you. Matthew 8:17 tells us that "He himself took our infirmities and bore our sicknesses." Therefore, we can declare "By His stripes we are healed." Agreeing with God's word is key; we must believe that God can, He

[54] Strong's Concordance #5061, https://biblehub.com/hebrew/5061.htm, accessed Aug. 23, 2018

wants to, and has already made the provision for our healing. Faith is active participation with God so that we can receive what we are believing to receive! God has made provision for every need you have. I guarantee you there is a specific promise for you in His word. You just need to ask Him what it is and begin to declare the blood of Jesus has made it possible. There are many other scriptures that help identify the spiritual roots to health issues but we must search them out. There are too many to list here, but I hope that I have sufficiently illustrated my point. If you have repeated difficulty in a particular area and can't seem to get the victory, you may need to consider that there is a spirit that needs to be evicted.

We have explored many various possibilities in blocks to prayer, healing and deliverance, but I hope that I have opened your eyes to some things that you may not have stopped to consider. Let us move on to the prayers.

CHAPTER NINE

PRAYERS FOR THE NATIONS

"Who has heard of such as this? Who has seen such things? Can a country be born in a day or a nation be delivered in an instant? Yet as soon as Zion was in labor, she gave birth to her children."
Isaiah. 66:8

There are many, many nations and I cannot possibly write a lengthy prayer for all of them, but I have included some for various nations. I have attempted to go about this somewhat strategically, so please allow me to explain the method to my madness before you go through the prayers.

In a 2006 article titled "What are the Most Widely Practiced Religions of the World? Dr. Stephen Juan states that the three **largest** groups of religious beliefs fall into several categories: Christian, Muslim and the third is a collection of both agnostic and those that declare themselves atheists. "Christianity and Islam are the two religions most widely spread across the world. These two religions together cover the religious affiliation of more than half of the world's population. If all non-religious people formed a single religion, it would be the world's third largest."[55]

According to Alan Cooperman, director of Pew Research, "As of 2010, Christianity was by far the world's largest religion, with an estimated 2.2 billion adherents, nearly a third (31 percent) of all 6.9 billion people on Earth," the Pew report says. "Islam was second, with 1.6 billion adherents, or 23 percent of the global population."

Those numbers are predicted to shift in the coming decades, as the

---

[55] Juan, Steven M.D.:What are the most widely practiced religions of the world? https://www.theregister.co.uk/2006/10/06/the_odd_body_religion/ accessed Aug. 16, 2018

world's population rises to 9.3 billion by the middle of this century. In that time, Pew projects, Islam will grow by 73 percent while Christianity will grow by 35 percent — resulting in 2.8 billion Muslims and 2.9 billion Christians worldwide."⁵⁶ "Around 62% of the world's Muslims live in the Asia Pacific region (from Turkey to Indonesia), with over 1 billion adherents. The largest Muslim population in a country is in Indonesia, a nation home to 12.7% of the world's Muslims, followed by Pakistan (11.0%), and India (10.9%)."[57]

I felt that one of the key factors of determining what prayers should be in the book ought to include not only geographic regions, but what they have in common. The Muslim population, for instance, originated in Saudi Arabia because they originated with the descendants of Ishmael. So, for many people that have their origin in the Middle East, renouncing the ancient gods of Saudi Arabia is very significant. Afghanistan and Saudi Arabia are grouped together. Some of the other prayers for Asia will also include things pertaining to Islam because of the high population of Muslims living in the Asia Pacific region. I tried to include some of the most important gods and goddesses in various regions, but there are so many I cannot possibly do them all. My suggestion is to invite Holy Spirit to speak to you before you go through them.

As I mentioned previously, many of the African, Caribbean Islands, Hatian, Cuban, Puerto Rican beliefs as well as Mexican and Native ancestry also mix together, having similar religious practices that tie them together through Catholicism, Voodoo and occult practices. I have tried to concentrate my prayers on these larger populations because I felt it would have a greater global impact.

Many nations today are a polytheistic society, which leaves the door open to many spirits in their lives and in the lives of their children and grandchildren. But beyond that, even when people don't 'worship' certain spirits, there can be spirits assigned to them to perpetuate a curse.

Ideally, a person should be able to go to their local church to find mature, experienced deliverance ministers, but that is not always the case. That is primarily the reason for this book. It is to help the individual

[56] Chappell, Bill: World's Muslim Population Will Surpass Christians This Century, https://www.npr.org/sections/thetwo-way/2015/04/02/397042004/muslim-population-will-surpass-christians-this-century-pew-says, accessed Aug. 16, 2018.
[57] "Islam by Country", Wikipedia, https://en.wikipedia.org/wiki/Islam_by_country, accessed Aug. 16, 2018.

understand the spirit realm so that they can work with God to achieve their own path to freedom and healing. The church has failed to adequately teach, train and equip others in this area. Sometimes a person finds themselves without the help of others that are knowledgeable in this area and they struggle to figure out the issues. Self-deliverance does have its limitations when we're operating in the dark. God designed us to need the gifts and ministry of others because sometimes He puts the answers we need in them. However, even if it is just you and God, He is will see you through the process. If you sincerely cry out for your healing and deliverance, He will answer. He always does!

In the ***Deliverance and Spiritual Warfare Manual*** by John Eckhardt, Eckhardt writes, "Every believer has authority over evil spirits, including the ones in his or her own life. Jesus tells us to cast the beam out of our own eye. The phrase "cast out" in Luke 6:42 is *ekballo,* which means to drive out or expel. It is the same Greek word used in reference to casting out devils (Mark 16:17)." [58] This issue often is our perception. We feel the demons are stronger than we are, but in reality, sometimes the deeper issue is that we have not yet made up our mind to fully surrender to God and reject what the enemy is offering us. Truth will displace the lie. Go looking for the truth and it will set you free.

Spirits can be known by the fruit of what they produce. "Rejection," "Fear," "Shame," "Abuse," and "Regret" are just a few. There are many more, and they all need to be sent back to the abyss! Jesus came to set the captives free. The Bible teaches in Romans 6:12 that we should not let sin reign in our bodies. If there is difficulty in overcoming a particular issue or something that stands between us and our healing, then often times it is an indicator that a spirit is withstanding us. True freedom comes as a result of removing those things. Renouncing a lot of various names of gods and goddesses or various spirits seems strange, I know, but let me remind you of the testimony I shared earlier in the book about the woman minister that also had Mayan Indian in her ancestry. She was completely unfamiliar with the names of various gods listed in the prayer, yet she did it in faith. Lo and behold, as she took that step of faith, she felt a demonic presence leave! This just proves that even if we have not personally worshipped particular gods or goddesses, those spirits can be still connected to us through generational curses and familiar spirits. Even if, in our generation, we do not recognize the names of some of these gods, if you were to ask your parents, grandparents or great grandparents, many of them would be familiar with

---

[58]Eckhardt, John: Deliverance and Spiritual Warfare Manual, Charisma House Publishers, pg. 237

certain names included in the prayers in this book. Many of our ancestors worshipped all sorts of spirits that they knew by name, and that means they can still be connected to us through familial spirits assigned to our families.

What has God said? **"You shall have no other gods before Me."** If you worshipped the demon god Baphomet, or Molech or some other Satanic idol and then you decided to come to Christ, there would be a need to renounce those demonic gods. You would need to confess the sins that opened a door to those spirits before you could command those spirits out of your life. This is just a principle of scripture, and we have covered that in previous chapters. James 4:6,7 reminds us that we must first submit to God before we can effectively exercise authority over evil spirits. Knowing this principle of scripture, it makes sense to renounce other demonic spirits that may be hiding somewhere in your life. Demons are squatters and must be forced to leave.

Before you speak the prayers out loud, ask Holy Spirit to cause the enemy to reveal himself through blocked memories, names, or other things that will reveal where he is hiding. Pay attention to any sense of resistance or sudden thoughts that may pop into your head. Sometimes a memory may rise to the surface, a particular word or thought that helps identify what spirit is at work. If a memory suddenly appears, then ask yourself what emotions or feeling is attached to it. Emotions can be powerful indicators of a particular spirit at work. Pause and take a moment to ask Holy Spirit to reveal what He wants you to understand about that particular event or memory. Ask Him to show you where Jesus was at that moment. Holy Spirit will help you to clearly identify what spirit is at work so that you can renounce it and command it to go.

You may not feel that some of these prayers are necessary for you, and that's ok, but there are other people who live in nations where this information will prove to be quite significant for them because of their culture, ancestry or religious traditions. There may not be a specific prayer covering your particular ancestry or nation, however, it is not difficult to do some of your own research. Everyone should know what is in their personal history through their family's involvement in certain things as well as what is connected to your ancestry. You can search the internet for the gods of your nation or particular region where your family originated. If your family had involvement in secret societies, the occult, or other things that you know are ungodly, repent for yourself and your ancestors, renounce those spirits and activities, then close the door by applying the blood of Jesus to them. These prayers have been constructed for those that don't know what's in their family line, but I cannot stress enough that the most important factor is seeking revelation through relationship with Holy Spirit, for He knows all things.

Please let me emphasize the fact that these are not to be viewed as some sort of religious ritual. Although there are demonic spirits that should be renounced, the focus isn't on them. Some of these prayers are a one-time deal, not intended to be done religiously. The focus is on what the shed blood of Jesus Christ has made available so that you can obtain your freedom and healing. Many years ago when I was struggling to obtain freedom, I found myself very frustrated at the fact that I had no idea what sort of doors were opened to the enemy. Scripture tells us "My people perish for lack of knowledge," and that is true. It is our responsibility to learn from scripture and Holy Spirit so that we do not suffer from our own ignorance. Far too often we choose to do nothing but that leaves people vulnerable at the hands of the enemy. The Bible tells us that we should not be ignorant of the enemy's schemes because he wanders around seeking whom he can devour. At that time in my life, I definitely felt that we were being devoured, but I was blocked by my own ignorance. I simply had no idea what to do next or how to close a door that I didn't know existed. What I did understand was my family was suffering at the hands of the enemy and we were stuck until we figured out how to close the doors and lock him out. The Holy Spirit began to teach me. I began by renouncing Voodoo, because that is where the Lord started with me. I didn't know that existed but then I had to ask myself what else could I be missing? My husband and I started to renounce everything we could think of that the enemy might be using against us. That is where our Breakthrough Prayer came from. It is a detailed prayer that covers many areas of a person's life all at once and it is great for people of any nationality or background.

I do a lot of research that I incorporate into the prayers. I do make them comprehensive because many people would never think to do this sort of thing for themselves, and they may not have any idea what demonic attachments and curses could be lurking somewhere in their family history. There is one thing I understand very well and that when it is regarding a possible open door to the enemy it pays to be thorough. The prayers for various nations are a great starting point to help eliminate some of the surface level demons, but as you continue throughout the chapter you will also see prayers written to help with deeper levels of healing, and prayers to help restore intimacy in your relationship with your Heavenly Father.

Prayer to Renounce the Gods of Afganistan and Saudi Arabia
(The Arab Gods)

Father, on behalf of myself and my ancestors, I renounce the following gods and goddesses of my native country. Please forgive any sins committed by myself or my ancestors, their idolatry, and rebellion to You.

I renounce the spirits of rejection, rebellion, lawlessness, religious pride and jealousy that came through Ishamel, son of the law.

I renounce the spirits of fear, terror and control associated with Allah, Islam and the teachings of Muhummad.

I renounce the evil inheritance I received through my ancestors and send it back to the abyss.

I renounce the goddesses Allat, Asherah and Athira. (goddesses of Islam)

I renounce Al-Uzza, also known as Aphrodite Ourania.

I renounce the goddess "Arom" that oversees contracts.

I renounce the god "Bagishi," god of flood waters and posterity.

I renounce the god "Dagan."

I renounce the goddess "Disani, " the fertility and mother goddess.

I renounce "Duzi," and all blood sacrifices made in his name.

I renounce "Gish," the god of war.

I renounce "Imra," who is known as a creator god.

I renounce "Indr," the tutelary and weather god.

I renounce the fertility goddesses known as "Kshumai," and "Kshumai Kafir", and all fertility rituals made in their names.

I renounce "Lunang or Lunang Kafir"" the patron goddess of the Prasun river.

I renounce Manat, chief goddess of Mecca.

I renounce "Marmalik, " god of the underworld.

I renounce the name "Mon," known as a warrior god.

I renounce "Munjen Malik," an earth god.

I renounce "Nirmali/ Shuwi," the goddess of childbirth.

I renounce "Nong, or Nong Zuzum" known as god of winter. I renounce all hatred and cold heartedness towards women that this spirit represents.

I renounce the deity known as "Panao," a creator god that controls the mountains, high places and the natural world.

I renounce the god "Paneu" and his seven brothers.

I renounce the goddesses known as "Poloknalai or ""Poloknalai Kafir" the goddess of animals.

I renounce "Prakde Kafir."

I renounce "Sanju Kafir," the harvest goddess.

I renounce "Sanu," and "Shomde," the god of the Hindu Kush.

I renounce "Sudrem," the weather god created from the breath of the god Imra.

I renounce "A'im," a deity of the Azd tribe,

I renounce "A'ra," the North Arabian tutelary god

I renounce "Abirillu," a North Arabian deity

I renounce "Allah", god of the Islam religion,

I renounce the supreme deity known as Al-Fals

I renounce the god known as Al-Kutbay, the god of writing

I renounce Almaqah, themain god of the Sabaeans

I renounce Al-Qaum, the Nabataean god of war and the night, and guardian of the caravans,

I renounce Al-Uqaysir;

I renounce Al-Uzza, daughter of Allah, equated to Aphrodite Ourania

I renounce Al-Ya'bub, a deity adopted by the Jadilah of Tayy

I renounce the moon god of Qataban

I renounce Atarquruma

I renounce Atarsamain, a North Arabian deity associated with Venus

I renounce Athtar, the South Arabian storm god

I renounce Awal

I renounce Awf, the great bird god worshipped in the Kaaba

I renounce Bajir, worshipped by the Azd tribe

I renounce Basamum, the South Arabian god of health and healing

I renounce Dai

I renounce Dhat-Badan, the South Arabian goddess of the oasis

I renounce Dhat Anwat, the West Arabian tree deity

I renounce Dhu al-Kaffayn,

I renounce Dhul Khalasa, the South Arabian god of redemption

I renounce Dushara, the chief deity of the Nabataeans

I renounce Haubas, the Sabaean oracular god

I renounceHaukim, the god worshipped in Qataban

I renounce Hilal, god of the new moon

I renounce Hubal, a god of divination,

I renounce Isāf and Nā'ila, deities located near the Well of Zamzam

I renounce Isis, goddess imported from the Egyptian pantheon

I renounce Inzak, the main god of Dilmun

I renounce Kahl, patron god of Kindah

I renounce Manaf, the Meccan god

I renounce Nasr, deity of the Quran, and all lying spirits, the perverse spirit that twists truth and all false teaching

I renounce Nuha, the North Arabian sun goddess

I renounce Nuhm, deity of the Muzaynah tribe

I renounce Qaynan, the South Arabian god

I renounce Quzah, the West Arabian weather god worshipped in Muzdalifah

I renounce Ruda, the North Arabian moon god

I renounce Sa'd, the West Arabian fortune god

I renounce Salman, the South Arabian god

Ii renounce Shams, the sun goddess

I renounce Sin, the moon god.

I renounce the symbols of the star and crescent moon associated with Islam, the moon goddess Hecate, also known as Artemis and the moon goddesses Selena, Luna and Diana.

I renounce Su'ayr, the deity of the 'Anazzah tribe

I renounce Suwa, a deity near Makkah and is also mentioned in the

Quran. I renounce all false teaching and lying spirits associated with Suwa.

I renounce Ta'lab, the Sabaean moon god of pastures

I renounce Theandrios

I renounce Wadd, the Minaean moon god of the Quran

I renounce Ya'uq, god of the Quran

I renounce Yaghuth, also mentioned in the Quran.

I renounce the birds of the air, evil spirits known as cranes, mentioned in the Quran.

I renounce the Satanic teachings of the Quran.

I renounce Yatha

I renounce the prophet Muhammed and all the teachings of Islam. I also renounce all soul ties to Imams and other teachers of Islam.

I renounce the false god Buddha and the teachings of Buddhism.

I renounce the teachings of the Quran.

I renounce the religious law and moral codes of the Hadith of Gabriel and all false teachings.

I renounce the false god Allah, his teachings and practices.

I renounce the spirit of Fear and Terror associated with retribution from Islam and Muslim brotherhood.

I renounce the spirit of shame.

I renounce the spirit of pride, racism, hatred and intolerance for other people and their beliefs.

I renounce the sins of rage, murder, and oppression associated with Islam.

I renounce and repent for sins of rape, incest, pedophilia and other sexual sins.

I renounce and repent for not showing love to others due to religious intolerance.

I repent for innocent bloodshed, human sacrifice and idolatry.

I repent for broken vows, covenants and agreements, and for making them with the wrong gods, goddesses and people.

I repent for hurting other people , whether it was done willfully or unknowingly.

I announce to the spirit realm that I divorce all these false gods and goddesses and any other idols by other names. I revoke all their authority and right to influence my life or that of my family. I accept and invite Jesus Christ to be my Lord and Savior. I confess I believe He is the risen Son of God, and through His shed blood on the Cross of Calvary, I have been redeemed from the curse. His blood atones for my sin, and through forgiveness of sins I now have acceptance as a child of the Most High God. I declare the blood of Jesus over every contract, covenant and agreements that has granted the enemy legal rights to remain in my life.

Holy Spirit, I invite you into my heart and ask You to baptize me in Your Spirit. Bless me with my heavenly language that allows me to commune spirit to spirit with my Heavenly Father. In the name and authority of the Lord Jesus Christ, I command all evil spirits to leave me now and never return. I command them to take all their evil works and go to the abyss created for them. Show me who I am in Christ. Turn me into an agent of healing for others. Thank you, Holy Spirit for revealing the truth that will make me free, healed and victorious, Amen.

This next section deals with African ancestry. There are three that deal specifically with African traditions and religious practices. I highly recommend the African prayers to anyone that has Native or Mexican ancestry, Cuban, Puerto Rican, Haitian, or ancestry in the Caribbean islands. I also suggest that people who have had Catholicism in their family line also do these prayers regardless of their ancestry because the same spirits are connected with involvement in Santeria, Lukemi, and other forms of Voodoo and occult practices. Catholicism is full of idolatry and the spirits of African witchcraft are syncretized with many of the Catholic saints. Please do the prayers to renounce the Catholic traditions as well. I realize it's a lengthy process, but these religious practices are all intertwined and it pays to be thorough.

Prayer to Renounce the Gods of Africa

Dear Heavenly Father,

I repent on behalf of myself and my ancestors for turning to false gods, idols, cults, and all forms of idolatry. I repent for rebellion to you, and I turn away from all worship and false religious practices that are forbidden in the Word of God.

Even though my culture has taught me otherwise, I choose to accept by faith that Jesus Christ is the Son of the One true God, my Creator and Father. I believe that Jesus Christ was persecuted, rejected, falsely accused, and innocent of all wrongdoing when He was crucified and died on the cross.

I believe Jesus died in my place, and took all my sins upon Himself so that I can have a personal relationship with God and eternal life. I believe that through the power of God's Holy Spirit, Jesus was resurrected from the dead in victory and has made a life of victory available for me through His sacrificial death and resurrection.

I thank You, Jesus for being my Lord and Savior. I thank You, Father, for eternal life and for forgiveness of sins. I ask that Your Holy Spirit would come live within me and baptize me with His Spirit.

Now, Father, I renounce and repent for any involvement with false gods, idolatry and occult practices. I renounce and repent for any occult activity, rituals, or witchcraft practices that I have done or that of my ancestors; including being dedicated to demonic spirits, initiation into witchcraft or ungodly religious ceremonies devoted to Satanic worship.

I renounce Satan as my spiritual father, as my god, and any spirits that represent the kingdom of darkness.

I renounce and DIVORCE the pantheon of gods and goddesses of my culture.

I renounce Adroa, also known as god in the sky, god on earth, creator god and river god that rules over social order, law and death;

I renounce Akuj, that rules over divination;

I renounce Ala, also known as Ale and Ane, known as creator goddess and queen of the dead that rules over community laws, morality, oaths and harvest;

I renounce Allah and the prophet Muhammed, and I break all agreement with rejection, rebellion, lawlessness, jealousy and pride that I received from my ancestors.

I renounce all evil inheritances from my ancestors.

I renounce the spirit of lawlessness that comes from rebellion and the spirit of Ishmael.

I renounce Anayaroli, the river demon that rules over wealth;

I renounce Asa, also known as father god or the strong lord, that rules over mercy, help and survival;

I renounce Asase, also known as Yaa, Aberewa, and Efua, "old mother earth" who is described as the goddess of creation and receiver of humans at their death, who rules over harvest and cultivation.

I renounce Behanzin the fish god;

I renounce Cagn, the creator god among the bushmen, who rules over shape-shifting and sorcery;

I renounce Chango, the god of thunder, transformations and revenge, the god of wrongful death, also known as the Santeria god and the Catholic saint Barbara.

I renounce Chiuta, also known as Mulengi, Mwenco, Wamtatakuya

Tumbuka, known as the creator god, the rain god, who rules over rain, help, agriculture and food;

I renounce Chuku, also known as Cheneke, known as creator, the earth goddess, the father of Ale, who rules over help and goodness;

I renounce Danh, also known as the snake god or the rainbow snake that rules over wholeness and unity;

I renounce Eleggua, and Eshu, patron of doorways, finder of lost things and Saint Anthony, worker of miracles.

I renounce En-Kai, also known as Parsai and Emayian, the sky god that rules over rain, vegetation and blessing;

I renounce Fa, that rules over destiny;

I renounce Famian, who rules over protection, health and fertility;

I renounce Guana, also known as Gawa and Gawama that lives among the bushmen, leads the spirits of the deceased, and rules over disruption, harrassment and death;

I renounce Ge, the moon god;

I renounce Gu, that rules over war, weapons and smiths;

I renounce Guruhi, the evil god that shows himself in meteors and rules over power and death over enemies;

I renounce Heitsi-Eibib, the sorcerer god that rules over shape-shifting and magick;

I renounce Imana, also known as Hategekimana, Hashakimana, Habyarimana, Ndagijimana, Bigirimana, "Almighty God " that rules over power, goodness, children and planning;

I renounce Ison, also known as Eka Obasi, Obasi Nsi, Ibibio, and Ekoi, the tortoise shelled goddess that rules over fertility of the earth;

I renounce water spirits known as Jengu, also known as Liengu and Miengu.
I renounce Juok, also known as the supreme god Shilluk that created

man;

I renounce Jok, also known as Jok Odudu and Alur that demands goats sacrificed in order to produce rain, and that rules over rain;

I renounce Kaka-Guia, also known as Nyami, that brings souls to the supreme god;

I renounce Katonda, a strongman spirit also known as Lissoddene, Kagingo, Ssewannaku, Lugaba, Ssebintu, Nnyiniggulu, Namuginga, Ssewaunaku, Gguluddene, and Namugereka that rules over help, judgment, divination and oracles;

I renounce Kwoth, known as the great spirit god that rules over nature, help, compassion and judgment;

I renounce Leza, the chameleon goddess that rules over protection and divination;

I renounce Mami Wata, also known as Mother of the Water, Mamlambo, NoMlambo, La Sirene, and any other water spirits.

I renounce Mbaba Mwana Waresa, that rules over rainbows, rain, crops, cultivation and alcohol;

I renounce Mawu, the supreme goddess and creator of all things, also known as a moon goddess;

I renounce Mukuru, known as the supreme god and creator that rules over agriculture, architecture and the harvest;

I renounce Mungo, the rain god;

I renounce Nenaunir, the rainbow snake known as an evil storm god;

I renounce Ngai, that rules over life and death;

I renounce Ngami, the moon goddess; I renounce Njambi, known as creator god that rules over protection, justice, help, forests and fertility;

I renounce Nyambe, that rules over restoring life;

I renounce Nyambi, known as the great god and the god over

everything;

I renounce Nyame, the god of fate;

I renounce Nyami Ama, the rain and storm god;

I renounce Nzambi, the god of justice;

I renounce Oba, the Santeria river goddess;
I renounce Obtala, patron of fathers.

I renounce Ochumare, the Santeria goddess of the rainbow;

I renounce Oddudua, the mother goddess;

I renounce Ogun or Oggun, the god of iron and warfare that rules over iron, warfare, removing difficulties, smoothing the path to a desired result, Justice, Smiths, Hunters, Barbers, Goldsmiths and Steel; also known as the Catholic Saint Peter, who is petitioned for success and employment.

I renounce Olorun, also known as Olofin-Orun and Olodumare, the sky god that rules over truth, control of the Elements, Foresight, Victory when the odds are against you, and Destiny;

I renounce Orisha Nla, chief of the dieties;

I renounce Osain, god of the forest, patron of healers and herbalists. Also known as the Catholic Saint Joseph.

I renounce Oshun, the love goddess who rules sexuality and pleasure, also money matters; also known as Our Lady of la Ccaridad del Cobre, patroness of Cuba, Our Lady of Charity and the Virgin Mary.

I renounce Pan, described as the son of the earth who rules over cultivation; the spirit that causes fear and panic, and the god of sexual temptation.

I renounce Rock-Sens, the sky god that controls thunder, lightning and rain;

I renounce Rugaba, also known as Ruhanga, Kazooba or Mukameiguru, described as creator god, sun god and sky god that rules over life, healing, death, sickness, and judgement;

I renounce Ruhanga, described as the great god that rules over fertility, abundance, children, animals, harvest, health, sickness, death, judgement, and rebirth;

I renounce Sakarabru, the god of medicine, justice and retribution;

I renounce Shango or Schango, known for carrying the double-headed axe. and rules over thunder, storms, war and magic;

I renounce Soko the creator god that rules over control over the elements, divination, (communication with the dead) and witchcraft;

I renounce Tilo the storm god that rules over sky, thunder and rain;

I renounce Unkulunkulu, also known as Nkulnkulu, the earth god of fertility, organization and order;

I renounce Utixo, the sky god that rules over thunder, rain, storms, rebirth and harvest;

I renounce Wele, also known as Khakaba or Isaywa, described as 'the high one,' or the sky god or creator god that rules over rain, storms, lightning, creation, prosperity, harvest and celestial phenomena;

I renounce Were, the father god or the great god that rules over Birth, Death, Nature and Judgement;

I renounce White Lady, knowns as the agricultural goddess that rules over agriculture and fertility;

I renounce Xevioso, the storm god with a thunder axe that rules over rain and fertility;

I renounce Ymoja, the river goddess that rules over women and children. Also known as Ymanja, Yemaya, Star of the Sea, the Virgin Mary, Our Lady of Regla and other names associated with Mary and the African Mother goddess.

I renounce any and all names of other gods or goddesses, false spiritual fathers and mothers, spirit guides, and familiar spirits that have had legal grounds to operate in my family.

I renounce all soul ties to former lovers, shamans, witch doctors, sorcerers, and those they have worked through. Let every part of my soul return to me, and any part of other people's souls return to them. I apply the blood of Jesus Christ to every sin that has been committed by myself and my ancestors, closing the door to these spirits and the assignments that they have had against me.

I renounce all lying spirits, all trickery, manipulation, fraudulent practices intended to deceive
and rob others. Let the blood of Jesus cleanse me from all unrighteousness.

I repent for the sins of shedding blood, human and animal sacrifice, selfishness, rebellion, jealousy, contention, evil speaking, pride, and every sin that was caused by disobedience and rejecting the Lordship of Christ. Let the blood of Jesus cover these sins in Jesus name.

Let my name now be removed from every ungodly altar and the evil altar destroyed in Jesus name.

Let every demon that has been assigned to carry out a curse be cut off and sent back to the abyss created for them in Jesus name.

Let the fire of God burn up every evil work in my life. Let the conviction of God's Holy Spirit keep me from reopening an old door that has now been closed in Jesus name.

Let the angelic hosts of heaven be assigned to fight on my behalf and release my restoration, in Jesus name.

I forgive all those that have been an instrument in Satan's service to cause pain, hardship or ruin to me and my family. I also forgive myself for anything I have done that has brought guilt, shame or condemnation upon myself. I ask You, Father, to bless those that have cursed me or treated me wrong. I cancel their debt and forgive their sin in Jesus name.

Father, I stand upon the principle of James 4:6,7. Now that I am submitted to Your authority, I command the enemy to take everything he has done to perpetuate a curse and leave me now in Jesus name. I also command the thief to repay the losses of previous years with no less than a 7-fold return according to Proverbs 6:31. I thank You for restoration, healing and revival to my heart and life in Jesus name, Amen.

Prayer to Heal African American Heritage and Cleanse Bloodline Curses

Dear Heavenly Father,

I seek Your help, the help that is only available to me through Jesus Christ, the blood of the lamb, and His Holy Spirit. I desperately want to be cleansed from demonic spirits, unbroken curses and familiar spirits that have been a part of my life, through my family members, from even before my birth. I ask You, Jesus Christ, Lord of all, to be my Lord and Savior. I ask You to cleanse me from all unrighteousness and set me free.

I repent for any way that I have knowingly or unknowingly given place to demonic spirits and allowed them to access my life. I renounce the sins of my parents, grandparents, and other ancestors; this day I divorce the enemy, Satan, and all other false gods and religions.

I renounce fear, self-will, lust, control and confusion. I break every ungodly covenant, oath and vow that may have been spoken by myself or any of my ancestors, knowing that this is forbidden by Your word. Lord Jesus, please let me be released from any ungodly alliances, covenants, or legally binding treaties that were enacted between me, my family, and demonic spirits.

I renounce and divorce the enemy, Satan, and any evil spirit that may have been called into my life. I renounce the spirits of Santeria, Lucumi, African gods and all familiar spirits associated with rituals, prayers, customs and traditions. I renounce the seven African spirits known as Papa Legba, Obtala, Oya, Oshun, Chango, Ogun and Yemmaya, in the name of Jesus Christ.

I renounce all Loas, mediums and familiar spirits, ungodly priests, priestesses, sorcerers and wizards.

I renounce African and cultural witchcraft, Yoruba traditions, shamans, witch doctors, their rituals and voodoo that have been practiced by my ancestors. I want nothing to do with those practices, rituals, and traditions and I renounce them all, in Jesus name.

I renounce divination and conjuring of all familiar spirits of the dead and those that my ancestors and family members have participated in. I renounce all soul ties to familiar and familial protectors, spirit guides, scribes and messengers, diviners and ungodly priests, false fathers and mothers, and those known as Babalawo,

I renounce all inanimate objects used for divining purposes, including casting of chains. Lord Jesus, I ask that You break every ungodly chain that has tied me to these things that I am now renouncing.

I renounce all animal and material sacrifices made on my behalf or those in my family line. I renounce all human involvement for the sake of divining information, the use of familiar spirits, spirit guides, and false gods. I renounce all blood that was shed from any source that was tied to my life through the use of occult practices. I renounce all herbalists and root workers that concocted medicines, potions, magic and incantations used in Ayajo.

I repent and renounce any participation of myself or those in my family line in the indoctrination, apprenticeship, spiritual journey, rituals or rites of passage of myself or others into occult practices.

I renounce all lying, devious, deceptive and manipulative spirits that were inherited as a curse.

I renounce the spirits of fear, suspicion, rejection, loneliness, inferiority, insecurity, poverty, death and hell that have come into my life. I renounce the spirit of abandonment, unloving spirits, guilt and condemnation. Lord Jesus, fill me with Your peace and love.

I lift up myself to You right now. I pray that You would help me embrace whatever traumatic or negative memories that I have either blocked out or forgotten, if recalling those memories can be used to release healing.

I repent for any sin or involvement of myself and my ancestors that opened doors to the occult through witchcraft and occult magic. I renounce Voodoo, the practices of making and wearing charms, amulets and making Ouanga. I renounce the works of evil associated with the bitter roots of the evil tree known as the figuier maudit, and any Ouangas made to practice witchcraft over others.

I renounce all soul ties, familiar spirits and bondages associated with Voodoo Kings, Queens, priests and priestesses. I renounce any and all covenants that were made with spirits of darkness and Satan himself. I hereby divorce the enemy and cancel any contracts that were made knowingly or unknowingly by myself or any of my ancestors.

I renounce and forsake any and all customs, traditions, practices and beliefs that are forbidden by God, that originated with West Africans, the French, Spanish, Creole and Caribbean people.

I renounce and break any soul ties now to the bondages, mindset, beliefs and emotional pain and bitterness that came through slavery, as a result of injustice, fear and oppression.

I renounce and break all associations with idolatry, familiar spirits, witchcraft and rebellion that originated with the Fon people and other groups known as the Bambara, Mandinga, Wolof, Ewe, Fulb, Narde, Minajjhhhjjii, Dahomean, Yoruba, Chamba, Congo, Ibo, Ado, Hausa, and Sango cultural practices.

I renounce all associations with the Haitian Maroon rebellion and massacre of other people. I renounce and divorce myself from all spirits of war.

I renounce the kinship, soul ties and solidarity of former slaves that has held anyone in my family in bondage. I renounce and break all covenants with the spirits known as Regret, Past, Bitterness, Bondage, Racism, Jealousy and the Perverse spirit.

I renounce the false God Allah associated with the Muslim religion, and all false teaching. I renounce all soul ties to ungodly religious teachers and send them back to their rightful owners.

I renounce all evil inheritances from my ancestors. I renounce the spirits of rejection, rebellion, jealousy and lawlessness that came through the seed of the law.

I renounce all mixture and perversity that came from Catholic traditions and religious practices, ancestor worship and African, Caribbean or Creole culture.

I ask You, Holy Spirit, to show me anything else that is significant to my life or family. I give You permission to dislodge memories that are stuck. I pray that You highlight any specific memories or situations, objects or possessions that are related to anything that is connected to a curse.

I pray that You would supernaturally remove the hurtful memories and the trauma of past events out of my mind, emotions, memories and out of my physical body. I ask that You would lift all remnants of painful events and the trauma that was created as a result of that pain. Lift it all out of the very cells of my body.

Let my ears not remember hurtful words spoken to me, about me, by me, or by others. Let my heart release all unforgiveness, anger, fear, rejection, pain and shame. I speak now and declare complete healing and freedom from every painful event in my life.

I declare that painful memories and hurtful words will not circulate in my mind and emotions any longer in the name and authority of Jesus Christ. I pray that no cell in my body would retain unforgiveness, bitterness, anger, hatred, fear, condemnation, regret, rejection or self-hatred. I pray that my physical body would no longer be in agreement with any negative emotions in Jesus name.

I release myself and others from the pain of their past, and the poor decisions they made as a result of their brokenness. I release them from guilt, shame, regret and bitterness now, in Jesus name. I forgive and release those who willfully and spitefully inflicted pain and suffering on me and my family.

I forgive and release those who had wicked intentions and gave themselves over to evil, in order to afflict, torment, and delight themselves in causing me or my family members pain. I give them over to You, Father, to do with as You choose; knowing that You are a just God and vengeance belongs to You. I choose to trust You in matters concerning justice and judgement towards others, knowing that as a matter of my will, I choose to forgive and am therefore free in Christ.

Let me remember only the good about those the enemy used to cause pain. I pray that my heart and mind would agree that I am in an entirely new day and I am able to graciously forgive those that treated me wrong. I forgive anyone that caused insult, offense, or physical injury to me, my family and those from my past. I take authority over the past and apply the blood of Jesus to every door the enemy has used to exploit pain, injury and injustice. I declare these doors are now closed and the enemy can no longer use them in Jesus name.

I ask Your forgiveness for any doors that I have accidentally opened to the enemy through trying to comfort myself with artificial means. I renounce and break every unintentional agreement that I may have made with spirits of fear, lust, anger, greed, gluttony, anger, bitterness, unforgiveness, unloving spirits, idolatry or a perverse spirit that also inflicts wounds on others. I submit to You, Holy Spirit, and command all ungodly spirits to leave me now, in the name and authority of Jesus Christ. I command all unclean spirits to go back to where they came from. I appropriate the blood of Christ over every part of my life, and others for whom I pray.

Let every weight be released. Let every hindrance be released. Let all that does not originate from the kingdom of heaven be released out of my mind, body, emotions and memories. Every weakness be filled now with wholeness and perfect soundness in the name and authority of Jesus Christ.

Holy Spirit, fill me now with Your fullness, strength and power in Jesus name. Fill me with joy, peace, and a release of supernatural healing that radiates from the inside out. I declare that by Your stripes I have been healed, according to Is. 53:5. Thank you for the blood You shed, Lord Jesus, that makes healing a reality. I thank You for revival, restoration, healing and complete regeneration in Jesus name.

Rituals are often performed when a new child enters the family, and sometimes the rituals are performed later in childhood as a rite of passage or indoctrination into shamanism and witchcraft. This next prayer is to break those ungodly alliances and demonic attachments that come from initiation into the occult. I used the testimony of a 4th generation witchdoctor turned Christian to write this prayer. Everything that this person mentioned as a practice in the occult, I turned it around to write a prayer to reverse it and renounce those practices.

Breaking the Power of Ancestral African Curses and Initiation Rituals into the Occult

Dear Heavenly Father,

I seek Your help, the help that is only available to me through Jesus Christ, the blood of the lamb, and His Holy Spirit. I desperately want to be cleansed from demonic spirits, unbroken curses and familiar spirits that have been a part of my life, through my family members, from even before my birth. I ask You, Jesus Christ, Lord of all, to be my Lord and Savior. I ask You to cleanse me from all unrighteousness and set me free.

I repent for any way that I have knowingly or unknowingly given place to demonic spirits and allowed them to access my life. I renounce the sins of my parents, grandparents, and other ancestors that have participated in witchcraft, all forms of sorcery and occultism. This day I divorce the enemy, Satan, and all other false gods and religions.

I renounce and divorce the enemy, Satan, all anti-Christ spirits, and any evil spirit that may have been called into my life.

I renounce the following spirits : Baal, Python, Lucifer, Jezebel, the spirit of Babylon and whoredoms, Bast, Ma'at, Nehebka, Seth, Isis, Zeus, Leviathan, Rahab, Beelzebub, Belial, Molech, Chemosh, Baphomet, Abaddon and all destroyer spirits, Lamia, Lilith, Lilu and all Lilin spirits. I renounce all vampire spirits.

I renounce all sun gods, moon gods, gods to the stars and planets;

I renounce all water spirits, mermaids and mermen spirits, all spirits that dwell beneath the sea, including sea snakes and the serpents of Sheol;

I renounce all unclean spirits;

I renounce the false god known as the god of fortresses;

I renounce bush and forest spirits, wind, sky and fire spirits;

I renounce high level ruling spirits known as Ascended Masters;

I renounce the spirits of Santeria, Lucumi, African gods and all familiar spirits associated with rituals, prayers, customs and traditions. I renounce the seven African spirits known as Papa Legba, Obtala, Oya, Oshun, Chango, Ogun and Yemmaya, in the name of Jesus Christ.

I renounce the demonic waters of initiation into the occult known as Adukrom Nsu;

I renounce the god of the graveyard, Baron Samedi, and the loa Maman Bridgitte, and all gods, amulets and practices of Haitian voodoo;

I renounce all witchcraft practices of juju;

I renounce the false god known as the Grand Master;

I renounce all Loas, mediums and familiar spirits, ungodly priests, priestesses, sorcerers and wizards.

I renounce fear, self-will, lust, control and confusion.

I break every ungodly covenant, oath and vow that may have been spoken by myself or any of my ancestors, even being dedicated to Satan from before my birth. I know that this is forbidden by Your word. Lord Jesus, please let me be released from any ungodly alliances, covenants, or legally binding treaties that were enacted between me, my family, and demonic spirits.

I renounce African and cultural witchcraft, Yoruba traditions, shamans, witch doctors, their rituals and voodoo that have been practiced by my ancestors. I want nothing to do with those practices, rituals, and traditions and I renounce them all, in Jesus name.

I renounce divination and conjuring of all familiar spirits of the dead and those that my ancestors and family members have participated in. I renounce all soul ties to familiar and familial protectors, spirit guides, scribes and messengers, diviners and ungodly priests, false fathers and mothers, and those known as babalawo.

I renounce all inanimate objects used for divining purposes, including casting of chains. Lord Jesus, I ask that You break every ungodly chain that has tied me to these things that I am now renouncing.

I renounce all animal and material sacrifices made on my behalf or those in my family line. I renounce all human involvement for the sake of divining information, the use of familiar spirits, spirit guides, and false gods. I renounce all blood that was shed from any source that was tied to my life through the use of occult practices. I renounce the practices of uniting the soul with demonic gods and goddesses through the use of sex, dance and mingling of blood.

I renounce all herbalists and root workers that concocted medicines, potions, magic and incantations used in Ayajo.

I repent and renounce for any participation of myself or those in my family line in the indoctrination, apprenticeship, spiritual journey, rituals or rites of passage of myself or others into occult practices.

I renounce all lying, devious, deceptive and manipulative spirits that were inherited as a curse. I renounce all evil inheritances.

I renounce the spirit of fear, suspicion, rejection, loneliness, inferiority, insecurity, poverty, death and hell that have come into my life.

I renounce the spirit of abandonment, unloving spirits, guilt and condemnation.

I renounce all spirits of infirmity.

Father God, Lord Jesus and Holy Spirit,

I want nothing to do with any of these spirits or their ungodly practices. This day I divorce the enemy and all false gods that have been a part of my life, whether through inherited curses, the sins of my ancestors or my own involvement. Please forgive me and those in my family line. Please wash us clean from this iniquity and let the blood of Jesus cover our sins, and close the doors to the enemy. I ask you to cleanse me from all unrighteousness according to Your word in 1 John 1:9. You said if I confessed my sins, You were able and just to forgive them and cleanse me from this unrighteousness. I submit to Your Lordship, Jesus, and the authority of Your Holy Spirit. You are the only God for me! I will not serve any other God but You! I ask You to restore my life, my health, my finances, my well-being, good, healthy and godly relationships, and bless me the way you want me to be blessed.

Father, I forgive my family members for the hurt they have caused me. I forgive them for releasing curses in my life. I ask You to bless them with revelation and understanding of the error of their ways so that they can find their salvation and deliverance in You, Jesus. Please heal their minds, set their hearts free, and take good care of them. I release them into your hands.

Now, confident that I am forgiven of my own sins, I take the authority that You have given me, and I declare:

According to Revelation 12:9,the dragon, that old serpent called Satan and the devil has been cast out of me, and all his dark angels with him .

In the name and authority of Jesus Christ, I loose myself from all punishing, tormenting and vengeful spirits assigned to my life that would perpetuate a curse.

In the name and authority of Jesus Christ, I declare Jesus only to be my shield, protector, guardian, and refuge.

I command every demonic chain to be severed from my life in the name of Jesus.

(This next part is included for those seeking future mates or if you are praying for your children's future spouse).

I declare that death and hell no longer have the right to advance against my life or any future children or family members I may have. Father, I pray that you prepare the heart and life of my future spouse (As well as my children's spouses) to also be educated and informed about generational curses. Prepare him/her/them now also, to be cleansed from the iniquity of her bloodlines. Help us/them to be well prepared for one another, and I trust You to bring us together when we are adequately prepared for one another. Let us together raise a family without inherited generational curses, and train our/their children in the ways of the Lord.

I command every demonic spirit on assignment over my life to return to the place that Jesus made for you. Do not come back, I want nothing to do with you and I resist you! According to James 4:7 you must now flee from me, my home and everything that pertains to me. Get out in Jesus name!!

Let the curse over my home, myself and my family, and all that pertains to us be broken now, in Jesus name. I thank You, Father, for allowing us to receive Your restoration and the blessings that have been held back. I ask that Your Holy Spirit fill me with love, truth, wisdom, might, a spirit of understanding and enable me to live according to Your commands. Let the ruach, the breath of God come into me now, according to John 20:22 where You breathed on Your disciples and they received the breath of God. In Jesus name, Amen.

Prayer to Renounce the False Gods and Goddesses of Australia

Dear Heavenly Father,

I come to You and ask your forgiveness for the sins of my ancestors and myself. I repent for any involvement in our family associated with false gods, idolatry, rebellion, witchcraft and making agreements with other spirits. Forgive us for allowing the enemy to have a place in our lives to influence us. Forgive us for the sins of innocent bloodshed and releasing curses upon our families and our land. On behalf of myself and my ancestors, I repent and do renounce the following gods and goddesses:

I renounce "Anjea" the fertility Spirit and the spirit of reincarnation.

I renounce "Bagadjimbiri," known as two brothers and creator gods. I renounce all gender confusion and that comes from these spirits androgynous spirits.

I renounce "Baiamai,"   also known as a creator, and the spirit known as his son, Burambin.

I renounce "Baiame,"   a sky god of death, life, the god of rain and the shamans. A storm god who oversees initiation rites and collects souls of the innocent. I renounce his voice and declare I can no longer hear him. I declare his will shall not manifest through the wind.

I renounce "Bamapana," god of mischief and discord, an obscene spirit that uses profane and forbidden acts, a god of incest.

I renounce "Banaitja"   a creator god.

I renounce "Biame", the creator god.

I renounce "Bila," the cannibal sun goddess.

I renounce "Boaliri and Waimariwi," creator goddesses.

I renounce "Bulaing Karadjeri"

I renounce "Bumerali," goddess of physical prowess.

I renounce "Bunbulama," the goddess of rain.

I renounce "Bunjil" the god, represented as an eagle.

I renounce "Binbeal," the rainbow spirit.

I renounce "Birrahgnooloo and Cunnembeille," wives of Biame.

renounce "Daramulum" a sun and moon god.

I renounce "Djamar" a creator, the giver of the moral laws and of initiation rites.

I renounce "Djanggau and Djunkgao," sister fertility goddesses.

I renounce the goddess "Eingana," a snake-goddess defined as a world-creator, the birth mother, maker of all water, land, animals, and kangaroos.

I renounce "Erathipa," a goddess of reincarnation that takes the souls of dead children.

I renounce "Gidja," god of the moon and sleepwalking.

I renounce "Gnowee" a sun goddess.

I renounce the spirit "Harrimiah," that represents secrecy, shame, abuse, slavery and oppression.

I renounce "Imberombera" the spirit that multiplies spirit children, confusion and confused languages.

I renounce "Jar'Edo Wens" a god of pride, arrogance, self-reliance, earthly knowledge and physical might.

I renounce "Julana" a lecherous spirit who attacks people in their dreams at night.

I renounce "Julunggul" the rainbow snake fertility goddess, a sexual spirit who watches over boys coming into manhood. Also associated with rebirth and the weather.

I renounce "Junkgowa," a water spirit over marine life and also visits people in their dreams.
I renounce "Karora" a creator god that resides in lakes.

I renounce"Knaritja" a sky god.

I renounce "Kunapipi Alawa" god of male rites of passage into adulthood.

I reounce "Kunmanngur" the rainbow snake god of fertility and creation.

I renounce "Madalait," goddess of creation.

I renounce "Mangar-kunjer-kunja," a lizard spirit that is a god of war, weapons, division and rules over marriages.

I renounce "Nepelle," ruler of the heavens and a false father spirit.

I renounce "Ngunyari" the sky god.
I renounce "Nogomain," a god who gives spirit children to mortal parents.

I renounce "Numbakulla" the lizard spirit.

I renounce "Numma Moiyuk" the fertility goddess.

I renounce "Nurundere" a god of magick and wizardry, one that hunts others.

I renounce "Nyege" the supreme god over Fowler's Bay, Australia.

I renounce "Pallian" a god over Australia.

I renounce God name "Papang," the creator and sky god who lives in the moon.

I renounce "Pilirin" the god of fire.

I renounce "Pundjel" the creator god and overseer of religious indoctrination and rituals of manhood.

I renounce "Puru kupali," the creator god of the Jinini.

I renounce "Thurremlin," god of passage, from adolescence to manhood.

I renounce "Ungamilia," goddess of the evening star.

I renounce "Ungud" the snake God who is sometimes male and sometimes female. He is associated with rainbows, fertility, sexuality of shamans.

I renounce "Wagyl," a snake-like creature who created the waterways in and around the south-west of Western Australia. (Water spirit)

I renounce "Walo" the goddess of war and the sun.

I renounce "Waramurungundi"

I renounce "Wati-kutjara," a lizard spirit.

I renounce "Wawalag" and "Wiradyuri," patron god of the Kamilaroi, and creator gods.

I renounce "Wolaro," the creator god.

I renounce "Wollunqua," a snake-god of rain and fertility.

I renounce "Wuluwaid," an Aboriginal rain God.

I renounce "Wuriupranili," a sun goddess.

I renounce "Wurrunna," a culture hero of the Aborigines.

I renounce "Yurlunggur," a rainbow snake goddess, also a sexual demon who rules over sexuality, fertility, rebirth and the weather. Also known as Kalseru.

Lord Jesus, I believe You are the risen son of God who died in exchange for my sins. I believe Your blood cleanses me of all sin and unrighteousness. Let Your holy blood cover every sin, transgression and iniquity and close the door to the enemy. I declare the enemy cannot cross over the blood, and that these doors are forever sealed by the blood of Jesus. I renounce all evil inheritances from my ancestors and release all claim to them.

In the name and authority of the Lord Jesus Christ, I command all evil spirits to leave me now and go to the abyss created for them. Take all your evil works, the effect of every curse, and leave me now.

151

Father, give me wisdom to not re-open any of these doors, and to conduct myself with wisdom and integrity all the days of my life. Holy Spirit, I invite you to live in my heart, to sanctify me and baptize me with Your love. Baptize me in the fullness of Your Spirit and bless me with my heavenly language. I thank You for revealing more and more truth that will continue to lead me in paths of righteousness, freedom and healing. In Jesus name, Amen.

Prayer to Renounce Gods and Goddesses of Asia

(China)

I renounce the goddess Guanyin, also known as Guanyin Pusa, goddess of mercy.

I renounce the Jade Emperor Yuhuang Dadi, the highest ruler over Buddhists, Taoists and all other Asian religions.

I renounce Wangmu Niangniang, wife of the Jade Emperor, also known as Queen Mother and is also a god of happiness and longevity.

I renounce Yan Wang, the Chinese king of death who commands all the gods of the underworld.

I renounce Long Wang the dragon king of the sea. This water spirit also known as a storm god commands the rain and wind.

I renounce the Chinese goddess Nuwa, a creator and sky spirit.

I renounce the spirit Nezha, who rules over youth and is known as a general in the heavens (a strongman spirit).

I renounce the spirits known as the Eight Immortals, water spirits that are known as:

He Xian'gu
Cao Guojiu, or Cao Jingxiu
Li Tieguai
Lan Caihe
Lü Dongbin
Han Xiangzi
Zhang Guolao
Zhongli Quan

I renounce the god Caishen, a money god

I renounce Chang'e, Chinese goddess of the Moon and the wife of Hou yi.

I renounce the Ao Guange, Azure Dragon and all demonic spirits that take the form of the dragon.

153

I renounce Baimai Shen, the Chinese god of prostitution and brothels.

I renounce Budai, Hotei or Pu-Tai, a Buddhist deity.

I renounce the spirit of Chen Sheng, the spirit of war, rebellion and uprising.

I renounce Chenghuangshen, the city god of protection.

I renounce Xuanwu or Zhenwu, a water spirit.

I renounce the spirits known as Lords of the Three Mountains.

I renounce Menshen, also known as Shenshu, Yule and Qianliyan, door gods and gatekeepers, also known as clairvoyants and false prophets.

I renounce Shunfeng'er, the god who hears everything and keeper of doors.

I renounce the goddess Mi also known as Cybele, known as Great Mother, mistress of the beasts, and one that dominates men.

I renounce the sea goddess Mazu.

I renounce the goddess Phyrgia.

I renounce the gods of the three stars known as Sanxing, or Fu, Lu and Shou who represent prosperity, status and longevity.

(Indonesia, Bali Java, Maluku, Sunaese, Toraja)

I renounce Acintya, the supreme god

I renounce Batara Kala, god of the underworld

I renounce Dewi Danu, goddess of the lakes

I renounce the goddess Diana.

I renounce Dewi Ratih, goddess of the moon

I renounce Dewi Sri, goddess of rice and prosperity

I renounce Batara Guru, avatar of Hindu god Shiva and ruler of the Kahyangan, god of revelations

I renounce Batara Sambu, god of teachers

I renounce Batara Kala, god of the underworld

I renounce Dewi Lanjar, goddess who rules the North Sea

I renounce Dewi Ratih, goddess of the moon

I renounce Dewi Sri, goddess of rice and prosperity

I renounce Nyai Roro Kidul, goddess who rules the South Sea

I renounce Hainuwele, goddess who gives origin to vegetable crops

I renounce Nyai Pohaci Sanghyang Asri, goddess of rice and prosperity

I renounce Sunan Ambu, the mother goddess

I renounce Puang Matua, the creator god

I renounce Pong Banggai di Rante, god of Earth

I renounce Indo' Ongon-Ongon, goddess of earthquakes

I renounce Pong Lalondong, god of death

I renounce Indo' Belo Tumbang, goddess of medicine

I renounce Allah, the prophet Muhummed, the Quran, lying spirits and spirits of religious pride.

Father, on behalf of myself and my ancestors, I ask Your forgiveness for generational rebellion, the practice of false religions, opening doors to the occult realm and giving place to the enemy in our lives. Forgive us for rejecting Your gift of salvation, for any religious practices that involved shedding innocent blood, animal sacrifices, and occult magic. Show me if I have anything in my possession that You forbid so that I can rid my home and business of any idols.

In the name and authority of the Lord Jesus Christ, I renounce and repent for any contracts, covenants and agreements made with these spirits, and sins committed in their name. I divorce all false gods named above and any others by any other names. I apply the blood of Jesus to the sins of me and my ancestors and ask You, Father, to forgive them. I believe in my heart and I confess with my mouth Jesus Christ is the living Son of God that died for my sins and rose again on the third day. Thank you for accepting me as a child of God and for eternal life.

Holy Spirit, please fill me with the Spirit of God and baptize me with my heavenly language. Please lead me into the truth that will continue to make me free. Now, in the name and authority of the Lord Jesus I command all evil spirits to leave me now and take all evil works with you. Go to the abyss created for you and never return in Jesus name, Amen.

Prayer to Renounce the Gods and Goddess of Japan

Dear Heavenly Father,

In the name and authority of the Lord Jesus Christ, who I confess to be my Lord and Savior, I do renounce all false gods of my culture. Please forgive me and my ancestors for serving false gods, for generational rebellion, and for partnering with the occult in various religious traditions and practices.

I renounce Amano-Iwato, god of storms.

I renounce Ame-no-Koyane.

I renounce Azumi-no-isora, a water spirit

I renounce Daikokuten, god of great darkness, also known as god of five cereals and one of the Seven Lucky Gods (Fukujin) and the Indian deity Shiva and the Shinto god Ōkuninushi.

I renounce Dhṛtarāṣṭra, one of the four heavenly kings.

I renounce Fūjin, god of the wind.

I renounce Fukurokuju, god of wisdom and longevity.

I renounce Futsunushi, god of martial arts.

I renounce Hachiman, the god of war.

I renounce the familiar spirits of Kami.

I renounce Kangiten, god of wisdom.

I renounce Kompira, god of merchant sailors.

I renounce Mahakala, god of protection.

I renounce Myōken, god of the Northstar and one of the Seven Lucky gods.

I renounce Ōkuninushi, ruler of the unseen realm of magick, also known as the great land master.

I renounce Omoikane, also known as Ya-gokoro-omoi-kane-no-mikoto and

Toko-yo-no-Omoikane-no-kami which means "Many-Minds'-Thought-Combining Deity." I renounce the god of self, the spirits of confusion and double-mindedness and mind paralysis associated with these spirits.

I renounce Rāgarāja, associated with Buddhist traditions.

I renounce Suijin and Susanoo, gods of water, mermaids, and sea life.

I renounce the god Ugajin, associated with fertility, sexual confusion and demonic sexual spirits, that looks like a serpent.bearded man.

I renounce Vaiśravaṇa, a god of Buddhism.

I renounce Virūḍhaka, one of the four heavenly kings and a god of Buddhism.

I renounce Allah, the prophet Muhummed, the Quran, lying spirits and spirits of religious pride.

Father, on behalf of myself and my ancestors, I ask Your forgiveness for generational rebellion, the practice of false religions, opening doors to the occult realm and giving place to the enemy in our lives. Forgive us for rejecting Your gift of salvation, for any religious practices that involved shedding innocent blood, animal sacrifices, and occult magick. Show me if I have anything in my possession that You forbid so that I can rid my home and business of any idols.

In the name and authority of the Lord Jesus Christ, I renounce and repent for any contracts, covenants and agreements made with these spirits, and sins committed in their name. I divorce all false gods named above and any others by any other names. I apply the blood of Jesus to the sins of me and my ancestors and ask You, Father, to forgive them. I believe in my heart and I confess with my mouth Jesus Christ is the living Son of God that died for my sins and rose again on the third day. Thank you for accepting me as a child of God and for eternal life.

Holy Spirit, please fill me with the Spirit of God and baptize me with my heavenly language. Please lead me into the truth that will continue to make me free. Now, in the name and authority of the Lord Jesus I command all evil spirits to leave me now and take all evil works with you. Go to the abyss created for you and never return in Jesus name, Amen.

Prayer to Renounce Gods and Goddesses of the Philippines

(Tagalog Gods)

Dear Heavenly Father,

In the name and authority of the Lord Jesus Christ, who I confess to be my Lord and Savior, I do renounce all false gods of my culture. Please forgive me and my ancestors for serving false gods, for generational rebellion, and for partnering with the occult in various religious traditions and practices.

I renounce Aman Sinaya - god of the sea, fishing, and seafaring

I renounce Amanikable - god of the hunt, the protector of huntsmen

I renounce Anitun Tabu - goddess of the wind and the rain.

I renounce Apolake - god of the sun, lord of war, son of Bathala, patron of warriors

I renounce Bathala - king of the gods, ruler of the heavens, creator of humanity, father of Apolake, Mayari, and Tala

I renounce Dian Masalanta - goddess of love, pregnancy, childbirth, also known as "Maria Makiling" and a protector of lovers. I renounce all demonic sexual spirits, lust, perversion, gender confusion and the spirit of jealousy.

I renounce Hanan - god of the morning

I renounce Hayo - god of the sea and the ocean

I renounce Hukloban - goddess of death. I renounce the spirit of enchantment and all lying spirits.

I renounce Idianale - goddess of good deeds and hard work

I renounce Lakambuwi - god of gluttony, food, and eating

I renounce Lakapati - deity of fertility and cultivated fields, protector of crops and farm animals, also known as "Ikapati" or "Lakanpati."
I renounce Linga - god of disease

159

I renounce Malyari - god of strength and bravery, pride and selfishness.

I renounce Manggagaway - goddess of disease

I renounce Mangkukulam - the fire witch

I renounce Manisalat - god of broken families, one that causes discord between husband and wife

I renounce Mayari -a moon goddess

I renounce Sitan - god of the afterlife, guardian of the realm of the spirits, has four follower gods

I renounce Tala - goddess of the stars

(Visayan Gods)

I renounce Alunsina - virgin goddess of the eastern skies

I renounce Bangun Bangun - god of time and cosmic movements

I renounce Bulalakaw - bird god, one who causes illness

I renounce Burigadang Pada Sinaklang Bulawan - goddess of greediness

I renounce Dalikamata - the many-eyed goddess, cures eye illnesses

I renounce Kan-Laon - the southern supreme ruler, whose counterpart is Bathala

I renounce Kaptan - supreme ruler of the gods, counterpart Bathala

I renounce Kasaraysarayan sa Silgan - god of rivers

I renounce Lalahon - goddess of harvest, fire, and volcanoes, sends armies of fleas to destroy crops when angered

I renounce Lisbusawen - god of souls

I renounce Lubay-Lubyok Hanginun si Mahuyokhuyokan - goddess of the night breeze

I renounce Luyong Baybay - goddess of the tides

I renounce Magdang Diriinin - god of lakes

I renounce Maguayan - goddess of the sea, wife of Kaptan

I renounce Maguayen - ferryboat god, ferries souls to hell

I renounce Maklium sa Tiwan - god of the valleys and plains

I renounce Maklium sa Tubig - god of the sea

I renounce Munsad Buralakaw - god of politics and affairs of men

I renounce Pahulangkug - god of seasons

I renounce Paiburong - god of the middle world

I renounce Panlinugun - ruler of the underworld, god of earthquakes

I renounce Ribung Linti - god of lightning and thunder

I renounce Santonilyo - god of graces

I renounce Saraganka Bagyo - god of storms

I renounce Saragnayan - god of darkness

I renounce Suimuran and Suiguinarugan - gods of hell

I renounce Suklang Malayon - goddess of homeliness

I renounce Sumalongson - god of the rivers and the sea

I renounce Sumpoy - god of the afterlife

I renounce Tungkung Langit - upper world and supreme god

I renounce Varangao - god of rainbows

I renounce Ynaguinid and Macanduc - gods of war, battle

(Bicolano Gods)

I renounce Aswang - god of evil

I renounce Bakunawa - the dragon/sea serpent, also known as "Moon eater."

I renounce Gugurang - supreme god, keeper of sacred fire atop the regional mountain

I renounce Haliya - protector of women and goddess of the moon

I renounce Nagined, Arapayan, Makbarubak - the "trinity deities," inflictors of pain and death

I renounce Oryol - the serpent goddess and shapeshifter with an enchanting voice. I also renounce all seducing spirits, all mind blinding spirits and the deaf adder spirit that closes the ears to truth.

Father, on behalf of myself and my ancestors, I ask Your forgiveness for generational rebellion, the practice of false religions, opening doors to the occult realm and giving place to the enemy in our lives. Forgive us for rejecting Your gift of salvation, for any religious practices that involved shedding innocent blood, animal sacrifices, and occult magick. Show me if I have anything in my possession that You forbid so that I can rid my home and business of any idols.

In the name and authority of the Lord Jesus Christ, I renounce and repent for any contracts, covenants and agreements made with these spirits, and sins committed in their name. I divorce all false gods named above and any others by any other names. I apply the blood of Jesus to the sins of me and my ancestors and ask You, Father, to forgive them. I believe in my heart and I confess with my mouth Jesus Christ is the living Son of God that died for my sins and rose again on the third day. Thank you for accepting me as a child of God and for eternal life.

Holy Spirit, please fill me with the Spirit of God and baptize me with my heavenly language. Please lead me into the truth that will continue to make me free. Now, in the name and authority of the Lord Jesus I command all evil spirits to leave me now and take all evil works with you. Go to the abyss created for you and never return in Jesus name, Amen.

Prayer to Renounce the Gods and Goddesses of Mexico
(Aztec, Mayan, Toltec, Olmec and other tribes)

Dear Heavenly Father,

On behalf of myself and my ancestors, I repent for having false gods, goddesses and the sins of idolatry. Please let the blood of Jesus cover these sins. Me and my family are guilty of rebellion and witchcraft. Please forgive us for our involvement in occult practices, for they are forbidden in Your word.

You alone are God, Lord Jesus. Only You can break the bands of slavery and deliver me from the power of the enemy. No other gods gave their life for me. They cannot redeem my soul from hell. No other gods can cleanse me from sin. You are the only true God, Jesus, and I renounce all false gods and goddesses. Your word in Exodus 20:3,4 tells me I am to have no other gods before you. Scripture says, "You shall not make for yourself any idol, or any likeness of what is in heaven above or on the earth beneath, or in the water under the earth."

Therefore, I renounce the false gods of my ancestors.

I renounce the god of the Mexicas and the Aztecs known as Huitzilopochtli or Tenochtitlan, the god of war. I repent for any involvement that me or my family members participated in that involved murder, bloodshed, sacrificial dismemberment, cannibalism, and human and animal sacrifice.

I repent for worshiping the sun, moon and stars. I renounce all sun, moon and astral gods and goddesses and the false religious practices associated with them.

I renounce the feathered serpent god, Queztzalcoatl and his twin, Xoloti; I also renounce these demonic spirits that represent the wind and wisdom. I renounce all animal spirits associated with these spirits such as snakes, crows, eagles, bears, jaguars and macaws.

I renounce the false god Tezcatlipoca that represents enmity, discord, rulership, divination, temptation, sorcery, war and strife. I renounce the spirit of pride, voyeurism, pretense and lying spirits that come from the spirit known as "Smoking Mirrors."

I renounce the matron goddesses of fertility, life, death and rebirth known as Chimalma and Coatlicue, Itzpapalotl and Xociticlicue. I renounce Tlazolteotl, goddess of lust, carnality, and sexual misdeeds.

I renounce Tonocatecuhtli and Tonocacihuatl, and all fertility rituals and worship associated with false gods associated with lust, carnality, sexual immorality and all unnatural sexual practices; the serpentine spirit, the spirit of Python, divination, and the sin of seeking power and immortality through occult practices. I ask your forgiveness for the use of phallic objects and other inanimate objects used in unnatural sexual and religious practices. I renounce the sins of adultery, prostitution, sex slavery, spiritual whoredom, and sexual immorality. I command the spirit of Lilith, incubus and succubus spirits, the perverse spirit and all familiar spirits to leave me now and never come back, in the name and authority of the Lord Jesus Christ.

Let all ungodly soul ties that came from former lovers or forbidden sexual encounters, rape, molestation, incest and other sexual sins leave me now in Jesus name. I ask You, Father, to command all fragmented parts of my soul return to me and the fragmented parts of other people's souls that have been attached to me, return to them. It is written in Psalm 23:3 that You restore my soul, and in Isaiah 53:5, "By your stripes we were healed." Lord Jesus, You took all my sins upon Yourself when You went to the cross. I ask You to please make me whole again by the power of Your Holy Spirit that heals me.

I renounce all shamanistic rituals and false prophecy, and all familiar spirits associated with dark magic, witchcraft and sorcery. I renounce all traditions and indoctrination rituals associated with occult ceremonies, their priests and priestesses.

I renounce all patrons of war: Huitzilopochtli, Mixcoatl, Tialoc and Xiuhtecuhtli.

I renounce Xipe Toutec, (SHEE-pay TO-tec) the god of agriculture.

I renounce the Lords of the Day and Lords of the Night, also known as water, fire, earth and sky dieties:

Xiuhtecuhtli, god of fire and time.

Tezcatlipoca, (Tez-cat-li-PO-ca) god of providence, the darkness and the invisible, lord of the night, ruler of the North.

Piltzintecuhtli, god of the visions, associated with planet Mercury, and healing.

Centeotl, god of maize (corn).

Mictlantecuhtli, god of the Underworld.

Mictecacihuatl, goddess of the dead, ruler of the Underworld.

Tepeyollotl, god of the animals, darkened caves, echoes and earthquakes. Also known as Tepeyollotl, associated with mountains and high places.

Tlaloc, (TLAH-loc) fertility god and god of rain, lightning and thunder.

Tecciztecatl, moon god, also associated with the innermost of the twisted conch shell.

Xiuhtecuhtli, god of fire and time.

Huehueteotl, also known as Xiuhtecuhtli or Ometoetl; ancient fire god and creator.

Patecatl, patron of medicines.

Mixcoatl, the cloud serpent.

Huitzilopochtli, known as the hummingbird, the personal God of the Mexica, or Aztecs, and a god of war.

Tlaltecuhtli, old god of earth.

Chalchiuhtlicue, goddess of water, lakes, rivers, seas, streams, horizontal waters, storms and baptism.

Tonatiuh, god of the Sun.

Mictlantececuhtli, god of the dead. (Nearly identical to the Greek God Hades).

Yohualtecuhtli, Lord of the Night and possessor of bones.

Quetzalcoatl, (pronounced Kayt-zal-CO-atl) god of the life, the light and wisdom, lord of the winds and the day, ruler of the West.

Tlahuizcalpantecuhtli, god of dawn.

Tzitzimitl, celestial demon goddess, goddess of the air.

Citlalicue, goddess of female stars (Milky Way).
Citlalatonac, god of female stars (Husband of Citlalicue) - And any other names regardless of what name by which they are known.

I renounce Satan and the works of darkness, all other gods by any name which they are known, all familiar spirits, indoctrination rituals into the occult, its traditions and practices.

I break every covenant made with any of the spirits that I have named as well as any other demons that may be in my life. I repent on behalf of me and my ancestors for any and all agreements made knowingly or unknowingly with demonic entities that may still be legally enforceable in the spirit realm. I ask You, Heavenly Father, to break the power of those agreements and apply the blood of Jesus to them. Let them be unenforceable from this day forward in Jesus name.

Prayer to Renounce Various Native Indian Gods and Goddesses

Dear Heavenly Father,

In the name and authority of the Lord Jesus Christ, who I confess to be my Lord and Savior, I do renounce all false gods of my culture. Please forgive me and my ancestors for serving false gods, for generational rebellion, and for partnering with the occult in various religious traditions and practices.

I renounce Ababinili (Chickasaw god)

I renounce Aguguq (Aleut god)

I renounce Ahone (Powhatan god)

I renounce Apistotoke (Blackfoot god)

I renounce Ataensic (Iroquois goddess)

I renounce Atina (Arikara goddess)

I renounce Atius-Tirawa (Pawnee god)

I renounce Bluejay (Chinook trickster god)

I renounce Breathmaker (Seminole god)

I renounce Caribou Master (Innu god)

I renounce Chebbeniathan (Arapaho god)

I renounce Chief Above (Caddo god)

I renounce Cuaygerri (Achagua god)

I renounce First Maker (Mandan god)

I renounce Ekeko (Andean god)

I renounce Evaki (Bakairi goddess)

I renounce Everywhere Being (Ioway dwarf god)

I renounce Gitchi Manitou (Anishinabe god)

I renounce Great Spirit (many tribes)

I renounce Gudatrigakwitl (Wiyot god)

I renounce Henon (Iroquois god)

I renounce Hutash (Chumash goddess)

I renounce Iya (Sioux primordial god)

I renounce Ioskeha (Huron Indian god)

I renounce Iriria (Bribri goddess)

I renounce Isa (Shoshone god)

I renounce Kami (Bakairi god)

I renounce Kanati (Cherokee god)

I renounce Keri (Bakairi god)

I renounce Kisulkw (Mi'kmaq god)

I renounce Ketanitowet (Lenape god)

I renounce Kudo (Bribri god)

I renounce Kujuli (Wayana god)

I renounce Kururumany (Arawak Indian god)

I renounce Lone Man (Hidatsa god)

I renounce Maheo (Cheyenne Indian god)

I renounce Makonaima (Cariban god)

I renounce Man'una (Hochunk god)

I renounce Masaw (Hopi god)

I renounce Mokat (Cahuilla god)

I renounce Mopó (Apalai god)

I renounce Natosi (Blackfoot Indian god)

I renounce Niottsi (Dene Indian god)

I renounce Nishanu (Arikara Indian god)

I renounce Niskam (Mi'kmaq Indian god)

I renounce Okee (Powhatan Indian god)

I renounce Old Man Coyote (Crow god)

I renounce Onatah (Iroquois goddess)

I renounce Orenda (Iroquois divinity)

I renounce Pachamama (Inca goddess)

I renounce Piai (Carib Indian god)

I renounce Raven (Northwestern Indian god)

I renounce Raweno (Iroquois god)

I renounce Sedna (Inuit goddess)

I renounce Selu (Cherokee goddess)

I renounce Sibo (Bribri Indian god)

I renounce Silver Fox (California Indian god)

I renounce Sipakmaat (Cocopa Creator God)

I renounce Sky-Chief (Carib Indian god)

I renounce Spider of Heaven (Arapaho Indian god)

I renounce Spider-Woman (Hopi Indian goddess)

I renounce Tabaldak (Abenaki god)

I renounce Taronhiawagon (Iroquois Indian god)

I renounce Tsááyaa (Beaver Indian god)

I renounce Tumaiyowit (Cahuilla god)

I renounce Unetlanvhi (Cherokee Indian god)

I renounce Unknown Woman (Choctaw goddess)

I renounce Utakké (Carrier god)

I renounce Wakanda (Omaha god)

I renounce Wakan Tanka (Sioux god)

I renounce White Buffalo Woman (Sioux goddess)

I renounce Yamoria (Dene Indian god)

I also renounce any spirits from Native Indian religion, culture and beliefs by any other name. I renounce the demonic spirits of hoodoo, voodoo, Satanism, and all spirits of witchcraft and magic in the name of Jesus Christ. I renounce all practices and demonic spirits associated with black magic, the Cherokee, Chickasaw, the Creek, Seminole, Choctaw, the Blackfoot, Cree, Crow, Pauite, Shoebone, Cheyenne,   Sioux, the Ute, Pawnee, the Navajo, Shawnee and Apache customs and traditions. I renounce African religions, the Catholic religion and their saints, patrons and patronesses; familiar spirit guides and any and all other false gods and deities of various religions that are syncretized with Native religious practices.

Father, on behalf of myself and my ancestors, I ask Your forgiveness for rejecting Your gift of salvation, for any religious practices that involved shedding innocent blood, animal sacrifices, and occult magick. Show me if I have anything in my possession that You forbid so that I can rid my home and business of any idols.

In the name and authority of the Lord Jesus Christ, I renounce and repent for any contracts, covenants and agreements made with these spirits, and sins committed in their name. I divorce all false gods named above and any others by any other names. I apply the blood of Jesus to the sins of me and my ancestors and ask You, Father, to forgive them. I believe in my heart and I confess with my mouth Jesus Christ is the living Son of God that died for my sins and rose again on the third day. Thank you for accepting me as a child of God and for eternal life.

Holy Spirit, please fill me with the Spirit of God and baptize me with my heavenly language. Please lead me into the truth that will continue to make me free. In the name and authority of the Lord Jesus I command all evil spirits to leave me now and take all evil works with you. Go to the abyss created for you and never return in Jesus name, Amen.

This prayer addresses certain sins that were committed against Native Americans by our nation's forefathers and others, such as the Indian Removal Act that resulted in the Trail of Tears and other injustices. As citizens of the United States, Native Americans have a dual role of utmost significance, because as intercessors, they can release forgiveness over the land for the injustices they suffered. There is also a responsibility to repent for the sins of their ancestors because of the pagan religious practices of worshipping other gods. This prayer is to be prayed from the perspective of identifying with the sins of the nation's forefathers as well as taking responsibility for generational curses that came through their natural ancestry.

Prayer for Healing and Deliverance for Native American

Father God, Lord Jesus and Holy Spirit:

I come to You on behalf of myself and all those in my ancestral line that came before me. I ask for Your forgiveness for our sins, and today I acknowledge that many of us sinned by never asking for Jesus Christ to be our Lord and Savior. Many of us committed sins and trespasses in rebellion to Your ways. Please hear my prayer and let the blood of Jesus cleanse my ancestral line from all unrighteousness. I take You as My Lord, and ask that You adopt me as Your child. You paid for me with Your blood, Lord Jesus, and I thank You that You went to the cross in my place.

Father, I also come to you as a citizen of the United States, and I ask You to forgive the sins of our forefathers. I ask You to forgive the sins of those that pioneered and settled this land, and the pagan practices, cultures and traditions brought in from foreign lands. Forgive, I pray, our presidential and political leaders that broke treaties and treacherously removed the boundary lines of Native Americans and others to claim them as their own. For it is written:

"Don't cheat your neighbor by moving the ancient boundary markers set up by previous generations." Prov. 22:28

Forgive us for encroaching on property that didn't belong to us and cheating rightful heirs out of their inheritance, for it is also written, "Do not move an ancient boundary stone or encroach on the fields of the fatherless," in Proverbs 23:10.

Forgive us for impoverishing Native American families, forcing them out of their homes, for making slaves of other races and nationalities; for causing others to feel overcome with jealousy, fear, anger and desire vengeance against those who treated them wrongfully. Forgive us for the grief we caused, the injustices and the bloodshed.

Forgive us for broken covenants, vows and agreements and for the curses that came as a result of those actions. Although I may not have personally taken part in these sins, I understand that there is a need to recognize the sins of those that came before us and I ask for the blood of Jesus to atone for these things so that this land can be cleansed. Please allow all those that have been affected by this generational root of bitterness, grief and poverty now find the grace to forgive, even generations of mistreatment and injustices. I choose to forgive anyone that I have been offended with. I choose to forgive those that I feel are responsible for my pain or bitterness. Please let Your restoration be upon us all. I pray for the blessings that have been blocked up, barricaded, unlawfully stolen, hidden or plundered - and I tell them, "Come back into your rightful generational line. Come back into those families and let the blessings flow abundantly in Jesus name."

Father, I renounce all false gods and masters. According to Your word, O God, in Deuteronomy 7:5, You commanded Your people to destroy ungodly altars and break down their sacred pillars. Let these prayers of renouncement accomplish the destruction of all ungodly altars in my family, in my generational line, and in this nation.

On behalf of myself, my generational line, the founding fathers of this nation and all political leaders in this land, I identify with these sins and the need to acknowledge them to You so that our land may be healed. Therefore, I renounce the demonic spirits of hoodoo, voodoo, Satanism, and all spirits of witchcraft and magic in the name of Jesus Christ. I renounce all practices and demonic spirits associated with black magic, the Cherokee, Chickasaw, the Creek, Seminole, Choctaw, the Blackfoot, Cree, Crow, Pauite, Shoebone, Cheyenne, Sioux, the Ute, Pawnee, the Navajo, Shawnee and Apache customs and traditions. I renounce African religions, the Catholic religion and their saints, patrons and patronesses; familiar spirit guides and any and all other false gods and deities of various religions.

I renounce the use of tobacco for ceremonial or ungodly religious purposes and any and all power associated with it to be rendered impotent, paralyzed and powerless, according to what You have already done on the cross, Lord Jesus.

I renounce all ungodly spirits that may be associated with Native American dances that involve the use of conjuring demons, the use demonic power, psychic energy, ancient witchcraft practices, sorcery, charms, spells, incantations and magic. Let all ungodly altars be silent and dismantled now. Let the blood of Jesus cover those individuals that have participated in demonic worship whether or not they participated knowingly or unknowingly. I ask You to deliver them and set them free from all deception, Lord Jesus. Let Your Holy Spirit reveal the truth that will free people from demonic oppression, possession, and deception. Let the blinders fall off. Give them a spirit of revelation and an understanding heart that they might come to know the One and True Living God, Jesus Christ.

I renounce all customs of speaking word curses on their enemies through traditional songs. Forgive us for things we did and practices that were accepted that had a spirit of death and cursing bound to the words that were spoken. Let all word curses be broken now in the spiritual and earthly realms. Let those words laced with death lose all power and cease to ring in the ears of those who have heard them. I bind the spirit of death that is associated with these customs and culture and forbid the spirits of death and hell from being released. I command them to go back now to the place where Jesus sends them and forever be bound into captivity. I declare that the spirits of death and hell will no longer advance in the name and authority of Jesus Christ.

On behalf of myself, my ancestors and the forefathers of this nation, I renounce demonic attachments associated with gambling and ceremonial gambling. I loose the demonic spirits and spiritual enforcers off of all objects used in gambling and command them to return to the abyss created for all demons. Let the spirits of lust, greed, selfishness and bondage be bound in the name and authority of Jesus Christ. I pray, O God, let the Spirit of Liberty be released to free all people that have been bound by sin and addiction. Let them be loosed from their bondage in Jesus name.

Let all demons be loosed off of individuals, out of homes, offices, businesses, churches, and expelled out of the land that You have given to Your rightful heirs. I ask You, Lord Jesus, to grant an order for eviction from the court of heaven that commands all encroachers, squatters, soothsayers, and those who practice demonic witchcraft off of the land. I command these demonic spirits to be sent back to the place prepared for all demons where they must be bound and confined until the day of their eternal judgment in the lake of fire.

I thank You, Lord Jesus, Heavenly Father and Holy Spirit for releasing Your power against the works of evil, that it might come to a quick and sudden end. I ask that You also release the power of Your Holy Spirit to bring forth forgiveness, compassion, grace and healing. Let there be signs, wonders and miracles, to the glory of the Son of God, Jesus Christ. I ask that You display Your power against the works of darkness, evil and Satan, that the workers of sorcery, demonic magic, witchcraft, spells, incantations, and every form of demonic power would be seen as inferior to that of Your Holy Spirit . I ask that the name of Jesus would be glorified and the enemy be put to an open shame. I ask that every thing the enemy has done to conspire, entrap, ensnare, falsely accuse, gain a false judgment by deceit, bribery or falsehood be overturned. Let all who oppress Your children and hinder them from their divine purpose and assignments be stopped and brought to justice. Let righteous judgment prevail. I ask that You would, according to this petition, grant victory and justice for those that have waited for Your intervention. Let the power of Christ be displayed, the name of Jesus glorified, as You destroy the works of the evil one. In Jesus name, Amen.

Prayer to Break Generational Curses
(Breakthrough Prayer)

Dear Heavenly Father,

I come to You on behalf of myself and all those in my ancestral line that came before me. I ask for Your forgiveness for our sins, and I acknowledge that many of us never asked for Jesus Christ to be our Lord and Savior. Many of us committed sins and trespasses in rebellion to Your ways.

Father, I also come to you as a citizen of the United States, and I ask You to forgive the sins of our forefathers. I ask You to forgive the sins of those that pioneered and settled this land, and the pagan practices, cultures and traditions brought in from foreign lands. Forgive, I pray, our presidential and political leaders that broke treaties and treacherously removed the boundary lines of Native Americans and others to claim them as their own.

Forgive all those in my family line as well as those who founded our nation and settled the land for making slaves of other races and nationalities; for causing others to feel overcome with jealousy, fear, anger and desire vengeance against those who treated them wrongfully.

Forgive us for the grief we caused, the injustices and the bloodshed. Forgive us for broken covenants, vows and agreements and for the curses that came as a result of those actions. Although I may not have personally taken part in these sins, I understand that there is a need to recognize the sins of those that came before us and I ask for the blood of Jesus to atone for these things so that we may be cleansed of all these unrighteous acts. Please allow all those that have been affected by this generational root of bitterness, grief and poverty now find the grace to forgive, even generations of mistreatment and injustices.

Father, You said that if I would humble myself, pray and seek Your face...If I would turn and repent from my wicked ways, You said You would forgive my sins. Whether other family members or myself have partaken of these sins knowingly or unknowingly, I ask Your forgiveness and I renounce:

All spirits of fear, the fear of man that brings a snare, self-pity, insecurity, and inferiority. Forgive me for the need to control or manipulate others out of a sense of fear, insecurity or inferiority. Forgive me for not trusting in your provision or your timing, and for failing to rest in Your love. Father, I thank you that Your perfect love casts out all fear according to 1 John 4:18. I come out of agreement with the spirit of fear and command it to leave me now, in the name and authority of Jesus Christ. Let the curse of fear and anxiety be broken now in Jesus name.

I renounce bitterness, jealousy, strife, anger, hatred, profanity, gossip, lying, slander and murder with the mouth. I repent for holding on to bitterness that comes from being hurt, mistreated or injustice that has occurred towards myself or others in my family. I renounce the spirit of Cain, which is a murderous spirit. I come out of agreement with these spirits and repent for my judgments against others. I command bitterness, jealousy, strife, anger, hatred, profanity, gossip, lying, slander and rage to leave me now in the name and authority of Jesus Christ. I willingly forgive all those that have hurt and offended me, from my heart. Let all curses of rejection, wandering and instability be broken now in Jesus name.

Forgive me and those in my family for any sins of hard heartedness, being critical or condemning, or showing lack of compassion towards others in their time of need. Forgive me and those in my family for turning a blind eye towards those in need and withholding good when it was in our power to help. Father, please let the hardness of my heart be changed. Let Your compassion fill my heart. Let the curse of greed that produces poverty be broken now in Jesus name.

I renounce the sin of abortion which is premeditated murder. Father, forgive me and anyone in my family for shedding innocent blood. Please let the spirit of abortion be broken off of my life. Let the blood of Jesus cover this sin and close the door to the curse in Jesus name.

I renounce all spirits of heaviness that bring depression, mental illness, obsessive compulsive disorders, schizophrenia, suicide, bi-polar disease and grief. I renounce the spirits of insanity, unbelief, double-mindedness, the cares of this world and all things that would give me give me divided loyalties in my heart and mind towards God. I renounce every seed that Satan has sown into my heart and mind that would cause divided loyalties and weaken my convictions towards Jesus Christ. I come out of agreement with the spirits of insanity, unbelief and doublemindedness and I command them to leave me now, in the name and authority of Jesus Christ. Let the curse of unbelief and double-mindedness be broken now in Jesus name.

I renounce all compulsive behavior and all addictions rooted in fear, rejection, or anxiety. I come out of agreement with spirits of compulsion, fear, rejection and anxiety. I command them to leave me now in the name and authority of Jesus Christ. Let the curse of all mental illness be broken now in Jesus name.

I renounce and forsake unforgiveness, including unforgiveness towards myself, retaliation, and vengeance. Forgive me, Lord, for any time that me or my family members have sown seeds of discord or caused pain to others. I repent for sins of judging or rejecting others, withholding love, acceptance or forgiveness. Forgive me for failing to show love, mercy, grace or compassion. Let the judgments I have spoken about others bear no more fruit in my life or theirs. Let the power of negative words I have spoken be broken now and I ask you to please release me from reaping judgment into my own life, in Jesus name.

I renounce and forsake spirits of self-hatred, self-rejection, unloving spirits, guilt, condemnation and shame. Father I thank you for your forgiveness. Your word says there is therefore now no condemnation for those who are in Christ Jesus. I come out of agreement with the spirits of self-hatred, self-rejection, unloving spirits, guilt, condemnation and shame, and command them to leave me now. Let all shame and condemnation be broken off my life now in Jesus name.

I renounce and forsake spirits of rejection and abandonment, all lying spirits and command them to leave me at once. I thank you Father that I am not rejected; I am accepted in the Beloved. I come out of agreement with spirits of rejection and abandonment and command them to leave me in the name and authority of Jesus Christ. Your word says You will never leave me or forsake me. I am loved and accepted according to Your word in Ephesians 1:6. Let the curse of abandonment be broken now in Jesus name.

I renounce and forsake all soul ties to illegitimate spiritual fathers or spiritual leaders, religious attitudes, and spirits of legalism, disrespect, self-righteousness, pride, , pretense, hypocrisy, masquerade, prejudice, controlling behaviors, manipulation, imposing my will on others, racism, disobedience, independence, critical spirits, arrogance, vain and judgmental attitudes. I come out of agreement with religious witchcraft, hypocrisy, pride, pretense, masquerade, control, guilt, manipulation and self-righteousness and I command them to leave me now, in the name and authority of Jesus Christ. Let the curse associated with these spirits be broken now in Jesus name.

Forgive me for not being able to separate the sin of those that have hurt me from them as human beings that have also been hurt and used by the enemy to hurt others. Forgive me for rebellion to authority and the times when I have not honored nor shown respect to those in authority, parents, spouses or others. Forgive me for not humbling myself or apologizing when I should have done so. I come out of agreement with the lies and the spirit of rebellion, insubordination and pride, and I command them to leave me now. Let every curse associated with these spirits be broken now in Jesus name.

I renounce and repent for all broken covenants, unfulfilled vows and promises, betrayal and divorce. I ask you to forgive me for any way that my actions may have provoked jealousy or pain in others. I pray that You heal any wounds in others that I may have caused. Let the curse of miscarriage, fertility problems, jealousy, and broken relationships be broken now in Jesus name.

I ask You to forgive me for making agreements with the wrong people. Please disentangle me and release me from ungodly covenants, vows, and unrighteous agreements. I ask You to break me free from agreements and relationships where I am yoked with things of the kingdom of darkness, evil and wrong relationships, in Jesus name.

I repent of all sexual sins. I renounce and divorce all spirits of lust, the spirit of Pan, the god of sexual stimulation; covetousness and witchcraft. I renounce and forsake all soul ties to former lovers, and any soul ties that were formed through trauma, pain, shame, abuse, deep disappointment and broken vows. Let the fragmented pieces of those people's soul return to them, and let the fragmented pieces of my soul return to me. Please heal the fragmentation in my soul and spirit. I renounce the perverse spirit. I renounce and forsake incubus and succubus spirits, ungodly fantasies, spirits of voyeurism, perverse sexual practices and homosexuality. I ask You, Holy Spirit, to purify my eye gate, my senses and desires. Help me be diligent to guard these places of my heart and mind so that the enemy cannot use these things as a temptation to ensnare me. I come out of agreement with these spirits and command them to leave me now, in the name and authority of the Lord Jesus Christ. I ask You, Holy Spirit, to help me come back to my senses. I thank You, Father, that you have created me to be holy and blameless according to Ephesians 1:4. Let every curse associated with these things be broken now in Jesus name.

I renounce and forsake all false gods, masters and all evil inheritances that have come through family line. I renounce African religions, the false practices and traditions of other religions and their saints, patrons and patronesses and spirit guides. I renounce and repent, on behalf of myself and my ancestors for any covenants or agreements made with the seven African spirits known as Papa Legba, Obtala, Oya, Oshun, Chango, Ogun and Yemmaya. I declare there is no other God except for Jesus Christ and I break any connections or agreements that have been made through candle burning, calling on the names of false gods or saints, and invoking their assistance. I come out of agreement with these familiar spirits and I divorce all gods and masters of various names. I command them to leave me now in the name and authority of Jesus Christ. Let every curse associated with these things be broken now in Jesus name.

I renounce the demonic spirits of hoodoo, voodoo, Satanism, and all spirits of witchcraft and magic in the name of Jesus Christ. I renounce the god of the graveyard, Baron Samedi, and the loa Maman Bridgitte, and all gods, amulets and practices of Haitian voodoo. I renounce all witchcraft practices of juju. I come out of agreement with any covenants and invitations of these spirits made by myself or my ancestors and I command them to leave me now in the name and authority of Jesus Christ. Let every curse associated with these spirits be broken now in Jesus name.

I renounce and repent for any involvement with secret societies and the ungodly covenants they demand. (If you know which ones are involved in your family history, name them).I renounce and forsake all pledges, oaths and involvement with Freemasonry, lodges, societies or crafts by my ancestors and myself. I renounce and forsake all false gods, false doctrines, unholy communion and abominations. I renounce and forsake the Luciferian doctrine; I renounce and forsake the oaths spoken to pledge loyalties to man or idol that violated the commands of God and conscience. I renounce all false masters associated with Freemasons, Shriners, Mormonism, Paganism, the Klu Klux Klan and other lodges and secret societies. I renounce and forsake the false god Allah. I renounce and forsake all words and phrases used as secret codes and I break agreement with all curses that were once agreed to be placed upon any and all family members, including myself and future generations. I come out of agreement with these covenants and evil spirits, and command them to leave me now in the name and authority of Jesus Christ. Let every curse associated with these abominations be broken now in Jesus name.

I renounce all lies and false teaching that blinds me to truth and mocks and resists God. I renounce all ungodly symbols that connect me to false teaching, false gods, ungodly alliances and pagan symbolism. I accept and receive no inheritance from evil sources, only that which my heavenly Father permits and allows. Let all evil inheritances be broken off of me and my family. Father, forgive me and my ancestors for resisting truth and resisting Your authority. Holy Spirit, I ask you to forgive me for grieving You and mocking the things of God. I renounce the spirits of mocking, scoffing, the deaf and dumb spirit, the spirit of blindness and all mind blinding spirits. I renounce the anti-Christ spirit and the spirit of pride. Let the power of Leviathan be broken off of my life. I come out of agreement with these spirits and command them to leave me now in the name and authority of Jesus Christ. Let every curse associated with these sins be broken now in Jesus name.

Lord, let there be a release of every curse that has come against me or my generational line as a result of these things. I decree a cancellation of every form of witchcraft and curse that has resulted from my involvement or that of my generational line. I ask You, Lord Jesus, to come and deliver me and my family from all demonic spirits that have come as a result of a curse. I ask that You restore all the years that the enemy has stolen according to your promise in Joel 2:25,26. Let the blessings that have been held back, stolen and hidden by the enemy be released into my hands now, in Jesus name. Let all demonic attachments be severed from me and my family line, both in the heavenly places as well as in the earthly realm. I declare that every seed that was sown by Satan in order to perpetuate a curse or cause myself or someone else in my family line to reject my heavenly Father, the Lord Jesus Christ and Holy Spirit must now shrivel and die immediately. Jesus, I give You permission to change what You know needs to change in my life and to convict me if I resist your Holy Spirit.

Father, I repent for these sins on behalf of me and my family to the tenth generation back. I thank You for Your forgiveness and cleansing of these sins. I declare that when I am tested, the Spirit of God will arise within me and bring me into a place of victory. I give You permission in advance of any situation I may encounter that You and Your Holy Spirit may change my actions, words and responses so that I honor You. Please reign and rule over my emotions.

Enemy, according to the scripture in James 4:7, as I am now submitted to God, you must flee from me. I command you to take everything that you have put on me, everything that you have tormented me with, every sickness and GO! I command you to pay restitution at no less than a 7-fold return, according to Proverbs 6:31 in every place that you have brought poverty, defeat, robbery or death and destruction.

Today I declare that the enemy is defeated where I am concerned. You are my Master, my Lord and my Savior. Please come with Your Holy Spirit and heal my mind, my emotions, my thoughts, my confession and my memories. Please heal my trust issues with you and others. Please heal the issues related to my past, my present and my future. Heal my hope, my faith and my love. Heal any areas of grief, heaviness, unbelief, and let the renewed mind of Christ be strengthened and formed in me each and every day. Thank You for releasing into me a spirit of Faith, a spirit of Obedience, the spirit of Adoption, the spirit of Revelation and Truth. Now tell me Lord, what I need to do as an act of faith that will release my breakthrough. Confirm it and convict me that I will not neglect to do whatever You tell me to do. Thank You for eternal life, health, and victory, and for restoring my life and my future, in Jesus' precious name, Amen.

Prayer to Renounce False Religious Practices
(Catholicism & Mexican Traditions
Occult Involvement & Satanic Worship)

Heavenly Father,

I repent for any way that I have knowingly or unknowingly enthroned Satan and spirits of darkness, given place to demonic spirits and allowed them to access my life. I renounce the sins of my parents, grandparents, and other ancestors that have participated in all forms of witchcraft, sorcery and occultism. This day I divorce the enemy, Satan, and all other false gods and religions.

I renounce the following spirits : Baal, Python, Lucifer, Jezebel, the spirit of Babylon and whoredoms, Bast, Ma'at, Nehebka, Seth, Isis, Zeus, Leviathan, Rahab, Beelzebub, Belial, Molech, Chemosh, Baphomet, Abaddon and all destroyer spirits, Lamia, Lilith, Lilu and all Lilin spirits. I renounce all vampire spirits.

I renounce all spirits associated with Santeria, Lucumi, African gods and all familiar spirits associated with rituals, prayers, customs and traditions. I renounce the seven African spirits known as Papa Legba, Obtala, Oya, Oshun, Chango, Ogun and Yemmaya, in the name of Jesus Christ.

I renounce the god of the graveyard, Baron Samedi, and the loa Maman Bridgitte, and all gods, amulets and practices of Haitian voodoo;

I renounce all witchcraft practices of juju;

I renounce the false god known as the Grand Master;

I renounce all Loas, mediums and familiar spirits, ungodly priests, priestesses, sorcerers and wizards.

I renounce fear, self-will, lust, control and confusion.

I renounce all Loas, mediums and familiar spirits, ungodly priests, priestesses, sorcerers and wizards that are syncretized with Catholic saints, and any other names which they may be called.

I renounce idolatrous worship to Mary, Queen of Heaven; Mary, Star of the Sea; Mary, Our Lady of Rule, and the Virgin Mary, also known as Our Lady of Mercy.

I renounce the patron saint of wrongful death and the storm god, Saint Barbara.

I renounce the patron saint of doorways, Saint Anthony. I renounce the act of seeking miracles through patron saints instead of the Lord Jesus Christ and His Holy Spirit.

I renounce the patron saint Joseph and all familiar spirits that may have been invoked in that name.

I renounce the spirit known as Our Lade of Charity, which is also known as the Cuban goddess Our Lady of la Caridad del Cobre that rules pleasure, sexuality, marriage, the arts and money.

I renounce the patron saint Peter, and any petitions made for the sake of monetary gain, success and employment.

I renounce I renounce all water spirits, mermaids and mermen spirits, all spirits that dwell beneath the sea, including sea snakes and the serpents of Sheol.

I bind any and all inanimate objects from being used in any sort of witchcraft, voodoo, hoodoo or other form of demonic practices and loose all evil spirits off of individuals, objects, and evil altars. I command them to go to the abyss that was created for them in Jesus name.

I repent and renounce all participation in Day of the Dead, All Saints Day and All Souls Day celebrations;

I repent for making ungodly altars during any celebrations or offering worship on defiled altars to false gods;

I renounce lighting candles and praying to any saints, gods or goddesses other than in the name of Jesus Christ.

I repent for all these practices and ask that the blood of Jesus cover these sins. Father God, let these doorways in the spirit realm be permanently closed and sealed by the blood of Jesus.

I renounce divination and conjuring of all familiar spirits of the dead and those that my ancestors and family members have participated in. I renounce all soul ties to familiar and familial protectors, spirit guides, scribes and messengers, diviners and ungodly priests, false fathers and mothers.

I renounce all animal and material sacrifices made on my behalf or those in my family line. I renounce all human involvement for the sake of divining information, the use of familiar spirits, spirit guides, and false gods. I renounce all blood that was shed from any source that was tied to my life through the use of occult practices.

Father God, Lord Jesus and Holy Spirit, I want nothing to do with any of these spirits or their ungodly practices. This day I divorce the enemy and all false gods that have been a part of my life, whether through inherited curses, the sins of my ancestors or my own involvement. Please forgive me and those in my family line. Please wash us clean from this iniquity and let the blood of Jesus cover our sins, and close the doors to the enemy. I ask you to cleanse me from all unrighteousness according to Your word in 1 John 1:9. You said if I confessed my sins, You were able and just to forgive them and cleanse me from this unrighteousness. I submit to Your Lordship, Jesus, and the authority of Your Holy Spirit. You are the only God for me! I will not serve any other God but You! I ask You to restore my life, my health, my finances, my well-being, good, healthy and godly relationships, and bless me the way you want me to be blessed.

Father, I forgive my family members and others for the hurt they have caused me. I forgive them for releasing curses in my life. I ask You to bless them with revelation and understanding of the error of their ways so that they can find their salvation and deliverance in You, Jesus. Please heal their minds, set their hearts free, and take good care of them. I release them into your hands.

Now, confident that I am forgiven of my own sins, I take the authority that You have given me, and I declare:

According to Revelation 12:9,the dragon, that old serpent called Satan and the devil has been cast out of me, and all his dark angels with him .

In the name and authority of Jesus Christ, I loose myself from all punishing, tormenting and vengeful spirits assigned to my life that would perpetuate a curse.

In the name and authority of Jesus Christ, I declare Him only to be my shield, protector, guardian, and refuge.

I command every demonic chain to be severed from my life in the name of Jesus.

I command every demonic spirit on assignment over my life to return to the place that Jesus made for you. Do not come back, I want nothing to do with you and I resist you! According to James 4:7 you must now flee from me, my home and everything that pertains to me. Get out in Jesus name!!

Let the curse over my home, myself and my family, and all that pertains to us be broken now, in Jesus name. I thank You, Father, for allowing us to receive Your restoration and the blessings that have been held back.

I ask that Your Holy Spirit fill me with love, truth, wisdom, light, a spirit of understanding and enable me to live according to Your commands. Let the breath of God come into me now, according to John 20:22 where You breathed on Your disciples and they received the breath of God. In Jesus name, Amen.

Decree to Dismantle Evil Altars

Father,

In the name and authority of the Lord Jesus Christ, I hereby release a decree against all ungodly altars and evil thrones.

Whereas, the enemy, hereafter known as Satan and all those under his influence, has conspired to perpetuate a curse against the people in this city and geographic region, including me and my family;

Whereas, the enemy has refused to leave these people alone, but has continually harassed, tormented, afflicted, robbed, deceived, murdered, accused, divided and destroyed;

Whereas, Satan and demonic spirits has made corporate covenants with people in order to terminate the life and spirit of Your people and those called into sonship with You;

Whereas, the enemy has plotted to tempt people to greed, rebellion and idolatry so that they would sin against You, thereby hindering You from drawing close to them;

Whereas, the enemy has contracted with services from unholy priests and unrighteous ministers in order to invoke curses upon Your people, to weaken them and make them susceptible to failure and defeat;

Whereas, the enemy and adversary has strategized how to deceive Your people through divination and fraud;

Whereas, the enemy has made strategies to bring division, discord and disunity in families, churches, ministries and throughout this geographic region so as to cut off a move of Your Spirit;

Whereas, the enemy has exalted himself as a god and erected altars to himself, thereby depriving You of worship;

Whereas, these ungodly altars include abortion clinics, where the blood of innocent lives are shed, thereby further empowering Satan and demonic forces to carry out evil plans;

Whereas, these ungodly and evil altars are for the sole purpose of perpetuating torment and affliction upon Your people and those in this geographic region;

Whereas, ancient covenants and ancestral traditions have empowered the enemy to continue to enact curses upon Your people so that they are carried away with grief, torment of soul and unbelief towards You;

Whereas these ungodly covenants have handed our families, the citizens of our cities and this geographic region over to bondage, making the citizens thereof serve ungodly kings and rulers, and have made people slaves to demonic spiritual powers;

Whereas, the result of these actions by the enemy and his followers produces captivity, slavery to sin and judgment from God;

Therefore, I ask that as the Just Judge of Heaven and Earth, You charge the enemy with the aforementioned crimes against humanity. I request that he be brought up on charges, chained, and brought to the court of heaven.

I petition the court in a class action suit against the evil one known as Satan, the Father of Lies, the Deceiver, the Thief, the Accuser of the Brethren, Diablo, the one who Divides, the Murderer, and any and all names by which he is otherwise known. Let all evil princes, warlords, witches, wizards, satanic priests and those practicing demonic sorcery also be named as defendants.

In Your law, Father, it is written in Deuteronomy 12:2-4, "You shall utterly destroy all the places where the nations whom you shall dispossess serve their gods, on the high mountains and on the hills and under every green tree. "You shall tear down their altars and smash their sacred pillars and burn their Asherim and you shall cut down the engraved images of their gods and obliterate their name from that place. "You shall not act like this toward the LORD your God."

It is also written in Deuteronomy 7:5, Exodus 34:14, Leviticus 26:30 and Numbers 33:52 that we, Your people, are to tear down ungodly altars and destroy the high places where evil thrones rule.

Again, in Exodus 23:24 it is written: "Do not bow down before their gods or worship them or follow their practices. You must demolish them and break their sacred stones to pieces."

Therefore, please send out Your angels to destroy all evil altars, that they may be permanently silenced. Let the spirit of python, witchcraft, familiar spirits and divination be bound and sent back to the abyss created for them in the name and authority of the Lord Jesus Christ.

Let all those that practice witchcraft and sorcery against others lose all power and effectiveness to carry out their plans, in Jesus name.

Let the enemy and all adversaries be set upon themselves in confusion, so that they cannot communicate, form plans or strategize in Jesus name, according to Genesis 11:7-9, 1 Samuel 14:20 and Judges 7:22.

Let praise and worship arise to Jesus Christ that sets ambushes and routes the enemy, for it is written in 2 Chron. 20:20 that when Your people began to praise You, You set ambushes for their enemies which caused the enemy to turn upon himself. Let the enemies of God be completely defeated in Jesus name.

Let all sacrifices to false gods cease immediately in Jesus name, for Your law states that man shall have no other gods before You, as it is written in 2 Chronicles 20: 3. I also request (in the name of Jesus Christ) that all abortion clinics where human sacrifices are made and all altars where the blood of innocents is shed must close down immediately.

Let Your fire be kindled upon the foundations of evil mountains and burn into the lowest hell according to Deuteronomy 32:22.

Let the foundations of evil altars hear Your shout, O God! Let their walls be torn down and her towers fall according to Jeremiah 50:15.

Let the sword of the Lord be released against evil foundations and altars where Satan is worshiped, according to Jeremiah 46:10.

Let evil foundations and demonic altars be shaken according to Acts. 16:26.

Let Your hand be stretched out against the destroying mountains that destroy the earth according to Jeremiah 51:25.

Let the foundations of deception and idolatrous beliefs be torn down, according to Ezekiel 30:4.

Let the wealth of the wicked be transferred into the hands of the righteous, according to Prov. 13:22.

Let all those that are involved in making sacrifices to false gods, satanic worship and involved in demonic sorcery immediately become disillusioned and disappointed in their false gods, reject and renounce all covenants, contracts and loyalty to evil spirits. Let them burn their magic books and come over to the Lord's side, as it is written in Acts 19:17-19. "Many of those who had believed kept coming, confessing and disclosing their practices. And many of those who practiced magic brought their books together and burned them in the sight of everyone…"

Let the word of God grow mightily and prevail, according to Acts 19:20.

Let those who have been poisoned by bitterness and bound by iniquity repent and be saved according to Acts 8:13 and vs. 22-24.

Let every intended curse that the enemy wants to put upon Your people be turned into a blessing, in Jesus name, according to Deuteronomy 23:5.

Let every form of deception, fraud and intent to injure your people be unraveled and come to nothing, in Jesus name, for it is written that no weapon formed against us shall prosper according to Is. 54:17.

Let angels be released to tear down evil altars and unseat ungodly rulers, according to Ephesians 2:6.

Let principalities and powers be spoiled, according to Jeremiah 51:56 and Col. 2:16. Let the God of recompense, El Gmulot, destroy the works of evil in Jesus name.

Let God arise and Your enemies be scattered according to Psalm 68:1,2.

Let the covenants and ancient traditions of the enemy be halted now, in Jesus name. Let people return to making covenants with God their Father according to Exodus 24:7-8.

Let the fire of God consume the divination of the enemy according to 1 Kings 18:40, and let all ungodly altars be silenced and void of power.

Let altars to God Our Father be constructed in our homes, workplaces and throughout the land, giving glory to the Lord Jesus Christ.

It is also written in Proverbs 6:31 that when the thief is caught he must repay with a seven-fold return and may have to give up all the substance of his house. I petition the court for the full amount due, and ask that You make the thief give up his entire house full of goods.

You also stated in Proverbs 13:22 in the word of God that the wealth of the wicked is stored up for the righteous. I petition the court for compensation of the losses of previous years and that You would grant my request. I ask that the enemy must repay retroactive compensation for past losses, due and payable immediately by the amount set by the court.

Let it be known that it is also written that we are not slaves, but sons, daughters and heirs. For Jesus Christ, our Liberator, bought our freedom when he was crucified and resurrected on our behalf. I ask that the thief must be declared guilty and a favorable judgment towards Your people would be granted. I also ask for angels to be put on assignment to administrate the distribution of wealth, blessings, healings, miracles, breakthrough, restoration and oversee that justice is brought to Your people.

I ask that all false judgments against Your people be overturned, and that Your people who have been falsely accused, slandered and shamed due to the evil plots of the enemy would be vindicated.

As a blood bought child of God, I petition the court to consider the charges brought against the defendant(s) and I call the LORD JESUS CHRIST to act as our defending counsel. I also petition the witness of HOLY SPIRIT to declare the truth in accordance to the aforementioned charges.

Please let it be recognized by the court that this appeal is not based on any righteousness or good deeds on behalf of the plaintiffs. In fact, we respectfully acknowledge that we have no personal merit by which we may stand before the court.

Your Honor, the plaintiffs should be acquitted of any counter charges brought by the enemy, based on the shed blood of Jesus Christ. I approach the court because it is written in Hebrews 4:16 that I may come boldly to the throne of grace to find help and mercy in the time of my need. I acknowledge that as plaintiffs, we are merely sinners that have been saved by Your grace, and we ask that You give consideration to the fact that the blood of the Lord Jesus Christ, our brother and Your Son, paid our debt in full with His very life. His sacrifice is not in vain.

Therefore, I request that any and all excuses or arguments made by the defendant(s) shall be upheld as an objection, rendered null and void, and be stricken from the court records, I also ask that Your people are granted the eviction notice that is immediately served upon the enemy which forces him out of my home, family, and the land in this geographic region. Let Your angels chain the enemy and render all adversaries paralyzed, silenced and impotent of all power.

I address every ungodly spirit, including Satan himself that may be hiding in the secret rooms of my heart, my soul and various body parts. In the name and authority of the Lord Jesus Christ, I bind you and forbid you to operate against me. Do not speak, do not forbid me to speak, and do not resist. I break every agreement made with you knowingly or unknowingly. I repent of any ways I have sinned against God, myself or others. I command every demonic spirit to come out from where you have been hiding and leave me now in Jesus name. Your authority and right to remain has been removed. Take everything you brought with you and go back to the abyss created for you and never return in Jesus name.

I speak blessing over every part of my body, mind, soul and beliefs where the enemy once occupied. I declare I am empowered with grace and compassion to forgive. I declare I am empowered with love and mercy instead of criticism and judgment. I declare I am empowered with humility instead of pride. I declare I am full of the Holy Spirit and His truth to continue to keep me free. In Jesus name, Amen.

Thank You Father for hearing my petition and for granting my request In Jesus name, Amen.

This next prayer is written by Attorney Elizabeth Nixon, who was referenced in chapter 5 of this book. This is the prayer that Ms. Nixon wrote and recited on Doug Addison's blog post **How to Reclaim What's Yours in the Courts of Heaven.** [59]

"…if you think about part of the territory that we're looking to get full ownership and occupation back over, it's our mental, our emotional, our physical, and our spiritual selves. This is going to bring that quietness that you need. I am going to bring it in the Hebrews 12:23 heavenly court, where it says the Court of God is where God is Judge over all things. I am bringing it in the subdivision—the Romans 5:9 blood court, the Court of Redemption— where it says that you have been made right in God's sight by the blood of Christ and He will certainly save us."

Petition To Quiet Title

" We bring a claim right now, Lord God, You who are judge over all things. And we bring it against the adversary, the accuser of the brethren.

Father, we say that there are personal, physical territories that he has been squatting on. There are emotional territories. We see this through trauma, depression and anxiety. There are mental territories where we see oppression, torment, mental illness, bipolar disorders. He is squatting on spiritual territories because of bloodline family issues, addiction, abuse and genetic illness. He squats on finance territories for business and family finances, contracts and even business opportunities. And he squats on geographical territories, whether that's a family ranch, a family home, or a city or a region that we are called to.

Lord God, we ask that the Adversary defendant be removed from our territories that he currently occupies, that he currently prevents us from having sole occupancy, possession, enjoyment and ownership of. This adversary has entered our territories via illegal trespass, and his presence is a continued occupancy that is illegal. He has no right to squat on our properties.

---

[59] Addison, Doug , How to Reclaim What's Yours in the Courts of Heaven, dated August 8, 2018. © Copyright 2018 Doug Addison and InLight Connection. All Rights Reserved . For more info on Elizabeth Nixon, please visit http://whitequillmedia.com/.

Father, we know that even though his trespass has nothing to do with our sin.

Father, there are areas where we are sin-free, where we are clean, but he still comes in. Father, we choose to begin this petition prayer request with Acts 3:19.

Father, we repent of our sins and we turn to God so that our sins might be wiped away. And Father, we come with a Psalm 51:17 contrite heart, that we know that You will not despise.

Father, we come according to James 4:7, that says we humble and yield ourselves before God. We resist the enemy so that he must flee. Father, we in all humility before You, rebuke and resist the enemy. We put Adversary on notice that we intend now to occupy all of our territories and, therefore, Adversary must flee.

Regarding personal territories, Father, we know that we have been made in Your image. We know that the Earth and all of its people are yours. We belong to You, and You have given us dominion over the Earth and over ourselves. So, Father, the enemy has no right to occupy those territories.

Father, we exercise authority over all power of the enemy. And we state in this case, again Luke 10:19, that we have liberty and the power of choice, the power to influence and change these situations. We have a level of governmental rulership and judicial decision-making power, which we now operate in over all the power and authority of the enemy.

Lord God, Your Word says that we have been given this power and authority so that the enemy cannot violate us anymore. He cannot cause unjust consequences against us anymore. He has no power to perpetrate crimes against us. Father, I thank You that according to Galatians 3:13, 1 Corinthians 6:20, and 1 Peter 1:18, that Your blood has paid the debt on all of our territories. Therefore, no debt exists on these territories and the enemy has no way to secure any ownership that trumps our authority. Moreover, according to Acts 4:12, there is no salvation in anyone else other than the Name of Jesus. And 1 Timothy 2:5–6, there is one God and one Mediator between God and mankind, Christ, who gave Himself to redeem us.

Father, we claim and decree the Name of Jesus and His redemption over all of our territories. And we petition this Court for an order that requires Adversary to leave with no ability to secure legal ownership in any of our territories, because he is unable to pay the debt, and the debt has already been paid.

Lord God, this is the order that we request—that You enter a judgment ordering the heavenly Recorder of Deeds and Titles to confirm our territories as belonging to us, and that You will require Adversary to be removed from all territories that he presently occupies, and that You would grant any other relief that the Court deems is appropriate.

We acknowledge that we have three witnesses to this prayer petition today. It is the Romans 8:16, the Spirit Himself who testifies with our spirit; it is the Revelation 1:5, Jesus Christ who is the faithful witness; and the Revelation 3:15, the Amen, the faithful and true Witness, the Originator of God's creation.

Father God, You have the right to rule in our favor according to Colossians 1:16–17, where it says, for by God all things were created, all things that are in Heaven and in Earth, whether they are visible or invisible, whether thrones or dominions or principalities or powers, all things were created by Him and for Him, and therefore they must serve Him. Father, we ask that You would cause our territories to be ours, our sole possession, and that they will serve us according to Your purposes.

Father, I thank You now that You have granted a judgment in our favor. Father, that You render judgment in our favor and that You order the immediate and complete removal of Adversary from our territories, and that You order a Proverbs 6:31 sevenfold reparation and compensation for lost access and for damage to our territories in addition to late fees, penalties and charges.

Father, I thank You that You are not only issuing that judgment, but that You are issuing the angelic hosts—the Hebrews 1:4 angels—who are purposed to minister and to serve us, the heirs of salvation. And that You release now those angelic hosts to do for us what we cannot do for ourselves.

Father, cause Your hosts to be released to enforce the immediate physical and forceable removal of Adversary defendant from our territories and the immediate enforcement of sevenfold reparations.

Father, You purposed this from before the foundation of the world and today

You affirm it again in this Court. Father, we thank You that You have restored to us the fullness of our territories. You have restored our physical bodies, You have restored our emotions, our mental abilities, our spiritual authority.

Father God, even the territorial lands and places and people groups that you have called us to. You have restored them to us, and the enemy has been removed. Father, we worship Your Holy Name. We thank You, in Jesus' Name."

Prayer to be Healed from Trauma

Dear Heavenly Father,

I lift up myself to You right now. I pray that You would help me embrace whatever traumatic or negative memories that I have either blocked out or forgotten, if recalling those memories can be used to release healing. I ask You, Holy Spirit, to show me what happened in my life right before I started feeling ill, or experienced fear, anxiety, or other symptoms manifested. I give You permission to dislodge memories that are stuck. I pray that You highlight any specific memories or situations that are related to my symptoms, illness or other physical and emotional issues. Help me pay attention to what You show me. Please give me understanding of what was going on in myself and others connected to those events, and grant me grace and compassion to be able to forgive myself and others. Help me to see from Your perspective.

I pray that You would supernaturally remove the hurtful memories and the trauma of past events out of my minds, emotions, memories and out of my physical bodies. I ask that You would lift all remnants of painful events and the trauma that was created as a result of that pain. Lift it all out of the very cells of my body. Let me remember only the good about those the enemy used to cause pain. I pray that my heart and mind would agree that I am in an entirely new day and I am able to graciously forgive those that treated me wrong. I forgive anyone that caused injury to my soul, spirit and even physically.

Let my ears not remember hurtful words spoken to me, about me, by me, or by others. Let my heart release all unforgiveness, anger, fear, rejection, pain and shame. I speak now and declare complete healing and freedom from every painful event in my life. I declare that painful memories and hurtful words will not circulate in my mind and emotions any longer in the name and authority of Jesus Christ. I pray that no cell in my body would retain unforgiveness, bitterness, anger, hatred, fear, condemnation, regret, rejection or self-hatred. I pray that my physical body would no longer be in agreement with any negative emotions in Jesus name.

I release myself and others from the pain of their past, and the poor decisions they made as a result of their brokenness. I release them from guilt, shame, regret and bitterness now, in Jesus name. I forgive and release those who willfully and spitefully inflicted pain and suffering on me. I forgive and release those who had wicked intentions and gave themselves over to evil, in order to afflict, torment, and delight themselves in causing me pain. I give them over to You, Father, to do with as You choose; knowing that You are a just God and vengeance belongs to You. I choose to trust You in matters concerning justice and judgement towards others, knowing that as a matter of my will, I choose to forgive and am therefore free in Christ.

I ask Your forgiveness for any doors that I have accidentally opened to the enemy through trying to comfort myself with artificial means. I renounce and break every unintentional agreement that I may have made with spirits of fear, lust, anger, greed, gluttony, anger, bitterness, unforgiveness, unloving spirits, idolatry or a perverse spirit that also inflicts wounds on others. I submit to You, Holy Spirit, and command all ungodly spirits to leave me now, in the name and authority of Jesus Christ. I command all unclean spirits to go back to where you came from and appropriate the blood of Christ over every part of my life, and others for whom I pray.

I speak now to my physical body and command all illness, disease, infirmity and weakness to be uprooted and removed now in Jesus name. I command complete release in every cell of my body of any and all residual effects of trauma. By the name and authority of Jesus Christ, I lift the remnant of trauma out of my body and ask that Holy Spirit, which is the Spirit of Life, release healing into every cell of my body. I speak to the hormones, organs and systems of my body and command them to come into balance and normal function. I command my body to be healed at the cellular level. Everything that has been retained that does not exist in the kingdom of heaven, be released out of my cells now in Jesus name. Let every weight be released. Let every hindrance be released. Let all that does not originate from the kingdom of heaven be released out of my mind, body, emotions and memories. Every weakness be filled now with wholeness and perfect soundness in the name and authority of Jesus Christ. Holy Spirit, fill me now with Your fullness, strength and power in Jesus name. Fill me with joy, peace, and a release of supernatural healing that radiates from the inside out. I declare that by Your stripes I have been healed, according to Is. 53:5. Thank you for the blood You shed, Lord Jesus, that makes healing a reality. I thank You for revival, restoration, healing and complete regeneration in Jesus name. Amen.

Commanding Prayer

Father,

I choose to forgive those that came before me that opened a door to evil spirits. I forgive those that did harm to my family and myself. I forgive the injustices that occurred. I know that my path to healing must occur through forgiveness and letting You be Lord over every hurtful word, every act of cruelty, injustice and sin against me and my family.

I have renounced the sins of my ancestors and myself, therefore I stand with confidence before you and declare that every evil spirit must now leave and go to the abyss You created for them. In the name and authority of Jesus Christ:

I command the spirits of abuse, abortion, addiction, alcohol, annoyance, anger and assault leave me now.

I command the spirits of abandonment, isolation, rejection and loneliness leave me now.

I command all unloving spirits leave me now.

I command the spirits of Abaddon and Apollyon, all spirits of witchcraft and divination leave me now.

I command all spirits of enchantment, magic, pharmakos, delusion, familiar spirits and fortune telling spirits leave me now.

I command all destroyer spirits, spirits of complaining and cursing, all devouring spirits and spirits of death leave me now.

I command all affronting, accusing and attacking spirits leave me now.

I command the spirit of prostitution, adultery, idolatry and lust leave me now.

I command the spirits of disloyalty, unfaithfulness, fornication, worldliness, and dissatisfaction leave me now.

I command the anti-Christ spirit, the spirit of mocking, sneering, unbelief and blindness to leave me now.

I command the spirits of criticism, backbiting spirits, spirits of evil speaking, slander, defamation, gossip, spirit of vengeance, murder and shame leave me now.

I command the spirits of brokenness, disapproval and disappointment to leave me now.

I command the spirits of indignity, injury and offense leave me now.

I command the spirits of corruption, exploitation, confusion, selfish ambition and envy leave me now.

I command the spirits of delusion, deception , distrust and doubt, alll lying spirits leave me now.

I command the spirit of bondage and affliction leave me now.

I command the spirit of jealousy, murder, rage, revenge, cruelty, covetousness, unforgiveness, comparison and greed to leave me now.

I command the spirits of strife, division and contention leave me now.

I command the spirits of heaviness, depression, oppression, grief, disillusionment, suicide, despair and despondency leave me now.

I command the spirit of sorrow, self-pity, dejection, rejection, hopelessness, tearing spirits leave me now.

I command all serpentine spirits and the Kundalini spirit leave me now.

I command the spirit of divorce leave me now.

I command the perverse spirit, the spirit of error, pride, the Leviathan spirit, and the spirits of or rape, trauma and pedophilia leave me now.

I command the spirit of Lilith, incubus and succubus spirits, spirit of incest, spirit of pornography, homosexual spirits, spirits of voyeurism and fantasy, spirit of impurity and spirits of compulsion leave me now.

I command all unclean spirits leave me now.

I command the spirits of bitterness, witchcraft, rebellion and control leave me now.

I command the spirit of haughtiness, arrogance, insubordination, heresy, lawlessness, humanism, idolatry and self-righteousness leave me now.

I command the spirit of infirmity, including spirits of weakness, impotency, spirits that cause lameness, scoliosis, arthritis and spirits of torment leave me now.

I command the deaf and dumb spirit, spirits of mental illness, insanity, double-mindedness, unbelief, spirits of seizures, epilepsy, spirits of tearing, suicide, crying, and mute spirits leave me now.

I command the spirit of fear, anxiety, terror, the screech owl that brings terror by night, spirits of phobias, and fear of death leave me now.

I command all seducing spirits, spirits of false prophecy, false signs and wonders, deception, wandering, and all soul ties to satanic messengers disguised as angels of light leave me now.

In the name and authority of the Lord Jesus Christ, I command every name above and below the earth, in the earth and in the sea, in my home and family – BOW and submit to the name of Jesus, I command you to take every evil work, every curse, sickness, disease and go back to the abyss that God created for you. I also command the thief to repay me and my family at no less than a seven fold increase according to Proverbs 6:31.

I release the Spirit of God, the Spirit of Revelation, the recompense and restoration of God. I release the Holy Spirit to heal, revive and restore areas of my soul and spirit that have been oppressed.. I release the Spirit of Liberty, the Spirit of Adoption, and the Spirit of Purity into my life and family. I release the Spirit of Might, the Exousia and Dunamis of the Holy Spirit to break every chain of the enemy. I release the Spirit of Holiness, Humility and Grace. I release the Spirit of Reconciliation, Mercy and Forgiveness to be poured out upon myself and my family and to go throughout the world. In Jesus name, Amen.

This prayer can be prayed over oneself or with others praying over someone else. Parents praying over children are encouraged to take responsibility for generational sins that could be contributing to a health issue due to a spirit of infirmity. Insert the person's name where appropriate.

Prayer to Heal Blood & Bone Disorders

Father,

Forgive me for the sins of idolatry and iniquity that has been in my bloodline. I/We renounce and repent for any sins I/we have committed as well as those of our ancestors. I/we repent for any rebellion towards your laws and the sins of bloodshed, murder, abortion and even accidental death. I/We repent for the sins of slander, criticism, bearing false witness, and cursing others. I/We repent for any involvement with forbidden practices involving occult magic. I/We repent of retaining judgments, offenses, unforgiveness and bitterness. I/We forgive all those that have spoken negatively about me (or our family) and I/we ask You to bless them in Jesus name. I/We repent for ourselves and any family members that did not demonstrate the fear of the Lord nor show honor to Your name, Lord Jesus. I/We repent for anyone that sinned by rushing to evil and following the ways of evil to harm others. Let every ungodly covenant and agreement made knowingly or unknowingly with the spirit realm be broken now and the blood of Jesus applied to those contracts, severing any bloodline covenants that may exist. Please let the blood of Jesus cover every sin and cleanse me/us from all unrighteousness in Jesus name.

I/We ask that You cleanse (insert name of person) the blood, bones and bone marrow from any contamination and let Your life flow into (insert name), Lord Jesus. I/we command all spirits of infirmity, unclean spirits, spirits of shame, envy, guilt, condemnation, fear and grief to leave _____'s body and bones right now in Jesus name. I/We command any demonic spirits assigned to the bones, the bone marrow and the blood to exit _____'s body now in Jesus name. Father, let _____'s bone marrow become fat, healthy and be filled with perfect soundness. Let the resurrection life found in Your Holy Spirit recreate new healthy bone marrow and red blood platelets in great quantities, and continue to reproduce health, life and strength to _____'s body now in Jesus name. I/We thank you, Father for hearing and answering our prayer. Amen.

Scripture Verses for Healing

When the doctors give you the facts, you tell them the truth – the WORD of GOD! Insert the name of the person you are praying for and make the scriptures personal. It will lift your faith as you declare these over the situation!

GOD, YOU ARE FOR ME, NOT AGAINST ME! Your word says in Romans 8:31,32 "If God is for us, who can be against us? He who did not spare His own Son, but delivered Him up for us all, how shall He (God) not with Him (Christ) also freely give us all things?" God's desire is to freely give us all things – and that includes healing. Don't let the enemy lie to you and tell you anything different!

God, You are not a man that You should lie. I choose to trust You for my healing. (See Numbers 23:19)

Father, You are Holy and bound by Your covenant with us. You cannot deny the nature of who You are: Jehovah Rophe, our Healer.

I declare according to Psalm 124:8, "Our help is in the name of the LORD, who made heaven and earth." MY HELP COMES FROM YOU!

Your word must forces the situation to change because Isaiah 55:11 tells us, "So shall My word be that goes forth from My mouth, it shall not return to Me void, but it shall accomplish what I please and it shall prosper in the thing for which I sent it." LORRD, thank you for changing my situation!

God's word cannot return to Him void, or empty, of accomplishing the very thing that He meant that word to do. It is anointed with supernatural power to produce exactly what God has purposed. BUT! They key here is that we must declare the word and RETURN it to Him by reminding Him what He said. That is how we activate our faith and send the word forth to accomplish what we tell it to do!

Isaiah 53:5 tells us that "By His stripes we ARE healed." We ARE ALREADY HEALED because Jesus accomplished that victory for us when He died on the cross and overcame for us all.

Jesus said in Revelation 1:18, "I AM He who lives, and was dead, and behold, I Am alive forevermore. Amen. And I HAVE THE KEYS OF HADES AND DEATH."

Satan no longer holds the keys of death, and it is not his right to take your life. Do you realize that the Bible says that every day of your life has been written ahead of time? God has an appointed time for each person to die, and He has a purpose for each one to fulfill before they are taken home. You just tell the devil, "GOD isn't done with me yet and I'm not going anywhere until HE takes me home! Devil, you don't have a right to my life, so go and take your sickness with you in Jesus name!" As a believer in Jesus Christ, Jesus holds the keys of your life. Jesus died to set you free, and He will not turn the keys of death over to the enemy. Let that give you confidence in knowing that JESUS is in control – not your illness, and not the enemy!

"By this I know that You are well pleased with me, because my enemy DOES NOT triumph over me." (Ps. 41:11)

Ask God to reveal if there is a root issue that needs to be resolved, such as unforgiveness or something else.

There may be a strongman that needs to be bound. Bind the strongman of infirmity, cancer, fear, death, etc. Jesus defeated the enemy with "IT IS WRITTEN…" Bind the spirit of infirmity and death over the person and loose the healing power of the Holy Spirit.

"I shall not die, but live, and declare the works of the Lord….He has not given me over to death." Ps. 118:17,18(b) You must fulfill your purpose here on earth before it is time for you to go home. It is not God's will that your life is shortened prematurely. Jesus paid the price for our healing on the cross. The debt was paid to redeem us.

By His stripes we have been healed and we are healed! (Isaiah 53:5) Therefore, you must stand in faith knowing that satan has no legal right to your life. This is a legal matter, not just a health issue. Go into the courts of heaven and settle the matter! The thief has taken what does not belong to him – your health! If God has not given you over to death, then Satan cannot take your life from you. It is not his to take. He must be ordered to loose his grip on your health!

"My soul clings to the dust; revive me according to Your word." Ps. 119:2 To REVIVE means to "cause to live." Lord, you have spoken and it is finished. Healing has been accomplished through the work of the cross, and by His stripes, we are healed! (Is. 53:5)

"But God will redeem my soul from the power of the grave, for He shall receive me. (Ps. 49:15)

"As for me, I will call upon God, and the Lord shall save me." (Ps. 55:16) It is absolutely His will to save you from this illness.

"Our God is the God of salvation; and to God the Lord belong escapes from death." (Ps. 68:20) He has provided a way of escape for you. Stand still and see the salvation of the Lord! Battles were won through praise and worship. (2 Chronicles 20:20)

"Also, Your righteousness, O God, is very high, You who have done great things; O God, who is like You? You, who have shown me great and severe troubles, shall revive me again, and bring me up again from the depths of the earth. You shall increase my greatness, and comfort me on every side." (Ps. 71:19-21) God's promise to revive you, bring health and restoration so that in the end, your testimony of His power in your life brings great glory to the Lord. He increases the greatness of your testimony and the anointing in your life to see others healed and restored!

"Establish Your word to Your servant, who is devoted to fearing You." (Ps. 119:38)

Read and declare Psalm 103.

Exodus 15:26 tells us that GOD does not put disease on people if we follow Him and live to honor Him. Declare this scripture and believe it!

ALL OF PSALM 91!

"He brought them out of darkness and the shadow of death, and broke their chains in pieces." (Ps. 107:14) When Jesus conquered death through the resurrection power of the Holy Spirit, because He was fully human, he defeated death for us all. He has brought you out from under the shadow of death and He HAS ALREADY BROKE YOUR CHAINS IN PIECES! Receive it by faith…the chains of death can no longer hold you. Ask Him for a new, deeper infilling of the Holy Spirit to give you resurrection power over death!

"Then they cried out to the Lord in their trouble, and He SAVED them out of their distresses. He SENT HIS WORD AND HEALED THEM, and delivered them from their destructions." (Ps. 107.19,20)

"Remember the word to Your servant, upon which You have caused me to hope. This is my comfort in my affliction, for Your WORD HAS GIVEN ME LIFE." (Ps. 119:49,50)

"Let Your tender mercies come to me, that I may live…" (Ps. 119:77)

"O Lord, revive me according to Your justice." (Ps. 119:149) Judge my case in the court of heaven, Father! Take the thief, the enemy, the oppressor, my adversary, to the court of heaven and Lord Jesus, plead my cause against this ungodly foe. Cause me to live – revive me! For You, Father, are a just judge. Thank you for making the thief, the destroyer, repay and restore my health. I belong to You, Father. It is not the enemy's rightful place to take my life. My life is hidden in You. Thank you for restoring me, even greater than before. And Father, thank You for a greater anointing so that I may see others set free and healed, also.

"Forever, O Lord, Your word is settled in heaven." (Ps. 119:89) Your word cannot return to You without accomplishing the very purpose for which You have written it and said it. (Isaiah 55:11)Your word tells me that death is under Your feet, so death is under my feet as well. Your word tells me that "by His stripes we are healed," so I thank you for Your healing power to flow through my body to bring a total and complete healing.

When the devil wants to present me with facts, I will tell him the truth. I am healed, in Jesus name! My body must align itself with truth, for the word of God is truth. I declare that I will live and not die, in Jesus' name! The things that are impossible with men and truly possible with God. He alone is my strength, my shield. My God is for me, not against me. He has saved me, redeemed me, and given life to my mortal body. I am not defeated because Jesus is not defeated, and His word tells me that He always causes me to triumph! (2 Cor. 2:14) As I have declared this healing in my body, it has been established for me, so that light will shine on my ways. (Job 22:28)

Father, Your word is truth. I believe it, and I'm putting my trust in the integrity of who You are. You are holy. You sacrificed your very own life for me, for my household...and for (insert name of person you are praying for). Your word says in Romans 8:32, He who did not spare His own Son, but delivered Him over for us all, how will He not also with Him freely give us all things? I believe in You, Lord Jesus. You would not have died in our place if You did not intend to give us what we ask for and need in order to live in health and wholeness.

You said in John 10:10 that You came to give us abundant life, so I am asking on (_____'s) behalf, that You give him/her the abundant life that You promised. I stand in faith and remind You of Your promises, and as I declare Your word to You, I ask that You release the power contained in Your word to accomplish all Your will and purpose. I ask You to release angels to carry out the fulfillment of Your promises.

Therefore, in the name and authority that You have given me as Your blood-bought child, and as a co-heir along with Christ, I do declare:

Psalm 68:20 - "Our God is a God who saves; from the Sovereign LORD comes escape from death."

Declaration: Father, I thank You that You have saved (_____) and delivered him/her from death according to Your word in Psalm 68:20.

Isaiah 38:16 - "O Lord, by these things men live, And in all these is the life of my spirit; O restore me to health and let me live!"

Declaration: Father I thank You that the life of Your Spirit lives in (_____). You have restored his health and let him live according to Isaiah 38:16.

Job 33:25 - "Let his flesh become fresher than in youth, Let him return to the days of his youthful vigor; "

Declaration: Father, I thank You that (_____'s) flesh is fresh and youthful, and You have restored his/her vigor according to Job 33:25.

1 Kings 19:7-8 - "The angel of the LORD came again a second time and touched him and said, "Arise, eat, because the journey is too great for you."

Declaration: Father, I thank You for sending Your angel and Your Holy Spirit to touch (_____) a second, third or even a fourth time, to tell him/her to arise and be healed. Touch them again as you did for Elijah in 1 Kings 19:7-8, for You are willing to do it.

Psalm 116:8-9 - "For You have rescued my soul from death, My eyes from tears, My feet from stumbling."

Declaration: Father, I thank You that You have rescued (_____'s) soul from death according to Psalm 116:8-9.

Ruth 4:14-15 - "Then the women said to Naomi, "Blessed is the LORD who has not left you without a redeemer today, and may his name become famous in Israel."

Declaration: Father, I thank You that You have not left (_____) or our family without a redeemer. Redeem his/her life from death so that Your name may become famous once again, according to Ruth 4:14-15.

Titus 3:5-6 - "He saved us, not on the basis of deeds which we have done in righteousness, but according to His mercy, by the washing of regeneration and renewing by the Holy Spirit…"

Declaration: Father, I thank You that You have saved (_____) from death not because of his own righteousness, but according to Your mercy, by regenerating his/her mortal body and renewing him through Your Holy Spirit, according to Titus 3:5-6.

1 Thessalonians 1:5 - "….for our gospel did not come to you in word only, but also in power and in the Holy Spirit and with full conviction; just as you know what kind of men we proved to be among you for your sake."

Declaration: Father, I thank You that the gospel of Jesus Christ is not only in word but in power of Your Holy Spirit. Let the power of Your Holy Spirit now raise (_____) up in complete health and restoration according to Your word in 1 Thessalonians 1:5.

Psalm 30:9 - "What is gained if I am silenced, if I go down to the pit? Will the dust praise you? Will it proclaim your faithfulness?"

Declaration: Father, I thank You that You do not benefit from (_____'s) death. Nothing is gained by silencing his voice and robbing him/her from being able to proclaim your goodness. Therefore, according to Your word, let his/her ability to speak and praise You be restored even better than before according to Psalm 30:9.

Jeremiah 17:14 - "Heal me, O LORD, and I will be healed; Save me and I will be saved, For You are my praise."

Declaration: Father, I thank You for healing (_____) and giving him/her the ability to praise you again according to Jeremiah 17:14.

Psalm 41:1 - "Blessed is the one who considers the poor! In the day of trouble the LORD delivers him;"

Declaration: Father, I thank You that because (_____) has been kind to the poor and has been a constant source of provision to our family and others, You remember him/her and have delivered him in his day of trouble. Let it be done for him/her now according to Your word in Psalm 41:1.

Jeremiah 39:17 - "But I will rescue you on that day, declares the LORD; you will not be given into the hands of those you fear."

Declaration: Father, I thank You that You have rescued (_____) and have not given him/her into the hands of death. We do not fear because you are in control. Deliver (_____) according to Your promise in Jeremiah 39:17.

Numbers 23:19 - "God is not human, that he should lie, not a human being, that he should change his mind. Does he speak and then not act? Does he promise and not fulfill?"

Declaration: Father, I thank You that You are so holy and pure that You cannot lie. You don't change your mind on what You've said. You don't make empty promises and then not fulfill them! I EXPECT You to raise up (_____) in health. I EXPECT You to restore his/her life better than before this health crisis occurred, because that's just who you are. You watch over Your word to make sure it comes to pass, so now according to Your word, let it be fulfilled this day for (_____) .

Isaiah 55:11 -"So will My word be which goes forth from My mouth; It will not return to Me empty, Without accomplishing what I desire, And without succeeding in the matter for which I sent it."

Declaration: Father, I thank You that Your word is anointed to bear fruit and it will not return to You empty. As I return Your word to You by speaking it out of my mouth, I thank You that it produces life. Let

Your word have good success and prosper to accomplish what You have desired it to achieve, in Jesus name, amen.

What God has promised, He is fully able to perform. As it was accomplished at the cross, and by His stripes I have been healed - this is God's promise to me. I was healed, I am healed, and somewhere in the future I am living in the manifestation of this promised healing. As it exists in the kingdom of God, I now call it into the natural realm and say, "Healing, come forth and produce health in my body now, in Jesus name!" I have called those things that do not exist and they have manifested by my declarations of faith. (Rom. 4:17) I receive my healing in Jesus' name, for all things are possible to those who believe!

Prayer to Experience the Father's Heart

Dear Heavenly Father,

I am not sure how to experience Your love. I feel so disconnected. I feel like I don't belong, and I lack a sense of identity and purpose. I have a deep sense of loneliness inside that has left me feeling like I have no real anchor of hope for my life.

Please bless me with a revelation of Your love. Please show me how You see me, and allow me to experience a true Father's love and acceptance. I need to hear your voice. I need Your reassurance that I am loved and accepted just the way I am. Please reveal Your heart for me. In Jesus name, Amen.

Prayer for the Lost

Dear Heavenly Father,

I ask Your Holy Spirit to minister to those individuals that feel lost, orphaned and in pain. Please send Your Holy Spirit to reveal truth that will unravel the lies that they are believing. Lead them back home, back to You.

I pray for those carrying an orphaned spirit to experience Your love in a profound way. Let the revelation of the Father's heart be poured out into their heart in such a personal, significant way that they will forever be changed by what they receive from You.

Let them come to their senses and run back to You. Bless them with undeserved mercy and favor. Bless them with the practical things they need to get back on their feet and to receive restoration. Drop Your words into their heart so they know how to pray. In Jesus name, Amen.

Prayer to Expose Demonic Spirits

Dear Heavenly Father,

Please show me if any evil spirits are hiding in any secret rooms of my body, mind or soul. Show me if there is something hiding that is resisting my freedom and healing. Show me what the enemy is currently doing to work against me.

Holy Spirit, I give you permission to lead me into greater levels of truth. Please show me the memories You want to heal. Show me where You were in those moments, Lord Jesus. Reveal to me whatever I need to know that will break the power of the enemy's lie. Flood me with truth that will displace the accusations that You abandoned me when I needed you. Give me the revelation that will break the power of my pain. Show me how You see me, Father. In Jesus name, Amen.

Prayer to Enter into God's Rest

Dear Heavenly Father,

I repent of selfish ambition, pride, and striving. Forgive me for trying to prove myself through constant striving. I renounce any and all agreements I have made knowingly or unknowingly with rejection, shame, insecurity, fear, pride and unworthiness. Forgive me for covetousness and envy. I repent for allowing my emotions to drive me into proving myself and trying to get ahead by self-effort. Help me separate who I am from what I do. I repent for putting my trust in my own abilities rather than putting my trust in You.

I have not trusted fully in Your provision. I have not been at rest, and though I have not seen it that way, You call it rebellion. My soul had corruption that I could not even recognize until now. Please forgive my sin and cleanse me from unrighteousness.

Father, help me to turn off the internal switch that has been motivated by fear, insecurity, pride, rejection, shame and ambition. Give me the revelation that I need that will quiet my soul and allow me to be at peace. I place my heart and my future in Your hands, Lord. I choose to trust You to take care of me, to open doors at the right time. Your favor can do more for me in a moment than all my striving. Thank you for helping me enter into your rest. In Jesus name, Amen.

A Prayer for Intimacy with God

Holy Spirit,

I don't know how to pray for what You want to give me. Bless me with a holy hunger for more of You. Bless me with a thirst to be in Your presence, to seek Your face.

Open my ears to hear what Your Spirit is saying. Open my eyes to see spiritual realities. Lead me into deeper waters of revelation and worship. In Jesus name, Amen.

Declaration to Open the Ears of the Spiritually Deaf

Father God,

I declare and decree over myself, my family and the inhabitants of this geographic region (name your city, state) will no longer turn aside from hearing and responding to truth. I bind the strongmen of the deaf and dumb spirit, unbelief and the perverse spirit in the name and authority of Jesus Christ. I bind up the spirit of heaviness that brings hopelessness. I forbid them from speaking, influencing, controlling or dominating others. By the authority of Jesus Christ I render them powerless, paralyzed and impotent. I command these spirits to be dismantled, torn down and sent back to the place God created for them in Jesus name.

I release the Joy of the Lord, a Spirit of Faith, Purity, Love, and Resurrection power by the Holy Spirit to go forth over this land in the name of Jesus Christ.

Lord Jesus, I ask You to release Your angels to surround my family, our cities and war against these strongmen spirits. I bind all interfering and assisting demons that try to enforce and support those being torn down, in Jesus name.

I declare that the ears that have been dull and without understanding, those that have sought comfort through denial, and those that have been under a spirit of stupor are opened now, in the name and authority of Jesus Christ, according to Mark 7:35. Lord Jesus, you said in Isaiah 61:1 of your word, "The Spirit of the Lord GOD is upon me, because the LORD has anointed me to bring good news to the poor; he has sent me to bind up the brokenhearted, to proclaim liberty to the captives, and the opening of the prison to those who are bound;"

Therefore,

I declare that every agreement with the enemy or works of darkness are now broken in the name and authority of Jesus Christ.

I declare that my family and those in my geographic region, in (city, state) have turned back to You, O God, that they may be healed.

I command the deaf ears to be opened now in the name and authority of Jesus Christ.

I command the dullness to come out of people's hearts, and they have been given a spirit of understanding from Your Holy Spirit, according to Matt. 13:15 and Is. 11:2.

I break the spirit of stupor and release clarity, focus, and healing to people's minds. I declare that Your words are clear to them according to Mark 7:14.

I declare that people everywhere hear the word of the Lord and are compelled to do what He says, according to Acts 10:33.

I declare that people will give up their other desires and pursue the Lord Jesus Christ, according to Mark 8:34.

I declare people will confess the Lord Jesus Christ and be saved, according to Romans 10: 9,10.

I declare that false brethren and lying signs and wonders will not deceive the righteous nor turn them away from the way of righteousness, according to Mark 13:22.

I declare the spirit and power of repentance is released now to make people ready to turn their hearts back to their heavenly Father, according to Luke 1:17 and Malachi 4:6.

I declare that people have cried out to the Lord for their deliverance and salvation, and the Lord has saved them from all their distress. He has brought them out of darkness and the shadow of death, and has broken their chains in pieces, according to Ps. 107. 13, 14.

I declare people are no longer dead in their trespasses but they have been revived according to Eph. 2:1.

I declare that people have turned away from their wickedness according to Acts 3:26.

I declare people have confessed their sins and received cleansing for their unrighteousness according to 1 John 1:9.

I declare people have confessed their sins one to another so that they can be healed, according to James 5:16.

I declare the generational curse of unbelief is broken according to

Malachi 4:6.

I declare our land, families and our cities are healed according to 2 Chronicles 7:14.

I declare and decree that people will be found watching and waiting for Jesus Christ according to Luke 8:40.

I declare that Jesus will find great faith according to Luke 7:9.

I declare restoration is released according to Ezekiel 36:29-36.

I declare the waste places are rebuilt and the breach has been repaired, according to Is. 58:12.

I declare rivers of joy are flowing in dry places, according to Jer. 31:9 and Is. 41:18.

I declare the head of the serpent that causes spiritual deafness is cut off, in the mighty name of Jesus Christ our Lord. Amen.

CHAPTER TEN

THE FATHER'S LOVE LETTER

For God so loved the world that He gave His only begotten Son, that whosoever believes in Him should not perish, but have eternal life. For God did not send His Son into the world to condemn the world, but that the world through Him might be saved.
John 3:16,17

My Child,

You may not know me, but I know everything about you.   Psalm 139:1

I know when you sit down and when you rise up.   Psalm 139:2

I am familiar with all your ways.   Psalm 139:3

Even the very hairs on your head are numbered.   Matthew 10:29-31

For you were made in my image.   Genesis 1:27

In me you live and move and have your being.   Acts 17:28

For you are my offspring.   Acts 17:28

I knew you even before you were conceived.   Jeremiah 1:4-5

I chose you when I planned creation. Ephesians 1:11-12

You were not a mistake, for all your days are written in my book. Psalm 139:15-16

I determined the exact time of your birth and where you would live.   Acts

17:26

You are fearfully and wonderfully made.   Psalm 139:14

I knit you together in your mother's womb.   Psalm 139:13

And brought you forth on the day you were born.   Psalm 71:6

I have been misrepresented by those who don't know me.   John 8:41-44

I am not distant and angry, but am the complete expression of love.   1 John 4:16

And it is my desire to lavish my love on you.   1 John 3:1

Simply because you are my child and I am your Father.   1 John 3:1

I offer you more than your earthly father ever could.   Matthew 7:11

For I am the perfect father.   Matthew 5:48

Every good gift that you receive comes from my hand.   James 1:17

For I am your provider and I meet all your needs.   Matthew 6:31-33

My plan for your future has always been filled with hope.   Jeremiah 29:11

Because I love you with an everlasting love.   Jeremiah 31:3

My thoughts toward you are countless as the sand on the seashore.   Psalm 139:17-18

And I rejoice over you with singing.   Zephaniah 3:17

I will never stop doing good to you.   Jeremiah 32:40

For you are my treasured possession.   Exodus 19:5

I desire to establish you with all my heart and all my soul.   Jeremiah 32:41

And I want to show you great and marvelous things.   Jeremiah 33:3

If you seek me with all your heart, you will find me.   Deuteronomy 4:29

Delight in me and I will give you the desires of your heart.   Psalm 37:4

For it is I who gave you those desires.   Philippians 2:13

I am able to do more for you than you could possibly imagine.   Ephesians 3:20

For I am your greatest encourager.   2 Thessalonians 2:16-17

I am also the Father who comforts you in all your troubles.   2 Corinthians 1:3-4

When you are brokenhearted, I am close to you.   Psalm 34:18

As a shepherd carries a lamb, I have carried you close to my heart.   Isaiah 40:11

One day I will wipe away every tear from your eyes.   Revelation 21:3-4

And I'll take away all the pain you have suffered on this earth.   Revelation 21:3-4

I am your Father, and I love you even as I love my son, Jesus.   John 17:23

For in Jesus, my love for you is revealed.   John 17:26

He is the exact representation of my being.   Hebrews 1:3

He came to demonstrate that I am for you, not against you.   Romans 8:31

And to tell you that I am not counting your sins.   2 Corinthians 5:18-19

Jesus died so that you and I could be reconciled.   2 Corinthians 5:18-19

His death was the ultimate expression of my love for you.   1 John 4:10

I gave up everything I loved that I might gain your love.   Romans 8:31-32

If you receive the gift of my son Jesus, you receive me.   1 John 2:23

And nothing will ever separate you from my love again.   Romans 8:38-39

Come home and I'll throw the biggest party heaven has ever seen.   Luke 15:7

I have always been Father, and will always be Father.   Ephesians 3:14-15

My question is…Will you be my child?   John 1:12-13

I am waiting for you.   Luke 15:11-32

Love, Your Dad.
Almighty God
60

ABOUT THE AUTHOR

Laura Gagnon is a woman that has been blessed with the gift of understanding God's restorative work through her own personal experience. Once bound by bitterness, witchcraft, rejection, shame, and anger, she now works with others to help them obtain their healing and deliverance. Laura is a witness to God's incredible love and knows firsthand the power of His grace. Through her insights and revelation, God has led Laura to influence many individuals into a restored relationship with Jesus Christ and has seen the power of God work miracles. She is a woman that stands on the promises of God, encourages others in an elevated expectation of the miraculous and declares the gift of His life.

Laura is married and lives in Winchester, California with her family. She also writes for her blog "Beyond the Barriers" located at: xpectamiracle.blogspot.com. She has authored Healing the Heart of a Woman, Prayers for Impossible Situations, Seduced into Shame, Healing the Heart of a Nation, Provision in Unexpected Places and Unmasking the Culture. She is also co-author of her husband's book, Room to Grow. You may contact Laura at: xpectamiracle@yahoo.com.

Acknowledgements

I would like to acknowledge the concepts of the various rooms of the body and soul as presented by Alaxander Pagini in his book, Secrets to Deliverance. (Charisma House 2018). Pagani's teaching on this subject is outstanding and I highly recommend it. He has many prayers for the various room of the body and soul that would greatly benefit others.

I would like to acknowledge the works and teaching of the late Dr. Martin DeHaan in his book, The Chemistry of the Blood. DeHaan presents the teaching on the purity of the blood of Christ from a medical perspective that is quite insightful and inspired me to write on this subject. His teachings can be found on Amazon.com.

I would like to acknowledge the teaching of John Eckhardt, especially regarding generational curses and deliverance. His teaching and years of experience in deliverance ministry is invaluable to the body of Christ. I highly recommend his book Deliverance and Spiritual Warfare Manual (Charisma House 2014).

Made in the USA
Monee, IL
19 October 2022

16221717R00134